"At a time when most news about the environment seems bad, a constructive impulse to restore ravaged ecosystems has lately materialized. . . .

"This book is about that impulse and about how some people are acting on it. Their efforts are fueling a rapidly growing new grass-roots environmental movement of potentially great breadth and force. They have given birth to a new scientific enterprise and have challenged some of the conventional scientific wisdom about the way in which natural ecosystems are put together. The emerging restoration movement, because it requires direct engagement with the natural world, has led many ordinary citizens to recast their perceptions of their own relationship to the rest of nature. Happily, the enterprise is also stimulating a new sense of wonder and delight among people who for the first time are beginning to understand how nature really works, close up. . . .

"While some environmentalists talk, the restorationists are discovering that they can make an important, exquisitely concrete difference. At its best, their effort is enabling rare and endangered species to reappear magically in habitats from which they had disappeared. All this is firing citizen volunteers with an extraordinary sense of mission and accomplishment, and is conferring on them a profound sense of satisfaction. . . .

"Restorationists are in it for the long haul. . . ."

D0877613

MIRACLE

UNDER
THE OAKS

The Revival of
Nature in America

WILLIAM K. STEVENS

Drawings by Patricia J. Wynne

Maps by Myra Klockenbrink

POCKET BOOKS
New York   London   Toronto   Sydney   Tokyo   Singapore

POCKET BOOKS, a division of Simon & Schuster Inc.
1230 Avenue of the Americas, New York, NY 10020

Copyright © 1995 by William K. Stevens
Drawings by Patricia J. Wynne
Maps by Myra Klockenbrink

Library of Congress Cataloging-in-Publication Data

Stevens, William K. (William Kenneth), 1935–
    Miracle under the oaks : the revival of nature in America/
William K. Stevens; drawings by Patricia J. Wynne; maps by Myra
Klockenbrink.
        p.   cm.
    Includes bibliographical references
    ISBN 0-671-78045-X
    1. Restoration ecology—United States.   I. Title.
QH541. 15.R45574   1995
333.7'153'0973—dc20   94-31436
                                                            CIP

First Pocket Books trade paperback printing May 1996

10 9 8 7 6 5 4 3 2 1

POCKET and colophon are registered trademarks of
Simon & Schuster Inc.

Cover design by Caroline Whang
Front cover photo courtesy Tony Stone Images

Printed in the U.S.A.

To
Joan, Jim, Elizabeth, and All Who Come After

Acknowledgments

Although it wasn't apparent at the time, this book had its origins in a conversation with Dr. Peter H. Raven, the director of the Missouri Botanical Garden, in late 1990. In the course of an interview for an article I was preparing for *The New York Times*, he mentioned that there was a movement afoot to restore damaged, degraded, and destroyed ecosystems, that the restorationists even had their own newly formed society, and that its director was a fellow named Bill Jordan. The result was another article for the *Times*, this one on the scientific efficacy and practical results of ecological restoration. It featured the work of Steve Packard and Dr. Robert Betz in Illinois. Soon came a telephone call from Claire Zion, an editor at Pocket Books, inquiring whether there might be a book in the subject. After several discussions that included Philippa (Flip) Brophy, an agent at Sterling Lord Literistic with whom I had been acquainted for some time, we decided that there was.

Working on the book has been a wonderful adventure. I have received much help and encouragement along the way, not least from my colleagues in the science news department of the *Times*. It is fast and delightful company to be in, and I feel privileged to be among them. Early in the game especially, John Noble Wilford, a productive and experienced writer of books, encouraged me to undertake the project and gave abundant and invaluable practical advice to a first-time author.

The editors of the *Times* provided support, advice, leeway, and encouragement, without which the project would have been extremely difficult if not impossible. These include David R. Jones, Carolyn Lee, John M. Lee, Cory Dean, Katherine Bouton, and most particularly Nicholas Wade, the paper's science news editor. Another experienced author, he was unfailingly positive about the project, generous in accommodating insofar as possible its demands on time, attention, and energy, and enthusiastic about the resulting manuscript.

Most of the sources contributing grist for the manuscript are quoted in the text; to all of them, a salute of gratitude. Those not quoted but to whom thanks are also due include Roger Anderson, William Cronon, William Franz, Russell Graham, Ardith K. Hansel, James E. King, E. C. Pielou, Ray Schulenberg, Stephen A. Spongberg, and Marjorie G. Winkler. I apologize for any inadvertent omissions in this list.

Kelly Cash of The Nature Conservancy was immensely helpful in putting me in touch with restorationists across the country and in assembling the list of Conservancy contacts for aspiring restoration volunteers that appears in Appendix I. Donald Falk, who in October 1993 became the executive director of the Society for Ecological Restoration, and Laura Lee Hoefs of the society's staff in Madison, Wisconsin, furnished most of the rest of the list in Appendix I. The knowledge, insights, contacts, and eager assistance of Dr. William R. Jordan, III, the guiding spirit of the restoration movement, were basic and irreplaceable. Sarah Blanchette and Sally Smith of The Nature Conservancy's California restoration team put me in touch with local volunteers, as did Tom Chase on Martha's Vineyard and Pauline Drobney in Iowa.

An extra-special note of thanks goes to past and present members of the North Branch Prairie Project and The Nature Conservancy's Volunteer Stewardship Network in Illinois, including especially John and Jane Balaban, Larry and Chris Hodak, Karen Holland, Susanne Masi, Laurel Ross, and Ross Sweeny; and to Dr. Robert F. Betz, who graciously shared his knowledge of prairie restoration.

Above all, the book simply could not have been written without Steve Packard's enthusiastic cooperation and generosity of time, thought, energy, and personal experience.

To everyone, to all who appear in the book and to all the restorationists who are themselves writing such an exciting new chapter in the history of conservation, goes my warmest gratitude. Whatever value this book has is because of them, while any shortcomings or errors are strictly mine.

I'm grateful also to Claire Zion and Flip Brophy, whose experienced nurturing of a rookie stripped the job of unnecessary anxiety, and to Patricia J. Wynne and Myra Klockenbrink, whose professionalism and talent as artists have added important notes of grace and illumination to the book.

Last and most important, I am grateful beyond words for the love, devotion, and encouragement of my wife, Joan Stevens.

—WILLIAM K. STEVENS
November 1993

CONTENTS

xi

PART THREE

MIRACLE
UNDER
THE OAKS

Mid-American Prairie-Savanna Complexes
Before Settlers Arrived

Adapted from Alan W. Haney

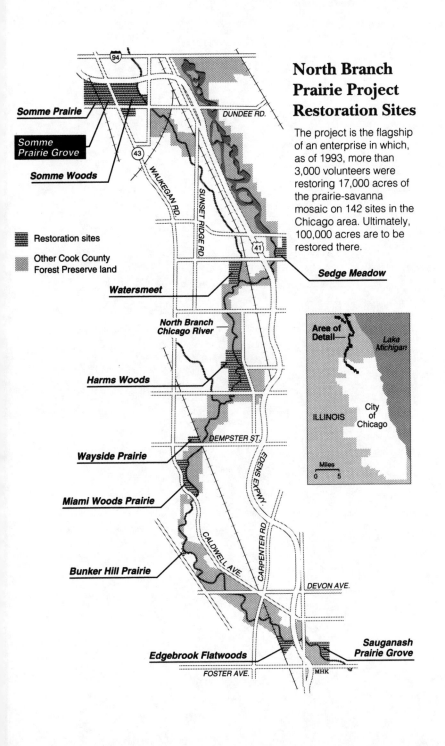

North Branch Prairie Project Restoration Sites

The project is the flagship of an enterprise in which, as of 1993, more than 3,000 volunteers were restoring 17,000 acres of the prairie-savanna mosaic on 142 sites in the Chicago area. Ultimately, 100,000 acres are to be restored there.

Somme Prairie

Somme Prairie Grove

Somme Woods

DUNDEE RD.

WAUKEGAN RD.

SUNSET RIDGE RD.

Restoration sites

Other Cook County Forest Preserve land

Sedge Meadow

Watersmeet

North Branch Chicago River

Harms Woods

Wayside Prairie

DEMPSTER ST.

EDENS EXPWY.

Miami Woods Prairie

Bunker Hill Prairie

CALDWELL AVE.

CARPENTER RD.

DEVON AVE.

Edgebrook Flatwoods

Sauganash Prairie Grove

FOSTER AVE.

MHK

Area of Detail

Lake Michigan

ILLINOIS

City of Chicago

Miles
0   5

INTRODUCTION

For tens of thousands of years, at least, humans have molded the earth and altered the surroundings—and thus the existence—of their fellow living creatures.

On the African savanna, early people set fires that transformed local ecosystems. Later, many scientists believe, human hunters helped drive the mammoth and the other big mammals of the Pleistocene to extinction. The ancient agriculture-based civilizations of Mesopotamia and Central America disturbed their environment so thoroughly, some archeologists say, that they fouled the natural resources on which their cultures were based and thereby brought about their own decline. The first Polynesians to reach Hawaii carried the seeds of plants from their original homelands. Reestablished in Hawaii, they soon crowded out and extinguished many native species. For centuries, the natives of the Amazon have rearranged the supposedly virgin rain forest in which they live, transplanting one wild species after another from one region to the next to make sure they have food and medicine wherever they go. Indians routinely burned the forests and prairies of North America, altering the face of the land and the ecological profile of much of the continent. And from the time Europeans first sailed the globe, they began redistributing the world's plant and animal species on a grand scale.

In our own era, when Homo sapiens seems about to overrun the planet, the technologies of the industrial and information ages have amplified beyond calculation the ability of humans to disrupt and transfigure the rest of nature. People now rank alongside titanic catastrophes like movements of the continents, volcanic eruptions, hurricanes, and even ice ages as one of the major agents of change that have kept the natural world in a constant state of turmoil—not balance—since the earth was formed. Human action is changing the composition of the atmosphere, threatening to raise the temperature of the planet to levels unknown since civilization developed. Homo sapiens, according to scientists' calculations, now appropriates to its use fully 40 percent of the products of photosynthesis, the very basis of most life. And if a majority of biologists who study the question are right, humans are destroying, degrading, and polluting natural ecosystems at such a rate that the earth could experience a mass extinction of species approaching in scope those of the remote geological past.

What does it matter?

On a purely utilitarian level, the diversity of living things represents a huge source of largely untapped wealth. Only a small fraction of the earth's plant, animal, and microbial species have been discovered, much less assayed for their value as food and medicine. This is true even in the United States, as widely explored as many of its natural areas are. Who knows what wild plant or microbe might hold the cure to cancer or AIDS? Or provide a major new food source for the world's exploding population? Scientists have given up for now their brave hopes that new drug cures can easily be synthesized from scratch in the laboratory. They must have something to go on, and only nature's medicinal compounds, produced by plants, animals, and microbes, can provide it. Only a few of the world's possible food plants have been converted from wild species into domesticated crops. If biological diversity is reduced, the genetic capital on which humanity's sustenance has always depended will be reduced as well.

More fundamentally, beyond utility, biological diversity—the product of millions of years of evolution—is the medium in which humans exist. Soil microbes and fungi, insects, reptiles, birds, fish, mammals—all play a role in the unfathomably complex web of energy exchanges that constitute the biosphere, the arena in which human life originated and to which it remains inextricably linked for its survival. Remove all insects and other invertebrates from the face of the earth, for instance, and the global ecosystem would collapse. Humans would probably last only a few months before being extinguished forever. In this sense, humans need the rest of the biosphere far more than it needs them: Remove people from the earth, and the rest of the biosphere would go on quite handsomely.

But while the biosphere would scarcely miss a beat if people disappeared from it, humans have the power to do it great harm as long as they are here. Destruction of other species' habitats, now proceeding apace throughout the world, inevitably reduces populations of some species to levels at which they are doomed to eventual extinction. Exotic species transplanted wholesale from one part of the world to another often find themselves without serious competitors or predators and run riot in their new homes, taking over entire habitats and choking out native species. When a landscape is disturbed by people, a few opportunistic "weedy" species tend to overrun the scene and dominate an ecosystem, reducing biological diversity and ecological complexity.

The upshot: Humans' impact on the natural world clearly works in favor of simplification and sameness

rather than complexity and variety, of biological impover-
ishment rather than richness. It is unlikely that rats, cockroaches, weeds, and other tramp species will join humans
as sole rulers of the earth, but things do seem to be moving in that direction. To whatever extent that is true, it
is because humans are substituting artificial selection for
natural selection: They are deciding, quite unconsciously
for the most part, which species live and die; and the
comparatively few weedy species that flourish in a continually disturbed environment have a better chance to
come out on top.

Species are always going extinct naturally as evolution
proceeds, and new ones are always arising, but at a slow
rate measured in thousands or millions of years. What is
different now is that technologically armed humans are
interrupting and dislocating these natural processes by
reducing wild populations rapidly and wholesale, setting
many species on the road to untimely extinction. Species
of plants that evolved millions of years ago and survived
ice ages and other severe climatic pressures by adjusting
their geographic ranges could vanish in a twinkling. The
vanished would be replaced only gradually, over millennia
or eons.

The biosphere in its natural state is not for the most
part fragile. Evolution has produced many species that
might fill a given niche in an ecosystem. But as diversity
decreases, the redundancies disappear, and the whole
ecosystem becomes more vulnerable to disease or climatic
stress. Emerging scientific evidence is beginning to confirm what conservationists have long thought: that the
fewer species an ecosystem contains, the weaker its de-
fenses are. The weakness appears to be progressive as
each species drops out, and scientists believe that sooner
or later what is called a "keystone species," one whose
presence holds the entire system together, is likely to go.
It brings down other remaining species with it, and the
whole system risks collapse. This can happen without a

single species' going globally extinct; the disappearance of enough species from a given ecosystem is sufficient. The bottom line is that a biologically diverse ecosystem is less likely to fail and weaken the larger biosphere.

Apart from the economic and ecological aspects of biodiversity, a biologically rich and various world is inherently a more beautiful and fulfilling one; an impoverished biosphere impoverishes the human spirit as well. And beyond all the implications of biodiversity for the human species, there is an ethical dimension, a growing belief that species have a right to exist for their own sake, that the natural world has intrinsic value all its own quite apart from its importance to humans.

Whatever the justification, a conviction has developed that biological diversity is better than sameness, that biological complexity is better than simplicity, that biological richness is better than poverty, and that humans must take active steps to insure that evolution—the fountainhead of biodiversity—can proceed as naturally as possible.

Humanity's negative impact on the environment stems from one source: the intelligence made possible by a large and complex brain, itself the product of millions of years of evolutionary interaction between hominids and the very surroundings they are now transforming. The same intelligence that has been willy-nilly disassembling much of the biosphere might well be applied to a more deliberate and organized effort to put it back together. Is that possible? Can humans put aside their divisions, look beyond next week, and reassemble Humpty Dumpty? The answer is by no means clear, although humans' track record so far does not appear to offer much encouragement. But at a time when most news about the environment seems bad, a constructive impulse to restore ravaged ecosystems has lately materialized.

This book is about that impulse and about how some people are acting on it. Their efforts are fueling a rapidly growing new grassroots environmental movement of potentially great breadth and force. They have given birth to a new scientific enterprise and have challenged some of the conventional scientific wisdom about the way in which natural ecosystems are put together. The emerging restoration movement, because it requires direct engagement with the natural world, has led many ordinary citizens to recast their perceptions of their own relationship to the rest of nature. Happily, the enterprise is also stimulating a new sense of wonder and delight among people who for the first time are beginning to understand how nature really works, close up.

The restorationists come from all walks of life: professionals, blue-collar workers, homemakers, retired people, students. Their pursuit is not one of advocacy, demonstrations, drumbeating or high-level policy making, but of green-thumbed work in the field. Some are gardeners who have found a way to apply their skills, experience, and feel for the land to a new and more exhilarating activity. While some environmentalists talk, analyze, lobby, sue, or protest, the restorationists are discovering that they can make an important, exquisitely concrete difference. At its best, their effort is enabling rare and endangered species to reappear magically in habitats from which they had disappeared. All this is firing citizen volunteers with an extraordinary sense of mission and accomplishment, and is conferring on them a profound sense of satisfaction.

Restoration efforts are also putting some of the ideas of academic scientists to the test of field experience. This has not endeared the restorationists to some professionally trained ecologists, who bridle at seeing some of their theories questioned by mere laymen. But other ecologists are realizing that they may have much to learn from what the green-thumbed field restorationists are turning up; that at the very least, new questions for investigation are being raised. In the past, the scientists have done most of the talking and very little listening. Now that is changing.

An active body of scientists has come to view hands-on restoration experiments as the ultimate test of their theories. They have even joined with field restorationists in a new organization, the Society for Ecological Restoration, dedicated to the mutual cross-fertilization of science and practice. If the effort ultimately succeeds, it will amount to a welcome bridging of a gap in American life between laymen and scientists, who all too often are perceived as high priests remote from the real world. In the infancy of the "hard" sciences like physics and chemistry, scientists relied heavily on the insights of craftsmen. Ecology is in a similar state of infancy today, and leaders of the restoration movement see the possibility of a new latter-day alliance between theory and practice. Restoration, they hope, will prove to be a powerful technique for ecological studies, leading to a stronger science whose principles in turn will lead to better restoration methods.

Restoration, in fact, thirsts for solid scientific guidance. Restorationists are working in all kinds of ecosystems, from prairies to forests to mountaintops to wetlands to lakes to deserts to alpine communities, even to coral reefs. But some of the work is being done sloppily, carelessly, in ignorance of the valid lessons that science has so far learned about how ecosystems assemble themselves and operate. Restoration of wetlands—thanks to government policies that allow landowners to destroy wetlands if they create new ones to replace what's been destroyed—has become a booming commercial business, but scientists who have investigated the projects say the results often turn out to be only cosmetic, or worse, and that failure is more common than success.

The new restorationists view their enterprise as a healing art. Some see themselves as physicians whose patients are ecosystems. Just as a doctor intervenes to treat a patient injured in an automobile accident so that healing can proceed, so restorationists intervene to repair the damage caused by other humans so that the natural evolutionary processes that generate biodiversity can resume. No one sees restoration as a substitute for the preservation of healthy ecosystems. For the restorationists are finding that putting nature back together is a daunting and humbling business. A surprising degree of recovery can be achieved in some cases. Essential ecosystem functions can sometimes be reestablished. Species diversity can sometimes be restored to an ecosystem, and with it stability and vitality. Habitats for endangered creatures can be re-created so that populations recover to healthy levels. Even so, most ecosystems probably can never be totally restored to their pristine condition.

So far, restoration amounts to a tiny counterattack when compared to the scale of ecological destruction that is taking place. And it has inherent limitations, some of them serious. Practitioners of this new art sometimes liken it to the building of cathedrals: It takes decades, even centuries, and several generations must participate. Restorationists are in it for the long haul.

They have in any case made a solid and encouraging start, and although the acreage under restoration so far is relatively small, it is not trivial. The acreage steadily grows, and restorationists are acquiring the knowledge and techniques to expand it farther. Few nature preserves in the wild are truly large compared with the vast biosphere, but all have the potential to preserve significant and perhaps critical populations of the plants, microbes, and invertebrates that undergird the biosphere's functioning. And even the smallest preserves provide an essential function that zoos and seed banks do not: a chance for species to engage with the rest of nature in the grand drama of evolution. Seeds in a bank or animals in a zoo are mere snapshots, examples of evolution frozen at a point in time. While seeds repose in cold storage, the world moves on, and evolution proceeds without them. It is only out on the land, back in nature, that species can make the adaptations to an inevitably changing environment that lead to the emergence of new species. The larger the nature preserves, the larger the evolutionary arena—and the greater the scope for evolutionary interplay among species and, more important, among genetically variable strains within species. Restoration provides a way to enlarge the arena, to expand protected areas, to go farther and farther beyond the limitations of the seed bank and the zoo.

It also offers the hope of not just halting or slowing habitat loss and ecosystem deterioration, but ultimately of reversing them. More and more, conservation biologists are coming to recognize restoration as an essential weapon in the struggle to head off the possibility of mass extinctions and collapse of ecosystems. Conservation and preservation, they say, may not be enough. There is a widespread view among veteran conservationists—it can be thought of as either pessimistic or realistic—that the human population explosion will roll over the rest of the natural world unimpeded before expending its momentum in the next century or two, and that every patch of viable habitat is therefore precious. If enough arks can be built, maintained, and kept afloat on the human tide, there will be enough raw material left once the flood subsides to "reclothe the earth," as it is put by Dr. Robert Jenkins, The Nature Conservancy's former vice president for science. Blue-sky talk? Not necessarily. American nature preserves, parks, and national forests, though many are deteriorating ecologically, have already been afloat for up to a century. Why shouldn't restoration not only bring them back to health but also expand their reach, create new ones, and extend their protective influence for another century or more?

Nowhere, perhaps, have the restoration movement's strands come together more revealingly and dramatically than in the northern suburbs of Chicago. Starting in 1977, a determined band of restorationists led by Steve Packard—a Harvard University graduate and onetime antiwar activist who was later to become the science director of the Illinois Nature Conservancy—set out to restore what they assumed were degraded, misused, beaten-down remnants of classic tallgrass prairie stretching along the North Branch of the Chicago River like an old string of pearls encrusted with grime. In trying to bring back their luster, the workers of what came to be called the North Branch Prairie Project rediscovered a long-lost ecosystem that no one even realized had existed. Today it has gloriously, fulsomely, returned from the edge of oblivion, a resurgent enclave of life populated by a number of rare and endangered species.

On any given weekend at each of the North Branch sites, one can find platoons of volunteers planting seeds, or collecting them, or beating back botanical philistines by cutting invasive and destructive copses of weedy brush, or otherwise doing the hard work of restoration. The volunteers include people like Larry and Chris Hodak of Chicago's North Side, he an architect and she an M.B.A. holder, who got into it simply because they were fascinated by prairies. And Preston Spinks, a union carpenter from suburban Morton Grove, now retired, and a championship gardener who once won prizes with his dahlias and then applied his extraordinary green thumb to prairie and savanna restoration at a time when the project sorely needed it. And John and Jane Balaban of Skokie, he a high school math teacher and she a pharmacist, who raised prairie plants from seeds in their backyard for transplantation to the restoration sites and became amateur plant taxonomists extraordinaire.

For many among the broadly based group of volunteers, representing a wide spectrum of backgrounds, occupations, and world views, their pioneering efforts in a new realm of conservation activity have opened broad new avenues to knowledge about the natural world and transformed their view of nature and the place of humans in it. Some have become amateur ecologists of no small accomplishment. Many have developed what can only be described as a bond with the ecosystems they have helped resurrect. "There's such a strong emotional component to it," says Jane Balaban. "In a way, it's almost like taking care of a child. It becomes very personal."

Over the years, the North Branch project evolved into a volunteer stewardship network that by 1993 included more than 5,000 volunteers working on more than 200 Illinois sites covering nearly 30,000 acres, more than half in metropolitan Chicago. It had become not only a model for community action in ecological restoration but also a spearhead of the restoration movement nationally. Exerting its influence through The Nature Conservancy, the largest private organization in the United States dedicated to setting aside, preserving, restoring, and managing natural ecosystems, it has helped revolutionize thinking about what the ends and means of conservation ought to be. It has touched off a lively scientific argument about the ecological character of savannas vis-à-vis prairies and forests. It has spotlighted important new ideas about the structure and functioning of ecosystems generally. And it has engaged the attention of a number of scientists who have joined in an intellectual alliance with Packard and the volunteers who work with him, even while raising the hackles of other academics who resent the intrusion of amateurs.

Some see the charismatic, quietly intense but often good-humored Packard—tall, dark, and lanky with medium-longish hair and rimless spectacles, looking younger than his fifty years—as something of a prophet. Not uncommonly, he captivates people with what is often perceived as an arresting combination of vision, passion for and knowledge of nature, and down-and-dirty political practicality. He is a genuine nonconformist in much the same way his fellow Bay Stater Henry David Thoreau was. And again much like Thoreau, he has become a respected

amateur ecologist even though he is without formal training in ecology. He is taken seriously by many academic
scientists, both those who have made common cause with
him and those who oppose some of his ideas. In breaking
old molds to create a brand-new enterprise, he has also
ruffled feelings and made enemies sometimes, and even
within his own circle he has had a few traumatic fallings-
out. Some people say he's a true creative genius; others,
that he's a manipulator and salesman. Pro or con, like
other innovators he tends to provoke strong feelings.

In any case, he has clearly emerged as a national leader
in ecological restoration, and a leader of a new kind: one
who is attempting to harness the hard-won ecological expertise of both professional scientists and field volunteers
to a groundswell of citizen enthusiasm, and to enlist the
potent combination directly in the cause of reviving
nature.

None of this could possibly have been foreseen when
the enterprise started out in 1977, a well-intentioned
but naive outgrowth of what began as Packard's hobby.
Nor was there any hint of the frustrations, difficulties,
and challenges—political, intellectual, and personal—that
would confront the undertaking. The would-be restorationists certainly did not know that the rediscovery of a
lost ecosystem awaited them.

Theirs is a story of perseverance in the face of multiple
setbacks, obstacles, and frustrations; of discouragement
and intellectual courage in the face of intellectual opposition. It is also a mystery story, a search for a Rosetta stone
that could unlock the secrets of a hidden ecological community. It is as much about the creation of a new sort of
environmental politics—perhaps even a new subculture—
as about restoration itself, and as much about readjusting
people's relationship to the landscape as about botany.
And it is the story of an enterprise through whose links

to other facets of an emerging national restoration movement the broader picture can be seen.

Most of all, it is a story about the building of a cathedral, its beauty already obvious but its completion a long way off.

PART ONE

1

VESTAL GROVE: PAST AND PRESENT

Vestal Grove has not always been the magical spot it is today.

The grove lies half an hour north-northwest of Chicago's Loop, five miles inland from the string of suburban gold-coast communities that stretch along Lake Michigan from Evanston in the south to Lake Forest in the north. It is the most precious pearl in a string of small surviving patches of central North America's original ecological mosaic that are coming back to life along the North Branch of the Chicago River. Big bur oaks, their heavy trunks and crooked, gnarly branches armored with rough bark so thick that twigs become as fat as a little finger, anchor this corner of one of the rarest and richest ecosystems left in the world. Neither wholly prairie nor wholly forest, Vestal Grove is part of a third sort of living community: an oak savanna. The web of life is so finely and intricately spun, the tolerances just so, that only certain plant and animal species live in the grove's dappled pattern of sunlight and shade. The mixture of species changes as one moves along an ecological gradient from the cozy enclave of Vestal Grove itself into a more open, parklike stretch of savanna where the trees are more widely spaced, and then to a treeless expanse of tallgrass prairie. All these interwoven elements, including Vestal Grove, are reemerging from near-oblivion on a publicly owned nature preserve called Somme Prairie Grove, which in turn is one of eleven restoration sites along the North Branch.

Once, the savannas were a far-flung confection of lush grasses, wildflowers, trees, butterflies, songbirds, turkeys, deer, elk, wolves, panthers, and innumerable other creatures from the magnificent to the microscopic. Bison trooped through the oak groves, and Indians hunted, camped, and foraged in them. The tallgrass savannas flourished for 8,000 years in the rich loam of what is now northern Illinois, southern Wisconsin, and parts of Iowa, blending seamlessly with both the open prairies to the south and west and the closed forests that pressed in from the north and east. Before Europeans arrived on the scene, the comely oak groves of the savannas were the characteristic ecological community in much of the region.

But by the early twentieth century, both the bur-oak savannas and the tallgrass prairies that intertwined with them had all but disappeared—cut down, overgrazed, or plowed under as European settlers and their descendants converted the grasslands and savannas into one of the world's most productive agricultural provinces. What remnants survived did so largely in urban and suburban areas, especially metropolitan Chicago, where they were in no danger of being broken up into furrows. Even there the actions and influence of humans brought the savannas so low, ecologically speaking, that they had virtually vanished.

When Steve Packard first saw Vestal Grove and its adjacent open savannas and prairies, at the Somme site, it was a dead ecosystem except for the dominant oaks and their attendant hickories; and not just dead, but lost to human ken. The classic tallgrass savannas had disappeared so quickly, before scientists could study them, that their ecological characteristics were almost unknown. Packard found the site strewn with mattresses, car seats, and milk crates that teenagers used as seats for outdoor parties. Bottles and cans were everywhere. Kentucky Fried Chicken take-out cartons, plastic buckets, and an automobile muffler decorated the ground. More serious from an ecological point of view, the site was choked by twenty-foot-high thickets of European buckthorn, an invader from abroad whose dense growth obliterated the original grasses and flowers, destroying not only the savanna ecosystem but also any possibility of knowing what it had been like.

Today, on the ninety-acre Somme tract tucked away along the tracks of the old Milwaukee Road railway in the northeastern corner of the town of Northbrook, where traffic roars by on Dundee Road a few feet away and jets from O'Hare International Airport fly by overhead, the savanna community is reassembling itself and revealing its secrets to the wondering eyes of its rescuers.

To Americans for whom forests represent the ultimate in ecological richness and complexity, the restored site is a revelation. Far from dull and one-dimensional, prairies and savannas erupt in color and biological variety when enabled to live naturally. In Vestal Grove, scores of native plants, many of them rare or uncommon, have come together in a tightly integrated assembly of life that in a good year blazes with color from May through October. Some of the names are wonderfully arresting: False dragonhead. Rattlesnake master. Golden Alexanders. Mad-dog skullcap. Yellow pimpernel. Seneca snakeroot. Cream gentian. Canada milk vetch. Meadow parsnip. Maple-leaved goosefoot. Small sundrops.

Plants that mature low to the ground rule Vestal Grove early in the growing year. The species change, with progressively taller types taking over as spring turns to summer and summer to fall. From March to June, short-stalked wildflowers poke their heads up under the protective oaks and less numerous hickories. Glossy yellow blossoms of the swamp buttercup and the bright yellows of the golden Alexanders mix with the big, waxy, three-petaled white blooms of the large-flowered trillium, the biggest of its genus in eastern North America; with spiky bristles of bottlebrush grass; with the tiny, white, five-petaled flower of the common strawberry, sweetest of all wild strawberries in North America; and with the fragile, cuplike white blossoms with golden-orange centers that open in full sun and close at night, identifying the bloodroot—a member of the poppy family whose underground stem exudes a red juice once used by Indians as dye for baskets, clothes, and war paint.

Midsummer's taller flowering plants bring a riot not only of whites and yellows but also of lavender, pink, violet, blue, and red against a bright green background. Feathery, creamy white masses of starry false Solomon's seal wave alongside the yellow blooms of small sundrops, a threatened species, and both nod in harmony with the snapdragonlike spike of the false dragonhead; the drooping yellow petals of the prairie coneflower, smelling like anise; the lavender tubular blossoms of the wild bergamot, whose aromatic leaves make mint tea; the sweet black-eyed Susan; the late figwort, which was used to treat insomnia and anxiety in the 1800s; the tiny, fragrant white flowers of the elderberry, famous as the stuff of jelly and wine.

From August through autumn, the twining vine of the hog peanut, advertised by its pale purple or lilac flowers, snakes along past spiny, greenish white flower heads atop six-foot-high stalks of rattlesnake master and the equally tall stalks of two kinds of Joe-Pye weed, spotted and purple. The former is known by its large pinkish, purplish, flat-topped clusters of fuzzy flower heads, and the latter by its dome-shaped cluster of dull pink flowers and its foliage that smells like vanilla when crushed. Folklore says that an Indian named Joe Pye used the plants to cure fevers. Sneezeweed, a member of the sunflower family with yellow daisylike flower heads whose petals droop backward, so-called because its leaves were used in making snuff, coexists with five different species of rare goldenrods. All these—and many more—strut their stuff against a sea of tall prairie grass pressing in from the adjacent open stretches. Two six-foot-tall aristocrats among Midwestern grasses dominate: big bluestem, whose fingerlike seed heads resemble a turkey's foot, and the shiny goldenbrown plumes of Indian grass.

It is a warm and friendly scene, luxuriating in botanical riches. Long-gone species of fauna, their habitat given back to them, are responding to the attraction. Intriguingly named butterflies like the great-spangled fritillary and the banded, striped, and Edwards's hairstreaks have reappeared. Birds such as the rose-breasted grosbeak, crested flycatcher, and peewee flit through the grove. The Cooper's hawk has returned. On one landmark day in 1989, a pair of bluebirds, their kind long absent from the area, showed up.

Vestal Grove is a work in progress, its unfolding controlled by nature's hazily understood laws of ecosystem assembly. But if the North Branch restorationists succeed, they will have restarted a natural process that enables as many species as possible not to die out but to survive, evolve, and adjust to a surrounding landscape drastically altered and fragmented by humans. As the restored ecosystem emerges, it will offer clues to what its presettlement incarnation looked like, what species of plants and animals composed it, and how it functioned. No one will ever be entirely sure. An air of expectation surrounds the site and animates the work nevertheless.

"Everything you see under these oaks is from seeds that we held in our hands," Steve Packard said as he surveyed Vestal Grove one day in 1991.

Any gardener knows how that feels. But for those who work at Vestal Grove, the experience is incalculably deeper because it ties them directly and intimately to titanic events that are of the earth's essence.

Twenty thousand years ago, just before the dawn of the relatively fleeting ecological era in which we live, the places that would one day become Vestal Grove and its sister restoration sites slept under a sheet of ice perhaps half a mile thick. Over the previous 2.5 million years, massive glaciers had repeatedly expanded their frontiers into and beyond what would become known, eons in the future, as northern Illinois. From time to time they would retreat poleward, and the northern climes would be warm again for brief intervals of 10,000 years or so before the ice began to build up and creep southward once more. These buildups began, according to prevailing theory, when periodic changes in the earth's orbit and tilt conspired with a regular wobble in its rotation to alter the angle at which the sun's rays struck the planet, allowing less sunlight to fall on the northernmost latitudes in summer. Summer after summer, millennium after millennium, the weakened sunshine failed to melt all the snow that fell in winter. The snows compacted under their own weight into ice that expanded and moved like a gigantic amoeba, undulating, twisting, plastic, overrunning everything in its path, covering most of North America, its leading edge advancing fast enough at times to bury whole forests alive.

In the latest of these surges, a river of ice flowed down the basin of what future inhabitants of the region would call Lake Michigan, filling the basin and covering the land where Chicago would some day rise. The ice stayed for 10 millennia, from about 24,000 to about 14,000 years ago. But even as this period of maximum glaciation settled in, the ever-changing tilt and wobbling rotation of the planet were entering another phase of their perpetual dance. More sunlight began to flood the far north. After perhaps

2,000 years of imperceptibly intensifying solar radiation, summers there started to get warmer. And slowly, the ice began to melt and retreat.

It was an uneven retreat. The ice fell back and then stopped, fell back and stopped, occasionally readvancing, again and again, as the earth's unfathomably complex climate system readjusted itself in fits and starts to the stimulus of the warming sun. All the while the ice sheet shrank, it remained dynamic. Ice continued to flow outward from huge central domes farther north, just as a river still flows when drought shrinks its volume. It ground and scoured the land, smoothing out hills and filling in valleys, preparing the flatland on which prairies and savannas would flower.

The flow of the ice also carried rocks, boulders, and soil toward its edges, where they were deposited on bare ground. Many rocks in and under the ice were ground into a fine flour that became the basis of the alkaline soil in which the ecosystem of the prairies and savannas would ultimately take root. Where the retreating ice front halted temporarily for a century or two, rocky, granular debris carried forward by the flowing ice built up into low hills, called moraines. Chunks of ice broke off from the glacier here and there and were buried in the moraines. The chunks melted as the climate warmed, and surface depressions formed where they had been. These eventually became bogs.

Vast quantities of water filled the increasingly exposed Lake Michigan basin as the ice melted, overflowing the modern-day shoreline and flooding the area where Chicago now stands. Near this expanded lakeshore, starting about 14,000 years ago, the retreating ice halted several times to form a series of five moraines. They materialized as small peninsulas extending southeastward like fingers into the expanding lake.

One of the fingers, the third in a series as one travels west from the present-day Lake Michigan shoreline, has been high and dry ever since. Modern scientists call it the Deerfield Moraine.

Vestal Grove adorns it today.

The melting icewater cut broad channels on each side of the moraine. What modern humans call the East and Middle Forks of the Chicago River's north branch would ultimately flow in these channels.

Gradually the lake began to shrink back toward its present confines. Among the earliest parts of the ancient lake bottom to be uncovered and become permanently dry was a stretch along the future North Branch of the Chicago River where, 11,000 years later, most of Vestal Grove's sister tracts in the North Branch Prairie Project would be situated.

As the glacier retreated, streams of cold air poured down its slopes, creating powerful gales across the newly bared land. The winds kicked up great clouds of dust, creating dust storms that may have been far worse than any today and rearranging the fine grains in dunes and thick layers that contributed to the bed of the ecosystem that was about to evolve. A few miles to the south, hairy mastodons roamed open, parklike forests of spruce dotted by marshes. Wind-borne seeds from this cold-weather ecosystem rapidly colonized ground left naked by the retreating ice. About the time the Deerfield Moraine was being formed, an open grassland with scattered spruce materialized in northern Illinois. It evolved into spruce forest within the geological eyeblink of perhaps two centuries. The cold-adapted spruce died off as the climate warmed, to be replaced by pine, birch, ash, and fir, migrating up from the southern refuges to which they had retreated in the ice time. Between 10,000 and 11,000 years ago, the area through which the North Branch would later flow looked much as the northern Great Lakes area looks today: a mixture of cool-climate deciduous trees with some evergreens thrown in.

The warmth reached its zenith some 8,000 or 9,000 years ago. With periodic spikes above and below the long-term trend, the world has gradually been cooling off since that long-ago peak, and scientists believe that the warm interval in which we live is surely only another relatively brief interlude between glaciations. This interlude is likely to end within another 2,000 or 3,000 years, scientists say, even if humans' burning of heat-trapping fossil fuels causes the global climate to warm significantly more than it otherwise would in the centuries immediately ahead.

The most recent peak of warmth in Northern Illinois nine millennia ago ushered in, at last, the era of the oaks. Analysis of fossil pollen grains makes it clear that they dominated the scene by about 8,000 years ago. The area around Vestal Grove might have remained a forest, as it did farther east and north, had the climate remained moist.

But it didn't, and one must look westward for the cause. That is the direction from which Pacific moisture, borne by winds off the ocean, spreads across the continent. Two great barriers, the Sierra Nevada and the Rocky Mountains, force the moisture-laden Pacific winds to rise to cooler heights, where the water condenses and falls as precipitation. Relatively little is left for the flatlands to the east. Forests, which require much moisture, have a hard time in this "rain shadow" cast by the mountains. But certain grasses and wildflowers thrive in drier conditions. The result is a "prairie peninsula" jutting eastward, stretching from the mountains to the middle of the continent.

The peninsula is bounded on the south by moist air swirling up from the Gulf of Mexico. It is bounded on the north by a jet stream that sweeps down out of Alaska and the Yukon and turns eastward. Today these are called Alberta Clippers, and the winter snows and rains they drop are responsible for replenishing the water table of the northern prairies. When the great ice sheet was in place, it diverted the Alberta Clippers southward, and the prairies with them. But with the removal of the ice, the path of the clippers moved northward once again.

As it happens, their general path crosses northern Illinois today. The big Alberta Clipper jet sails more or less directly over the North Branch Prairie Project sites. This means they lie on the boundary between the prairies to the south and the deciduous woodlands to the north. In that transition zone, the oak forest and the grassland engaged in a continual tug of war over the centuries as the climate oscillated between warmings and coolings of lesser duration and magnitude. Given one or two cooler, wetter decades, the oaks flourished and advanced. During warmer and drier intervals, the grasslands drove them back. Seldom was the line crisp and straight. The grassland-forest frontier was more like a crazy quilt, with patches and peninsulas and groves of trees, some of them densely spaced and some more open, intermixing with the treeless prairie.

In this ever-shifting vegetational pattern, trees, grasses, and wildflowers arranged themselves in associated communities according to a number of factors, including topography, soil, drainage, and light. The depressions caused by melting ice blocks became little dabs of wetland, called prairie potholes. The oaks were especially partial to moraines, as were the grasses and wildflowers that assembled under and around them. On the western slopes of moraines and other rises, the afternoon sun bore down more strongly than on the eastern slopes, which tended to be in shade. Only a smidgen of sunlight reached the shaded ground under the oaks compared with the nearby open prairies. This guaranteed a mixture of grasses and flowers different from that on the prairie. And given the infinitely variable combinations of growing conditions, each spot was different, vegetationally speaking, from every other spot.

Fires from time to time scrubbed the prairies and the savannas clean of invading weeds and trees. Without fire, in fact, neither the oaks nor the prairie and savanna grasses and wildflowers would have flourished. They would have been crowded out by brush like hawthorn and trees like ash and maple. Fire destroyed these competitors. But the thick carpet of tall grasses and wildflowers sent its roots deep into the ground. Most of a prairie or savanna plant lives underground, in fact, and after a fire, top growth springs up again, as thick and beautiful as ever. Oaks were also hardy in the face of fire. The fire would burn off their tops, but they would resprout like grasses from the surviving stumps. When the interval between fires was long enough, some oak trunks got big enough, and their bark grew thick enough, to let them survive to majestic proportions. Each bur oak, so named because the caps of its acorns are rough-fringed, commanded its own territory, holding its neighbors at arm's length, as its root system sent tendrils as deep as the tree was tall and as far outward as the longest branches reached. And there the big oaks reigned, each one living not just for decades but for three or four centuries.

Each patch of habitat within this grand mosaic supported its own characteristic, interdependent community of birds, insects, small mammals, reptiles, and microorganisms. And through each, in different climatic and ecological phases, passed a succession of bigger animals. Immediately in the vegetational wake of the retreating ice, mastodons roamed openings in the spruce parkland, browsing among the evergreen branches. There may have been woolly mammoths in a narrow belt of tundra immediately next to the ice. Scientists can't be sure on the basis of fossil finds, but the general pattern of the postglacial age leads them to believe that the area was also inhabited by caribou, musk oxen, dire wolves (larger versions of today's timber wolf), bison much bigger than today's, beavers as large as a modern black bear, the stag-moose (a sort of cross between a moose and an elk), the swift, savage short-faced bear, and the fearsome saber-toothed cat. All of these megafauna, as paleontologists call them, had disappeared by about ten thousand years ago. Scientists disagree on the cause of the mass extinction. Some say it was climatic and environmental factors, while others insist that the giant creatures were hunted to oblivion.

As the ancient megafauna disappeared, the oak savannas became home to an unusual combination of animals. Though not as numerous as farther west, modern bison migrated back and forth across Illinois, contributing to the ecosystem's constantly changing physiognomy by cropping back much of the grass and leaving well-worn trails and wallows across the prairie. Some of them visited the oak groves and savannas north of Chicago. Much more abundant there were white-tailed deer, a forest animal that also frequented the savannas, as did elk, wolves, coyotes, beavers, cougars, and bobcats.

But of all the mammal species found on the virgin prairie and savanna, none was more important from an ecological standpoint than Homo sapiens.

Humans arrived in northeastern Illinois close behind the retreating ice. It is uncertain just when their ancestors first fanned out into North America after crossing from Siberia on a broad land bridge uncovered when the ice locked up so much water that sea levels fell and gave them a clear passage from Asia. But by 11,000 years ago, people were probably living in northeastern Illinois. These nomads probably hunted caribou and mastodons as well as smaller animals like arctic hares. A favorite hunting strategy appears to have been to drive a mastodon into the muck of one of the many pothole swamps that dotted the landscape, then kill the mired animal.

By 10,000 years ago, as the spruce-and-tundra ecosystem was succeeded by deciduous trees and grassland, and as the mastodon was fading from the scene and the caribou and arctic hare were replaced by white-tailed deer, rabbits, and other species thoroughly familiar today, the hunting of deer had become the focus of human subsistence. It would remain so for the next 9 or 10 millennia.

The hunters themselves became increasingly settled, gathering in semipermanent base camps along rivers and establishing temporary outlying camps for use during hunting forays. It was an extremely durable style of life, lasting for some 8,000 years. Village society became increasingly developed and sophisticated. By the dawn of the Christian era in the far-off Mediterranean, the inhabitants of northern Illinois, southern Wisconsin, and northeastern Iowa were constructing spectacular "effigy mounds," some but not all used for burial, in geometric shapes and forms that suggested birds, lizards, bears, turtles, cougars, and sometimes humans. And as the present millennium dawned, the Indians of northern Illinois were living well. The growing of corn, squash, and gourds on family plots, coupled with the gathering of wild plants, added a new dietary dimension to the staple of venison, small game, and fish. A two-hundred-year dry period between about six hundred and eight hundred years ago enabled the prairies to win over the woodlands for a time, and bison became more numerous than before. With bison, deer, agriculture, and wild vegetables as food sources, the Indians who lived around Vestal Grove had the best of all possible North American worlds in the years when, unknown to them, the European explorers were beginning to stir.

A number of Indian tribes lived in the Chicago area at one time or another, but the most important, on the eve of the Europeans' arrival, were the Potawatomis. They combined the features of two classic Indian cultures, those of the plains and the eastern woodlands. Natural rhythms regulated the life of the Potawatomis. In warm weather they would live in bark-covered rectangular houses arranged in villages scattered throughout the Chicago area. Some of these villages undoubtedly were on the savannas because they were attractive places with open groves and fertile soil and good drainage. It is not known whether a village ever existed at Vestal Grove, even though it is near a stream, but the Potawatomis and their ancestors probably foraged for game and acorns there, at the least.

Potawatomi women would plant corn, beans, squash, and other vegetables in early summer, and once the crops were in the ground the villagers would move out to temporary camps, living in small, domelike wigwams. From these bases they would catch fish and hunt deer, bison, elk, and small game. They dried what meat they did not eat for use in the winter.

Come late summer, they would return to the permanent villages to harvest their crops and to gather the wide variety of nuts and fruits that gave balance and variety to their diet. Once all the crops had been harvested and cached away, the villagers would disperse again and go to winter hunting grounds. This was probably a favorite time for bison, but the villagers also continued to hunt deer. They would go back to the main villages again in late February or early March in time for the spring run of maple sap, maple sugar being not only an important condiment but also a substance used in rituals.

The Potawatomis, like their forebears in earlier millennia, affected the ecosystems in which they lived in numerous ways. They tilled the soil. Like other predators, they helped keep the population of deer and other prey species in check. But more than anything else, they were agents of the cleansing fire of the prairie and the savanna. The very name Potawatomi, in the Algonquian tongue, means "Keepers of the Fire," or "Fire Nation." They got the name because they were entrusted with perpetuating the council fire after the Chippewas, Ottawas, and Potawatomis, originally one tribe, split into three before the seventeenth century. But it could just as well describe their powerful ecological role.

The Potawatomis and their ancestors in many tribes probably fired the prairies and the savannas for a variety of reasons. Wildfires are a natural occurrence on the prairie, and once one starts it can be unstoppable. By firing the area around a village in advance, Indians provided a sanctuary for themselves. Firing the savannas, oak groves, and adjacent forests also made movement easier and more comfortable, aided in hunting, and enabled villagers to see the approach of enemies more readily. Indians, as a matter of fact, employed burning routinely from the Atlantic to the Rockies, and in this way exercised a major influence on the shape of nature.

Every autumn, after the grass had died and provided a trove of dry fuel, prairie Indians would torch it. In the millennia after humans first showed up in the region, the entire ecosystem coevolved with humans and their fire. Plants that thrived in fire, like big bluestem grass, survived the culling-by-fire and became dominant. Others disappeared. Farther west on the prairie, where it was drier, lightning may have been the main cause of prairie fires. But in the wetter east, humans were probably the main source of the burning that in large measure determined the composition of the prairie and savanna ecosystems.

While their impact on the shape of the system was formidable in some ways, humans at this stage of North American history were essentially an integral component of the natural order; just one element in a continuous process of natural disturbance and flux that keeps nature from ever settling into a static balance.

What this produced in the savanna belt that stretched across the northern edge of the Prairie Peninsula on the eve of the Europeans' arrival was an extraordinarily rich ecosystem whose grasses, sometimes tall enough to hide a man on horseback, took away the breath of the first settlers to gaze on them. Punctuating the open stretches were the sparsely scattered oaks of the open savanna and the cozier bur-oak groves, with their thick carpets of flowers, that reminded some early travelers of orchards and parks.

All—trees, grass, flowers, humans, and other animals—were part of an ecological whole, the end product of an assembly process that took some 15 millennia and made use of living materials that had previously evolved over millions of years.

Europe discovered the prairies and savannas of the Chicago area in 1673, when Père Jacques Marquette and Louis Joliet traveled through on their way back to the Great Lakes after exploring the Mississippi River drainage. Before long, French voyageurs and fur traders were moving confidently through the territory, winning the Potawatomis as allies in commerce. The Indians enthusiastically trapped beaver and other fur-bearing animals for the French in exchange for cloth, metal pots, firearms, powder, and shot. The French alliance and the firearms empowered the Potawatomis as never before, enabling them for the first time to stand up in organized fashion to the fierce Iroquois, who had once pushed them out of lands farther east.

It was the French who named the grasslands "prairies," and they who established the first European outpost along the Chicago River. The young United States Government built Fort Dearborn there in 1803. All its American inhabitants were killed or driven off by the Potawatomis, then allies of the British, at the outset of the War of 1812. The Army rebuilt the fort after the war, and it quickly became the focal point of a revitalized fur trade and of a small village inhabited by French and Potawatomis. Outside this American-French island, Potawatomi life went on much as it always had, and the prairie-savanna ecosystem remained essentially intact.

Both the cozy life of the fur traders and Indians and the integrity of the ecosystem were shattered with shocking suddenness. As early as 1804, the land hunger and expansionist pressures of a westering European-American population had resulted in a treaty in which other Indians—the Sacs, Foxes, and Kickapoos—ceded their lands in western Illinois to the United States Government. The government forthwith began selling the lands to settlers. Like the Potawatomis, these other tribes were accustomed to moving across the landscape at will in search of game. The bargain rankled, and in 1832, a band of Indians under the Sac chief Black Hawk tried to take back what had been ceded. Black Hawk, asserting a deeply ingrained Indian ethic, insisted that land could not be sold but belonged to all. The Army moved against him—Colonel Zachary Taylor, Captain Abraham Lincoln, and Lieutenant Jefferson Davis were part of the force—and the Indians were defeated.

Very little of the fighting took place in the Chicago area, but the campaign nevertheless was the beginning of the end for the Potawatomis, their way of life, and the ecosystem on which they depended. Soldiers who had taken part in the campaign returned to their homes with enthusiastic accounts of the richness of the prairie lands. Within a year of Black Hawk's defeat, a wave of farmers broke over the Chicago area. Almost immediately, the Potawatomis signed away their lands in the vicinity, and within two or three years they, too, had been forced by the government to move west of the Mississippi. Chicago's population had doubled by the spring of 1833. New streets were laid out. A real-estate bubble grew and burst. Yankee settlers from the East set off a land rush. Some of them settled in the prairie-and-savanna mosaic along the North

Branch, and by the 1840s they were joined by a new wave of immigrant farmers, this one from Germany.

Ecologically speaking, the arrival of the settlers was almost as cataclysmic as the arrival of the glaciers had been many millennia earlier. They plowed under the prairie grasses, cut down many of the oaks, and converted much of what was left to pasture. They "mined" some of the land, scraping off its topsoil for use elsewhere. They turned cattle loose to graze, with devastating results. And they suppressed fire.

In 1839, before any timber cutting, land clearance, plowing, livestock grazing, or introduction of exotic species took place, the federal government surveyed the natural features of what would later come to be called Somme Prairie Grove, including Vestal Grove, and Somme Woods (a forested area adjoining Somme Prairie Grove to the east). The survey survives today—ecological gold—and the picture it paints is that of the prairie-savanna-forest mosaic in almost perfect microcosm, a snapshot of the forest-prairie tension zone as it existed when white people arrived on the scene. To the east of what is now Waukegan Road, but was then a trail made by Indians, rose a forest dominated by oak and hickory. The trunks of the trees forming the forest canopy averaged fourteen to sixteen inches in diameter, but diameters of two feet or more were common. The timber was scattered in places, with openings and gaps in the canopy where prairie plants grew. Today this is the area called Somme Woods, and it remains forested much as it was then.

As one moved west across the Indian trail, into the area called Somme Prairie Grove where the North Branch restoration project operates today, the forest gave way to a more open landscape. Scattered trees created an open savanna in some stretches; in others, relatively dense groves of oaks punctuated the prairie to produce a more closed savanna—not quite forest, but a long way from prairie.

The 1839 survey stopped frustratingly short of any description or inventory of the plants that grew on the prairie or under the savanna trees, or of the fauna that attached itself to the vegetation. There was no science of ecology then, no driving need to record the details of what would eventually come to be called an ecosystem.

Three years after the survey, a man named John Kinsey Clark—Indian Clark, he was called, because he had married an Indian—became the first white man to buy a chunk of the Somme site. A mail carrier on the Chicago-to-Milwaukee route and a handyman, Indian Clark did little to the site except hunt deer on it. He sold it in 1853 to John Frederick Werhane, who had just fled from civil and political strife in his native Germany. He moved onto the Somme site with his wife and four daughters and began to farm it. At about the same time, two other farms began operating on the site, each of the farms spanning it from east to west in three parallel strips cutting across woodland, prairie, and savanna.

Over the next three quarters of a century, farmers turned the site into a prime example of what was going on all across the prairies and savannas. They plowed its open parts to plant corn and other crops. They installed drainage tiles. They turned pigs loose to forage for acorns under the oaks and set dairy cows free to eat the grass. Louis Werhane, the original landowner's great-grandson, recalled at the age of eighty that his father and grandfather generally suppressed fire on the site, but that sometimes sparks from locomotives on the Milwaukee Road tracks running along the western boundary of the site would set blazes. Sometimes the farmers themselves would use fire to clear small patches, and they would clear brush with axes to create open spaces in the woods, which they rented out to picnickers.

Decades of overgrazing would by itself have been enough to destroy the intricately webbed ecosystem. Settlers used a grazing regime much like the one they had learned in Europe, in which cattle were allowed to eat everything right down to the ground. The tall grasses that are the hallmark of the prairie can survive periodic fires, but continual grazing is too much for them, and they die. One by one, depending on their hardiness, wildflowers disappear as well. First one component of the ecosystem vanishes, then another, until all that are left are plants cattle won't eat, like vervain, with its horrible taste, and strongly flavored mints and spiny thistles. In the final stage of overgrazed pasture, native brush like hawthorn invades the land. What does survive is European bluegrass, and farmers commonly sowed it on pastureland to provide food for their animals.

As ecologically destructive as grazing was, it also turned out to play a key role in future efforts to save the Somme site and all the other North Branch restoration sites. In the progressive era just before World War I, there surfaced a movement to set aside and preserve surviving remnants of the forest-savanna-prairie system. The movement was hatched by Dwight Perkins, a Chicago architect. Perkins was a member of an informal downtown Chicago group, called the Committee on the Universe, that discussed the future of Chicago over lunches at the City Club. Jane Addams, the social worker famous for her settlement houses, was a sometime member. The idea of preserving remaining parts of Chicago's forests, prairies, and savannas came out of the sessions. Perkins spearheaded the drive to create a system of forest preserves. The plan passed the state legislature in 1913, but a number of legal challenges—the last one formally instituted by Perkins himself to clear away any shadow—delayed the project until shortly after World War I, when the Cook County

Forest Preserve District came into being as the first of a series of such districts across the state.

Over the next few years, Perkins scoured the county looking for likely sites to acquire as preserves. He "personally tramped every piece of property for the first 30,000 acres," said his son, Lawrence B. Perkins, a retired Chicago architect. The forest preserves were "my dad's bridge, his tennis, his social life," said Lawrence Perkins. "It was his love, his baby, and his reward." Without him, Vestal Grove and tens of thousands more acres would not have been preserved before it was too late.

At that time, most of the land outside the city itself was taken up as fertile truck farms. What open land existed was mostly pasture; so pasture, along with the remaining wooded areas, became the prime acquisition target. Much of the acquisition took place in the 1920s. In 1926 or 1927, the Werhanes and their neighbors sold land to the Forest Preserve District to create the Somme preserve.

For years thereafter, the district rented much of the land, including some at Somme, back to farmers, who tilled it and grazed cows on it from time to time. The last time Somme's open areas were farmed was 1936 through 1938, when the Werhanes leased part of the land back from the Forest Preserve District. After that, the district's managers began planting trees there as part of the Works Progress Administration's Depression-era employment programs. Most of the seedlings died the first year, Louis Werhane remembered, and rabbits ate the rest.

But at Somme and elsewhere, trees introduced by the Forest Preserve District eventually did take hold. Birch, European poplar, ash, black locust, oak, maple—all were planted successfully as part of a program to restore and restock the preserves. Many of these trees were not native to the area. Others were, but with natural fires suppressed, they flourished in stretches of savanna where they never could have hoped to survive in presettlement days. Native species like dogwood and hawthorn, no longer deterred by fire, also invaded the sites. So did exotic species like Tartarian honeysuckle and especially the number one scourge, ecologically, of the North Branch preserve sites: European buckthorn. This coarse shrub, much taller than a man, thick with thorns and so dense that a person can scarcely walk through it, was introduced to the United States as an ornamental hedge. Birds ate its fruit and distributed its seeds far and wide. It became a pestilential weed, easily and rapidly colonizing many disturbed areas, throwing up impenetrable walls of brush and monopolizing the land where prairie and savanna had once bloomed. Native plants had no chance in the face of this invasion.

Where buckthorn, hawthorn, foreign honeysuckle, dogwood, and introduced trees did not take over, the Forest Preserve District routinely mowed open areas that once would have been a thick carpet of prairie and savanna grasses and flowers. They did it partly to provide open spaces where people could stroll, picnic, and relax, partly to keep the brush from spreading, and partly to prevent what some people thought of as an eyesore. Natural savannas and prairies, for all their richness, can seem ragged and disorderly to people who are used to suburban lawns.

After World War II, suburbia closed in on the North Branch with a vengeance, making islands of the Forest Preserve sites. And there, with many of the oaks that had once been the spine of the ecosystem intact but the rest of the once-exquisite natural community degraded to the vanishing point, its glory long gone and the ecological secrets of its past hidden from modern eyes, Vestal Grove and its sister sites languished.

Waiting.

2

GRASSROOTS RESTORATION: BEGINNINGS

The antiwar movement was over. Richard Nixon was out of office. The army of young protesters who had worked to end the Vietnam horror and remake American society had disbanded with a collective political and emotional hangover. Some of its members had simply burned out. Others, already recovering, were drifting into conventional politics. Still others, their idealism dissipating in the toils of proto-yuppiehood, found themselves in the first stages of the Big Chill.

Steve Packard was rediscovering a kinship with nature that began in boyhood. Forced from the forefront of consciousness by the later turmoil of youth and rebellion, the bond would nevertheless resurface from time to time over the years, like an old friendship, then recede again.

In 1952, when he was a fourth-grader, a whole new universe of woods and fields and streams, of trees and plants and birds and animals, had opened up to young Steve when his family moved from the industrial city of Worcester, Massachusetts, to the bucolic adjoining town of Shrewsbury. Steve, the oldest of seven children, got top scores on the standardized Iowa reading tests, and like many other 10-year-olds he developed an all-consuming, single-minded interest. His was the natural world. His fourth-grade teacher set up a contest between the boys and the girls to see who could find, identify, and collect the most species of wildflowers. Except for Steve, the boys collected very few. They won.

As a shy boy and a new kid in town, Steve had trouble making new friends and "just latched onto this teacher's ideas." She was Mrs. Gudren Chamberlain, and she lived out in the woods with her husband, Owen, who kept himself informed on what was going on in the world, talked about it a lot, espoused Quaker values though not a Quaker himself, was very proud that his forebears had been stationmasters on the underground railroad—and loved nature's wild things. Steve spent many formative hours at the Chamberlains'. Mrs. Chamberlain was "very instrumental in getting him interested in nature, but I think Mr. Chamberlain was a very free thinker," says Mae Packard, Steve's mother. "I'm not entirely sure he was a good influence."

As a sixth-grader, Steve asked his father, a successful self-made businessman who had grown up in the Worcester slums, if he could establish a nature corner in the back section of their lot, where he would create a bird sanctuary by putting up feeders and planting some trees, and his father said yes. The eleven-year-old was particularly taken by the majesty of hemlocks, whose drooping branches, graceful lines, and delicate evergreen foliage suggested great antiquity. Could he dig up and transplant some young hemlocks he had spied on one of the solitary nature walks he had gotten in the habit of taking? Yes, he was told again, provided he found out who owned the land and asked permission. He went to the town hall, where a somewhat amused clerk helped him track down the owner, and then to the owner, who gruffly gave permission. "I never thought you'd do that," his father said, or words to that effect. "You've earned some trees; I'll take you down to the nursery and we'll get some."

Steve protested stubbornly, arguing that only wild trees would do. His father gave in, and they dug up and transplanted some small wild hemlocks and white pines. But the trees looked scrawny, and the father insisted once again, over the son's furious objections, that they get some better-looking ones from the nursery. They did, "and when you looked at their white pine by my white pines," Steve would recall years later, "you knew which one was going to kick sand in the other's face. Mine were skinny little trees, and theirs looked like it was full of steroids and had been pumping iron for a month." Rabbits ate his hemlocks instantly. And sure enough, his pine trees "just sort of sat there," while the nursery pine, to his disgust, became the very model of a robust Christmas tree. But vindication was his in the end: The big nursery-grown pine contracted disease and became a deformed intensive-care case, while his little wild pines slowly acquired a robust majesty.

In junior high school, he spent his summers at camps organized around nature study and ecology. In high school, he displayed a flair for scientific investigation that would one day serve him handsomely in ways he could not possibly anticipate at the time. "Student's Project Amazes Doctors," said a Page One headline in Worcester's *Evening Gazette* for April 20, 1961. The story began:

> An 18-year-old boy scientist from Shrewsbury astounded doctors at the last meeting of Worcester Medical Society with his prizewinning paper on "Factors Effecting Cancer Immunity." He is Stephen G. Packard, a high-honor student and senior at Shrewsbury Junior Senior High School.

It went on to describe how young Steve—working with scientists at the Worcester Foundation for Experimental

Biology, where the first birth-control pill was developed and where Steve had a student scholarship—performed variations on an experiment in which cancerous fluid was injected into healthy animals to induce an immune reaction. "If my theory is correct," the teenager told the newspaper, "a vaccine or some other method would stimulate proliferation of an antibody-producing cell, and these antibody cells would kill cancer."

The article also noted that Steve was "not absorbed only with things scientific"; that he was a member of the school's state-champion debating team; that he was a six-footer "who skis and enjoys swimming and sailing at his family's summer home in Dennisport"; that the previous summer he had caught a 450-pound swordfish; that he wrote and read poetry, with T. S. Eliot, e. e. cummings, and William Wordsworth among his favorites; that he wrote articles and poetry for the school magazine and liked "satire of an explosive nature"; that he was a member of the National Honor Society and had received that year's Harvard Club Award as an outstanding boy. The newspaper quoted Steve as saying he "might enter science, business, or law" as a career.

What makes a nonconformist? Packard himself believes that the roots of his alienation lay partly in an early conviction that much of what the Methodist Church was teaching him "was as false as Santa Claus and the Easter Bunny," a conviction that in turn "threw up for grabs the whole ethical basis of society and purpose of life." About the same time, all his male friends "started to spit and swagger," a form of machismo that thrilled the girls. "I did not at all know how to compete with this, or handle it in any other way," he remembered later. "It seemed false, not fun. So I retreated all the more into books and walks in the wilds." Another factor may have been an inherent shyness that made it hard for him to click with other people after the early move to Shrewsbury and that made him socially ill at ease as a teenager. His intellectual bent also set him apart, and he found it difficult to join in standard teenage entertainments of the day. Though he "got a tremendous amount of attention" at home as an infant, there was less as the six other children came along, and he "felt pretty much cast adrift as a teenager." Many of the adults on his block seemed to him not to have time for children—"they seemed like an alien occupying force, and I remember thinking I wouldn't like to be like any of them." Their lives, he thought, "seemed pressured and grim; I did not look forward to adulthood one bit."

He went off to Harvard University in 1961, the first person from his family ever to go to college. There he became one of the millions of young people of his time who expressed a growing repulsion from mainstream culture and institutions and a disdain for American materialism. He was part of the 1963 civil-rights march on Washington, when Martin Luther King, Jr., gave his "I Have a Dream" speech, but he remembers being there "with a sense of disquiet; black people were saying, 'We want to have what white people have,'" and "I hated to think that black people might strive to be something as empty and false as what I saw white culture to be."

He began thinking of himself as an artist. It seemed a respectable career that would satisfy the expectations that others had for him while not compromising his values. He avoided studying art at Harvard, though, because he thought the college approach corrupted things and would turn him against the very pursuit in which he was interested. Leaving Harvard after two years because he hadn't the remotest interest in any career that it could prepare him for, he gravitated to New York. He first thought he might try to be a playwright, then connected with the underground film scene, which was coming to focus on the antiwar movement and other activist causes of the day.

Those were days of searching for self and for purpose. And all that year, he would turn to nature as a sort of comforting best friend, taking the subway to Jamaica Bay to walk around in the marshes and look at ibises and rails and black skimmers and other wetlands birds, or hiking in the Catskills.

Neglect of his health brought on an illness that sent him back to the security of Harvard after a year. He studied social psychology and anthropology and graduated in 1966, then resumed his search for identity in New York. He worked on television commercials as a film editor for a time—Jif peanut butter was one account—and tried unsuccessfully to promote commercials he had written that were designed to subvert values "that to me meant sexual repression, youth repression, passion-for-life-and-justice repression." Drifting, he met a young woman who had studied film at Northwestern University but could get only a receptionist's job at the film company where he worked. The allure of the wild surfaced once more, and the two decided they would run off together to Madagascar and "wear robes and have dust on our skin and see lemurs and smell the jungle," as he later put it.

The relationship fell apart, but not before she told him about a "newsreel collective" that made propaganda films for various activist groups—the early women's liberation movement, the Black Panthers, Catholic priests who poured blood on draft files, the community-control-of-schools movement in Brooklyn—any group that the filmmakers thought was doing something radical that would lead to fundamental change in society. Wherever the action was, the filmmakers were there with their cameras. That was in 1968, the summer of the Democratic National Convention when the Chicago police assaulted antiwar demonstrators in what investigators later called a police riot. Watching the riot and the convention on television transformed Packard's life, and he became an instantly radicalized conscript for what was known as "the movement." He signed up in the newsreel collective eagerly, not only to oppose the Vietnam War but also, he said later, for a broader purpose: to help transform society into something more like what Thomas Jefferson or Thoreau would favor. "I felt that the adults I knew led empty, dreary lives," Packard would write later. "Selfish, harried, preprogrammed, humorless, pompous, etc." In 1968, he was "looking for community, an opportunity to do good work. We thought our values were better and would gradually take over everything."

The collective sent him and three other of its members to Chicago in 1969. They made no films, but rather plunged directly into the politics of the antiwar movement. "I supported him in that entirely," says Mae Packard. "I felt he was right. He really put his life on the line in that situation." For the next five years, until the fall of Nixon, Packard recruited movement members and organized demonstrations and strikes, learning tactical and organizational skills as he went. His views of what worked and what didn't evolved considerably during that time. Never an advocate of revolution-by-the-gun, he came to believe that even nonviolent confrontation often was counterproductive. He was jolted when some community-college students from blue-collar backgrounds rebelled against confrontational tactics because they considered such tactics to be "antipeople." It was a shock to one who had seen the movement's overriding purpose as that of benefitting people. He also took to heart the pragmatic views of some visiting antiwar activists from Sweden, who argued that it was better and more effective to build a broad societal consensus on a single issue, even if many of the disparate kinds of people who shared the consensus parted company on other issues. By contrast, Packard says, everybody in the American movement "had to be pure and perfect about everything; that meant we were infinitesimal" in numbers and influence. It was a lesson that would serve him well in the future; from then on, he became a consensus-builder.

These evolving views were reflected in Packard's work for what was called the Indo-China Peace Campaign, founded by Tom Hayden, one of the New Left's top leaders. The campaign eschewed strident confrontation and demonstrations in favor of grassroots organizing. "The focus was sort of on organizing local constituencies and pressuring Congress to cut off funding for the war," says Diane Horwitz, a longtime friend of Packard's who was closely associated with him in the movement and is now a sociology teacher at a Chicago-area community college. Packard concentrated his efforts on blue-collar Middle America. Earlier, he had worked in a Gary, Indiana, steel mill both to try to recruit steelworkers to the cause and to relieve his pennilessness. He organized a group called "Cubs Fans for Peace" that attended Chicago Cubs games, handing out leaflets, recruiting adherents, and getting signatures on petitions. At one game the group sat with the outfield Bleacher Bums and unfurled a "Cubs Fans for Peace" banner. "It was received incredibly well," Horwitz remembers.

Packard "was intense, very intense in a low-key kind of way," she recalls. "He was very, very hardworking, kind of single-mindedly focused in terms of his work. He was constantly on the phone. He's kind of passionate about his ideas." Horwitz also remembers that Packard believed that ordinary people could, if encouraged, become experts of sorts on complex questions—in this case Vietnam policy—and that this could energize grassroots efforts. This belief would be put into practice in more highly developed form in later years.

As Packard's thinking evolved, the movement was withering. And when it vanished, much of Packard's identity vanished as well. Lean and poor, just over the watershed age of thirty, knocking about Chicago at loose ends, teaching a little, working in the special collections library at Northwestern University, trying to write a book about the sixties, Packard found himself in the mid-1970s with what he would later describe as "this empty hole in my life."

Once again—this time for good—nature filled the void. A former member of the film collective, a woman to whom Packard happened to be attracted, introduced him to a copy of the Roger Tory Peterson-Margaret McKenny field guide to North American wildflowers. In the book, Peterson, the world-famous naturalist, talked about how he would drive around the countryside, searching for plants to illustrate the work. Packard decided he would fill his empty days by learning the flowers of the Chicago area. "They entranced me with their sexiness and their delicacy," he would say later, "and when you start to learn them, you discover new things about the world, the ecosystem, the landscape." This was not consumerism, not materialism; this was "life, poking up its pretty little face everywhere."

He began planting native wildflowers on small vacant lots in his North-Side Chicago neighborhood of bungalows and small factories near Ashland and Diversey, a locale then in some need of sprucing up. The same friend who lent him the Peterson-McKenny book also introduced him to a thin, beautifully illustrated little volume, *The Prairie: Swell and Swale.* It contained an essay on the characteristics, nature, destruction, and preservation of prairies by Dr. Robert F. Betz, an ecologist at Northeastern Illinois University who was rapidly becoming one of the world's authorities on the tallgrass prairies of the Midwest and who had recently embarked on an ambitious prairie restoration project. Betz wrote:

> To see a virgin Illinois prairie in the spring of the year covered with golden Alexanders and pink shooting stars; or to view the midsummer prairies blanketed in grayish lead plants mingling with the wispy-awned porcupine grass; or, in autumn, to be-

hold the tall waving expanse of big bluestem grass bedecked with aster, goldenrods, and gentians, are all unforgettable sights.[1]

Entranced, Packard was soon reading all he could about the prairies and visiting remnant prairie sites owned by the Illinois Nature Preserves Commission to learn about them and marvel in their glory. Or their potential glory. Many were substantially degraded and in need of better management, and Packard would wade out into them and try to imagine what they looked like before the appearance of high-tension wires and highways and factories and, in one case, a nuclear power plant. He could picture Betz's brilliant grasses and flowers marching off to the horizon, with buffalo ambling over the hill. He felt a need to do something about the degradation. He also felt helpless and unqualified.

About this time he compromised his resolutely antimaterialistic values with two acquisitions: a camera, with which he avidly recorded his wildflower gardens and the wild prairie plants he was tracking down, and a bicycle, so that he could expand his explorations. The explorations took him northward along the Chicago River into suburbia, and on June 22, 1975, he stopped, got off the bike, and made a fateful discovery.

There, on land owned by the Cook County Forest Preserve District, in the condition to which 14,000 years of slow ecological evolution followed by nearly a century and a half of degradation by humans had brought it, he discovered what appeared to be a remnant of original Illinois prairie in an opening of a few acres surrounded by thickets of brush. It was called Bunker Hill Prairie. He did not know it at the time, but the land had once been given to an Indian leader named Sauganash by Americans grateful that he had stopped the massacre at Fort Dearborn in the War of 1812. But by consulting Betz's little book, he did learn that seven species of honest-to-god prairie plants were growing there, and he saw three bobolinks, genuine prairie dwellers. Altogether he discovered seven such prairie openings strung out along the North Branch of the Chicago River, and they all seemed in sorry shape. Some were mowed occasionally by the Forest Preserve District to make them more usable for people and to keep the weedy vegetation that had grown up in them from spreading into neighboring communities. Some of the open areas had deep, scarring tire tracks all through them. Some were dumping grounds for garbage. In one, cars had been abandoned, stripped, and burned from time to time. All were being taken over by brush, and Packard knew from Betz's essay that in the absence of fire, brush kills prairie ecosystems.

It was the same sort of thing he had seen at the Nature Preserve prairie sites, and Packard feared that all of the North Branch prairie remnants, with their distinct mixtures of species, would ultimately vanish if they weren't appreciated and respected for what they were. Maybe, he thought, the authorities would let someone like himself, with no credentials, help out on these minor sites.

So far, all of this was still a hobby with Packard. He had by this time decided to cast his lot as an environmentalist and was taken on at $95 a week as Chicago representative of the Illinois Environmental Council, a fledgling environmental lobbying group. Packard calls it "the first worthy job I ever had," though he had unloaded fruit at the piers in New York. He envisioned his new role in life as that of fighting pollution—"It seemed sort of mean, hard. I didn't want to do birds and bunnies, as it was called at the time." While he loved planting prairie flowers and exploring prairie remnants and angling to try to save them, the work seemed trivial, almost embarrassingly so, after the events he had been involved in before: massive demonstrations, police stakeouts of the demonstrators' headquarters, tear gas, all part of a movement aimed at preventing the death or maiming of thousands of people.

But a realization was growing: Here, right under people's noses in the Forest Preserve prairie remnants, was a small world that deserved saving, and maybe he could help do it. He was rapidly learning a lot about prairies, and at a certain juncture he said to himself, "Okay, Steve, there's a decision point here. You know politics. You know how to organize people. If you do this, you're very likely to be drawn into a commitment that will last a very long time and take over your life." He would not, he knew, take it on only to give it up anytime soon. The decision to go ahead, he felt, was potentially as serious as deciding to get married or have a child.

Packard does not remember exactly when he made the commitment. But once he did, the obstacles seemed enormous. His initial overtures to the Forest Preserve District had been less than an overwhelming success. He was assured that there was no problem and was thanked for his interest. Taking a leaf from his activist days, Packard decided that what the neglected prairie remnants needed was a constituency. He thought, "I can bring people up here and show them." And then one day it dawned on him that, no, if the prairies were to survive, they needed congregations, as he started calling them, of people who could interact with the land—who could develop an emotional bond with it. The way to achieve that, he thought, was to get people to come out and work on the land and help restore it to health.

So he called up the Forest Preserve District's superintendent of conservation at the time, Roland Eisenbeis, and asked, he recalled later, "if we could do something to make the sites a little nicer; sort of adopt these little prairies, pick up some trash, cut some brush where it's grown over and covered the prairie plants, and throw some seeds around. I'm not quite sure where the throwing of seeds came from, though I suppose it was from throwing them around my gardens." Eisenbeis said yes. "He had no idea how this was going to unfold," Packard says, "and I did."

The Forest Preserve District itself had been attempting, through sowing seeds, to restore some of its lands where farming had destroyed the prairie. But time and money were limited, and only a few small experiments involving the planting of grass seed from Nebraska were tried. Eisenbeis, who has since retired, was nevertheless cautious when Packard made his proposal. "In managing public lands," he recalled, "there's always this hesitancy to get involved with outside forces" for fear that volunteer enthusiasm cannot be sustained. "But Steve is of a different caliber," Eisenbeis says. "You had there a man who could spend . . . time at it, and he was very sincere, and I soon sensed it. We got along well, although there was a reluctance among some people higher up in our organization."

Using phone numbers of environmentally interested people he had been building up in his new job with the Illinois Environmental Council, Packard began to create a constituency. One night he went to a Sierra Club meeting at the Chicago Academy of Sciences and asked if he could have five minutes to show slides and announce that he, as a Sierra Club member, was going to start this restoration project and that it was going to start this weekend.

"They gave me two and a half minutes," he said. Steve Packard can be a very persuasive person, and it was enough. The North Branch Prairie Project was born.

From the start, Packard's goal was to restore the North Branch sites, insofar as possible, to the condition in which the first European settlers found them. To him, that meant allowing the ecosystems to resume the long, ancient evolutionary process of ecological assembly that had taken place since the last ice age, before it was interrupted by European settlement. "Nature," he would say later, "is something that's changed slowly over long periods of time so that the complex, highly evolved web of life is still there.

If you change it too quick, that's not nature anymore; it's destruction or cultivation."

The effort began modestly enough. The start of work is recorded in a handwritten journal that Packard kept, partly as a means of documenting the seriousness of the project for potential supporters. The first entry, dated August 6, 1977, reads: "Twelve Sierra Club members gather about 2,000 seeds of smooth phlox just west of Somme prairie." Most of the seed gatherers, Packard recalls, were "secretaries and men interested in the secretaries." One taught at the University of Chicago. None were with the project long—the volunteer membership has changed over the years even as it has expanded, although the first among a core of long-term stalwarts would soon join the effort.

Packard's research had revealed that the pink-flowered prairie phlox was one of many plants suited to the medium-moist soil of the three sites they had targeted for early action, and a wild stand of phlox was ripening at Somme prairie.

At this point, Somme Prairie Grove, as it came to be called, and what the North Branchers would eventually name Vestal Grove did not yet figure prominently in Packard's plans as a restoration site. The concept of "savanna" was one they had not yet dealt with.

It took the volunteers four hours to gather the 2,000 seeds, and a week later they planted them in three enclaves of degraded prairieland called Wayside Woods Prairie, Miami Woods Prairie, and Bunker Hill Prairie. Kneeling in dense vegetation, the volunteers planted the phlox seeds one by one, a quarter of an inch deep. But the phlox, unlike other prairie grasses and wildflowers they subsequently planted, would not come up for some time—it eventually took five years, in fact, for the blossoms to appear in a thrilling affirmation—and Packard knew he would not be able to hold the volunteers if no results could be seen soon. So in an effort to enlarge the

restoration area—to expand the beachhead, as it were—
they began cutting the brush that had choked out the
original vegetation. Packard would point out the genuine
surviving prairie plants, and together they would use
common garden loppers and handsaws to remove the
thickets of European buckthorn, hawthorn, and gray dogwood that were choking them out. It was tedious, back-
breaking, sweaty work, but at the end of the day you could
see results. In the morning, tall, thick brush would obscure parts of the prairie; by afternoon, the walls of brush
would be gone and bare ground would emerge, some of
it to be filled in naturally by prairie plants and some of it
requiring replanting.

The group gradually settled on Sunday morning for its
work sessions, and the three activities—brush removal,
seed gathering, and planting—became staples of the restoration effort. A number of other people in the Chicago
area besides Betz, both scientists and amateurs, had also
been experimenting with prairie restoration, and botanists
had a good handle on the prairie flora. Packard assidu-
ously picked the brains of all these people to find out
where to prospect for seeds and what techniques to use.
Later, as the North Branch group gained in experience
and new knowledge, information would flow the other
way, too.

All that late summer and fall of 1977, the North Branchers combed snippets of surviving prairie remnants, often
along railroad rights-of-way, stripping the plants of seeds
for their newly adopted restoration sites. They took seeds
of a given species from as many sites as possible to help
ensure that a full gene pool was represented, and they
limited the search to within fifteen miles so that the plants
would be truly indigenous. They worried that they would
be criticized for "stealing" the seeds, but it turned out
later that it was a good thing they had taken them: Many
of the donor sites vanished, victims of development. In
any case, the North Branchers persisted. Packard would

tell each seed gatherer what species to concentrate on, be it blazing-star or wild quinine or prairie dock or hoary puccoon or purple prairie clover or bastard toadflax or dropseed or any one of scores of other prairie plants that had been driven by agriculture and development to their scattered refuges. Then the crew would hike along, stripping the seeds and putting them in paper bags, often tied around the neck.

"Everyone loves to gather Indian grass," says Packard, "because it feels so good when it comes off. When it's ripe, you just pull your hand up the stalk, and you have this big handful of seeds, and you dump them in the bag. With rattlesnake master, on the other hand, the seed is spiny and tough. One way to do it is to wear gloves and wrench the heads off. Later on, we developed better methods. With rattlesnake master, for instance, we cut the heads off with garden snippers and throw them in a box with a screen on the bottom. Someone rubs the heads, and the seeds separate and run through the screen, and you catch them in another box."

For all seeds, it is critical to get them as they ripen. Most prairie plants ripen in the fall, but those that ripen earlier are often buried in a sea of taller grasses and flowers and are difficult to find and harvest. The North Branchers would eventually solve this problem by growing those plants for seed in their own gardens.

That first winter, Packard's living room was heaped with bags of "all these wonderful seeds," he says. "I just loved to look at them. I felt like Silas Marner." But that's a very poor way to store seeds, because houses are hot compared to the cold outdoors where the seeds would normally be in the winter, and to which they are adapted. So the North Branchers began to store them in unheated garages. To keep mice from eating the seeds, the restorationists would hang them in bags from the ceiling or put them in sealed plastic garbage cans. One member of the burgeoning group kept great numbers of mousetraps all over his garage. "When we came to remove the seed," Packard recalls, "everyone was being snapped constantly by this barrage of mousetraps."

In the wild, the cold and moisture of winter set off certain chemical changes in the seeds of plants that mature in the late summer or early fall, as most prairie plants do. These changes enable the seed embryos to "break dormancy" in the spring and resume their growth. Nursery operators had long since developed a technique of mimicking natural conditions by storing collected seeds in cold, damp conditions. The technique is called "stratification" because seeds originally were stored between layers of damp sand in boxes or pits. Today, a more common procedure calls for mixing the seeds with at least an equal volume of damp fine sand and storing the mixture in plastic bags in a refrigerator with the temperature set between 32 and 38 degrees Fahrenheit. This is what the North Branchers did.

Despite all this meticulous work, a number of experts were dubious that seeds could successfully be sown in the degraded turf of the North Branch sites. The only way to do it, some said, was to plow the ground and start fresh. Some said that the only way was to grow little plants in a greenhouse and then put them out one at a time. Plowing was out; no spare tractors could be found. So the North Branchers settled on their strategy of what might be called miniplanting, in which they would dig up their little bits of ground, remove the roots of weeds, and leave a patch of loose dirt about two inches deep. That first fall, using this method at Wayside Woods Prairie, they planted the seeds of the pale coneflower, rattlesnake master, wild quinine, Indian grass, switch grass, dropseed grass, Culver's root, blazing star, thimbleweed, New England aster, nodding wild rye, big bluestem grass, little bluestem grass, and prairie cinquefoil—classic prairie plants, all. They also began to experiment with the setting out of young plants. Over that first winter of 1977–78, they made arrangements to grow prairie plants in local conservatory and university greenhouses. And Packard did his own experimenting, growing seeds in petri dishes to see if they would really germinate. Some did, others did not.

The restorationists also developed a technique of transplanting what they called "rootlings." Most prairie plants, because they are perennials whose tops die and are destroyed by fire, invest an inordinate amount in their roots. A blazing star, for instance, might produce one little grasslike leaf in its first year while putting the rest of its energy into a root that might be a foot or more long. In the second year, a full-sized plant develops. The North Branchers found it possible to plant seeds in a garden, water them, tend them, and weed them, and in the space of a square yard raise a thousand baby plants. Then the roots could be dug up and transplanted with little or none of the trauma that comes with transplanting a fully grown plant. A year later, it is too late because the roots have gone too deep. The way they transplanted the rootlings was to use a common gardener's bulb planter, a tin-can-like tube on the end of a handle that removes a coring of dirt from the ground. They sliced the dirt coring in half lengthwise, laid the rootling on one half, closed it up like a sandwich, and stuck the coring back in the ground.

In a handwritten New Year's card that winter of 1977–78, Packard was able to report to his small band of workers and supporters that, among other things, 88 prairie species had been identified at the restoration sites, that 56 volunteers had spent a total of 341 hours gathering literally millions of seeds from more than 50 species of prairie plants in 1977, that the next year's planting had started, and that the Forest Preserve District had assured him that the prairies would no longer be mowed during the growing season.

Mowing, if allowed to continue, would frustrate the North Branchers' efforts. It wasn't just that the work itself would be set back. Volunteers might become discouraged and drop out, threatening the entire enterprise before it had built up enough momentum. One day in the early summer of 1978, Packard arrived at Miami Woods Prairie, which had been shaping up as a major experimental plot for the North Branchers' efforts, to find that it had indeed been mowed despite the official assurances. "It took a while to get the word out," Eisenbeis later explained, and there may have been some resistance: "Someone comes in and says don't mow here anymore, and here's a man who maybe has been working there for fifteen or twenty years, and this division [of the Forest Preserve system] is his little fiefdom. And particularly if some guy is coming in from the outside and telling him what he shouldn't be doing, it raises hackles."

Packard had by this time developed a strong emotional attachment to this reemerging ecosystem, and the mowing came as a shock. At the same time, with a great sense of exhilaration, he realized that the Forest Preserve District had handed him the solution as well as the problem. Working the telephone, he rallied all the volunteers and supporters—by this time he had enlisted the support of a number of groups, including garden clubs and neighborhood improvement associations, not to mention the director of the Academy of Sciences—and they made themselves heard and felt. One outraged protest reached a local ward committeeman, a person not lightly ignored in Chicago politics. He called up the Forest Preserve District to ask what was going on. Why were his constituents so unhappy? The result, Packard said later, was that "these sites were then secured; no one wanted to mess with them again."

But now that so much attention had been called to the North Branch project, officials of the Forest Preserve District seemed to be getting nervous. "They apparently thought we would do a little work and go away," Packard says today. But now "it was sort of getting too big too fast, and they wanted to do the right thing." That July, Forest Preserve officials invited him to join them on a tour of the sites with the intention of deciding, now that the restoration effort was picking up steam, whether it was really a good idea to go ahead. "I questioned whether the sites were worth the effort," Eisenbeis says, "so we went out to look at them to satisfy our own mind. We still weren't sure we were dealing with people who had a true sense of a prairie."

Packard and the officials, including Eisenbeis, had already arrived when a car drove up, and, in Packard's memory, "this guy with a bushy beard gets out and starts walking over, a little ominous looking." "We invited Dr. Betz to come along," one of the officials said, to Packard's surprise and shock.

Betz. The very ecologist whose pioneering work on prairies and prairie restoration had inspired Packard and whose insights had guided him. Soon Betz would become a mentor to Packard, and their relationship would flower into one of mutual respect and cross-fertilization of ideas. But at the time, although Packard had talked with Betz on the phone and sent him the New Year's card, the two had never met. Packard didn't know whether Betz was friend or foe that day, and he thought: "Goddamn it, I see what they're doing. They're going to ask him whether these are prairies or not." Packard knew enough to realize that the Forest Preserve sites were still pretty dismal versions of prairies, and that in their present state their very identity as prairie could be challenged. The preponderance of prairie vegetation is tall grass, and there was none at the North Branch sites. If Betz said no, it might mean that the venture would end right there, and Packard's heart sank. Eisenbeis says he invited Betz "because I thought maybe I was being too choosy; so you bring in an arbiter."

It was a beautiful day. At Bunker Hill Prairie, blazing star was blooming—big, tall, purple spikes, and a lot of them. In the middle of this luminous midsummer display, the Forest Preserve officials kept asking Betz, "Is this a prairie? Is this a prairie?" He didn't answer for some time, while Packard held his breath. "He has this sort of Old Testament prophet way about him," says Packard, "and you sort of know when he's ready to make a proclamation. He turned to them and said, 'These are incipient prairies.'" He even chimed in with suggestions on how to manage the sites most effectively.

Betz's imprimatur was critical; it gave the North Branchers a credibility they had never had up to that point. And largely on the basis of his say-so, the Forest Preserve officials decided that the North Branch sites were to be managed as prairies and gave the restorationists formal permission to sow seeds and clear brush and trees. These included ashes, dogwoods, cottonwoods, and hawthorns that, although they were native American species, did not belong on a prairie and would never be there if fire were allowed to have its natural way.

So the North Branchers proceeded, concentrating heavily on Wayside Woods and Miami Woods prairies. By now, a nucleus of more or less permanent volunteers with a long-term commitment was beginning to coalesce. Among the earliest was Larry Hodak, then a twenty-six-year-old architect not long out of the University of Illinois, who had accompanied Packard on the critical tour of the sites with Betz. Hodak and his wife-to-be, Chris Olsen, a year younger and the holder of an M.B.A. from the University of Illinois at Chicago, had long been drawn to prairies as an aspect of the Illinois landscape they loved, and Larry had even helped gather seed for an early prairie restoration project carried out by Betz. "The real hook was that so much of Illinois was [once] prairie, and there was so little left," Larry said later. "We were just kind of seeking it out because it really seemed like it was all going, that there wouldn't be anything left."

Packard, in a constant search for support and volunteers, by this time was making the local lecture circuit and showing slides, and Larry and Chris showed up for one of his presentations at the Chicago Academy of Sciences. "There is one thing I distinctly remember about that lecture," Chris Hodak recalls. "Steve showed pictures of, I think, a Michigan lily, close-up, and referred to it as being sexy. It changed the whole slide show for me. It was a good word, a nonbotanical word, but it was so apt. It really *was* sexy. The pollen. The anthers." Looking at it this way brought plants out of the mental pigeonhole in which she had put them and connected her to the living prairie, which up till then had been an object mainly of historical interest to her. But mostly, in the beginning, Chris gravitated to prairies, and the North Branch project, "because it was a real passion for Larry." His passion and involvement would in time make him an authoritative amateur ecologist in his own right—and it would also place certain strains on the Hodaks' young marriage.

Chris remembers the early prairie work as being onerous, "but in a perverse way there was some fun in it. It was beastly hot, and always on Sunday, when I'd much rather have stayed in bed rather than getting up and going out and walking around in raspberry thickets." To her, "fall has always been the more magical time, when we get to go out and collect seeds. The work is real easy, you don't have to bend over so much, you're not getting wet. And the colors, the fall colors, a range of tones that's very subtle."

A pleasant ritual grew up around the Sunday work sessions. "It was a neat mix of people, and we would have these great lunches," nice, warm interludes after a morning of sacrifice and discomfort, after which the group might do more work or just get lazy and make nature-study forays nearby. Mim Desmond, Packard's lover and future wife, "really was an insect freak, and she taught me a lot," recalls Chris. Once, after Chris and Larry got married in 1978, they brought leftover champagne and everyone "sat around and got silly" after lunch. "There was a lot of respect and trust," she says.

For all the hard work and thinking and organizing, Chris Hodak's intuition told her not to expect too much in the way of results. "I enjoyed the people I was out there with, but didn't put a lot of credence in the thing surviving. I didn't feel like there was much hope at all. We'd plant these two-inch little green babies that somebody had grown with a lot of love over the winter, and with back-breaking work, and they died within hours."

The project's first systematic survey of results, in August 1978, was indeed sobering, though not uniformly bleak. Where dogwoods had been cleared, bare dirt was left. There, six-inch-tall rattlesnake masters planted by the North Branchers had sprouted. The plants didn't look like much, but they were there. Transplanting small plants turned out not to work, however, even if they could be watered. Animals ate them. Digging up little circles of turf, freeing them of roots, and sowing seeds was a flat failure; the weedy turf around the circles grew vigorously, while the circles turned dry and sterile-looking.

"We weren't discouraged," Packard would say later. The prairies were no longer being mowed, prairie plants that had been there originally were spreading into areas where the brush was cut back, and the tender young rattlesnake masters gave cause for hope. "But the bulk of it," Packard conceded, "was a disaster."

"The early victories we claimed may not have been that huge," Larry Hodak said years later. "The first couple of years took a lot of vision on Steve's part, and I give him a lot of credit for convincing people that it was worthwhile and that it was working."

But clearly, it was not working well enough.

Without fire, it never would.

3

POLITICS, FIRE, AND BUCKTHORN

Burning the prairies had been a straightforward enough proposition to the Potawatomis. But in the late 1970s and early 1980s, the very idea unnerved and upset lots of people.

There was precedent for the concept of burning as a restoration tool. The University of Wisconsin Arboretum in Madison had long been burning its prairies as part of a pioneering restoration effort begun by the renowned naturalist Aldo Leopold in the 1930s. In the Chicago area, Bob Betz had since become convinced that if prairies were to be preserved and restored, fire was essential. At hearings held by the Illinois Nature Preserves Commission, he had argued hard for prescribed burning. Commission scientists were leery. How do we know the fire won't kill some of the rare things we're trying to protect? What about the tiny thrips? Or the snakes? Or the butterflies? Go slow, the scientists urged. Get grants. Do research. Find out what would really happen. Betz argued that if burning were put off until the necessary money was in hand, the ecosystems themselves would be gone and the question would be moot. He pointed out that the Indians burned the prairies, and lightning set them afire, and they always came back. Betz persisted, and ultimately the scientists agreed that at least some prairies needed to be burned.

By 1979, Steve Packard was working as a field representative for the Natural Land Institute, a private, nonprofit environmental organization that provided staff support to the Illinois Nature Preserves Commission. A number of prairies were being burned by then, and the Land Institute was deeply involved in the effort. Capitalizing on his role as an institute employee, Packard was learning the techniques of burning with the intention of applying them to the North Branch project. "We knew, partly from Dr. Betz and partly from our own experience, that the prairie doesn't thrive if it isn't burned," he says. Despite the North Branchers' strenuous efforts to cut back the hawthorn and dogwood that choked a number of their restoration sites, for instance, the brush just kept coming. "In some of these sites," Packard recalls, "every square yard would have two or three young brush sprouts." Over the long haul, this would have meant that the restorationists would spend so much time clearing brush, just to keep it from reclaiming the small areas they had planted, that it would be impossible to expand the restored area. "We wanted prairies large enough so that the prairie birds would come back," Packard said, but it was difficult to imagine "snipping back the brush forever with our little loppers." Even had that been possible, it would have been unthinkable to control alien weeds, particularly bluegrass, without fire—unless, Packard said, "you trained tens of thousands of grasshoppers to tell the species of plants apart." Earlier controlled experiments at the arboretum in Madison had found that when a prairie is cleansed by fire, it produces twice as much vegetation by weight as it would if left unburned for a number of years.

But a formidable philosophical obstacle remained. For Packard, it surfaced in particularly poignant form one day during a burn at Sand Ridge Nature Preserve, under the supervision of Dr. Marlin Bowles, a professional ecologist with whom Packard worked at the Natural Land Institute. The group was burning a narrow swath to create a fire-break, controlling it carefully by beating its edges. "All of a sudden there was another guy in there," recalls Packard, "and he was trying to put the fire out. When I explained that we were actually trying to burn the site, he started to cry: 'This is my favorite place; you can't burn this up.' He didn't understand the ecology. There was a good reason why it was his favorite place. It was so rich in plants and animals, but they were fire-dependent plants and animals, and he didn't understand."

The man's anguish reflected a clash between a common, intuitive view of nature as being fixed, balanced, and immutable, and a newer, more generally accepted paradigm among ecologists in which nature is seen as dynamic, ever-changing, subject to constant disturbance, and in a perpetual state of flux and disruption. To most people, "nature is what they experienced when they were thirteen years old," says Dr. Michael E. Soulé of the University of California at Santa Cruz, one of the country's foremost ecologists. What most people experience at age thirteen is not pristine nature at all, but rather an altered form of nature shaped largely by the hand of Homo sapiens. At the North Branch sites, the thickets of buckthorn, hawthorn, and dogwood that overran the prairie and savanna in the absence of natural fires became, in the minds of most people, true nature. Packard and his associates said to themselves, "That's not nature, that's an artifact of human disturbance."

At the North Branch sites, Packard believed, European settlers had essentially interrupted and suppressed a long, ancient, postglacial evolutionary progression that had produced the wondrously diverse biological assemblages of the prairies and savannas. The goal of restoration, he felt almost from the beginning, was to allow that evolutionary progression to resume. This meant it was necessary, in the restoration areas, to undo the effects of postsettlement human activity and allow presettlement ecological processes to reestablish themselves. This required the removal of both alien invaders like buckthorn and homegrown woodland-edge species like dogwood and hawthorn that were taking over the prairie remnants in the absence of fire. It also required, as things turned out, the replanting of native prairie species where they would not come back on their own—and the reintroduction of fire.

From day one, Packard and his volunteers took pains not to attract the opposition of people whose sensibilities about nature, however uninformed, might be offended. "A very big part of what we did," says Packard, "was to be perhaps boringly cautious about things. We went to the most extreme lengths so that the Forest Preserve District would not have to deal with complaints about what we were doing." Not long before, the district had spent several thousand dollars on a massive clearing of brush in another part of the Chicago area, igniting a furious public outcry. "It really made them gun-shy," said Packard. "The Boy Scouts were after them—'You're destroying the habitat of the animals'—and the neighbors were after them—'We bought this property because we wanted to look at these beautiful trees, and you're cutting them down.'"

So the North Branchers trod lightly, even sneakily. Their brush-clearing and planting operations took place as discreetly as possible. As a screen for their activities, they would leave a wall of brush in place along the bicycle trail or roadside. Behind the screen, they would cut a little brush here, and little there, and make their plantings. Eventually the plantings would flower and everything would look stable and lovely, and only then would they cut away the roadside screens. After the vegetation had grown up, they removed unwanted invading trees (always called brush by the North Branchers, to deflect criticism) by girdling them below the vegetation line, where the killing cut could not be seen. Then the tree would slowly fade away and no one would notice. The whole idea was to keep people from becoming upset about destroying "nature" so that nature could actually be restored.

Fire was the ultimate point of sensitivity, not least in the minds of the Forest Preserve District officials. It is one thing to cut brush and plant seeds in a heavily populated suburban area, but quite another to set a fire there. On top of that, the chief forester of the district apparently saw some of his handiwork threatened. Sam Gabriel—"a wonderful old-time conservationist," Packard calls him— "had spent his career planting trees in the forest preserves, and he had just the hardest time understanding why someone would want to go and burn them down. And some of the fires we proposed were going to kill trees; that was one of their primary purposes."

The question had come up at the crucial meeting in July 1978 when Packard and Hodak toured the North Branch sites with Betz and Eisenbeis and eventually got permission to manage them. Gabriel, since retired along with Eisenbeis, was on the tour as well. "Every time I would mention burning," Packard recalls, "Gabriel would sort of reach for his heart. Betz finally dragged me aside and said, 'Steve, go easy. You've got 'em. You're gonna get it.'"

Betz remembers it similarly: "Gabriel's eyes were rolling in all directions, and I said, 'Steve, we're going to get it, but they're really upset. Just cool down on it and don't say any more.' And he didn't say any more." The upshot was that Eisenbeis and company agreed, as part of their overall assent to the North Branchers' request to manage the sites and to allow the use of fire as a management tool—under close supervision. Gabriel insisted that Sauganash Prairie, where valued swamp white oaks grew, be exempt from burning.

From the North Branchers' viewpoint, actually putting fire to work was an agonizingly slow process. The Forest Preserve officials insisted that they be on hand to supervise the burns, but their officials and workers had many other things to attend to, and it was some time before any actual burns took place. Meanwhile, Packard and his associates were learning the technique of the controlled burn.

In the standard Illinois method, it works like this: On the extreme downwind edge of the plot to be burned, a natural firebreak is found or an artificial one is created. A natural firebreak could be a footpath or a stream or a street. If there is none, a swath five to ten feet wide can be cleared by raking dead leaves, brush, and other flammable material to the side. The fire is started on the upwind edge of this break. A "drip torch" is typically employed to do this. The torch is a cylinder filled with a mixture of kerosene and gasoline. Attached to it is a tube with a wick on the end. You turn the torch upside down, light the wick, and walk along dropping little drops of fire on the ground. This "backfire" burns into the wind, moving slowly at perhaps a foot a minute, which means it can be easily contained. It is controlled by volunteers who wield "flappers," each a long pole with a big piece of flexible rubber on the end, to swat the fire and put it out. Water sprayers are sometimes used as well. (This is perhaps the most ticklish part of the procedure, since backfires in the hands of inexperienced crews can easily get out of control and send up five-foot-high flames that are too much for flappers. "Managing a fire is like driving a car or changing a baby," says Packard. "It's not difficult for an experienced person, but it's also not something you do easily the first time.") The backfire is extended up the two sides of the plot, creating a U-shaped strip of burned ground enclosing three sides of the overall area to be burned. In the last step, the fourth side of the plot, the upwind side, is fired with the drip torch. This headfire races downwind across the site, meets the burned strip created by the backfire, and goes out. The burn is complete.

Burning actually began in 1980, but not in the way just described. From the start, for Packard, it was an exercise in frustration. The Forest Preserve supervisor and employees who appeared to conduct the burn, with the help of North Branch volunteers, seemed supercautious and slow. The supervisor "would get there, and the crew would get there, and we'd sit down and drink a cup of coffee from a thermos, and talk and check the tools," says Packard. "The volunteers were not used to all this sitting around, and they were taking time off from work." (Burns, once they started, invariably took place on weekdays. The wind and weather conditions had to be right, and this could not be guaranteed on weekends. Also, fewer people noticed the burning on weekdays, and this was important in the early years. "We thought it would upset them and they'd write crabby letters to the Forest Preserve District," Packard says.) District officials also insisted that fire trucks be on hand. They would drive out into the middle of the prairie while the North Branchers gritted their teeth at the soil compaction they caused. Many times, according to Packard, one of the trucks would get stuck, "and we would have to take the crew off everything they were doing to come protect these wretched fire trucks" from the fire.

Moreover, the district supervisor's caution led him to insist that only backfires be started. And instead of creating a thirty- to fifty-foot stretch of backfire at a time, as the North Branchers would later do, he would fire perhaps five feet at a time and stand there and watch it while one or two people beat the downwind edge out, and then fire another five feet. As for results, progress was excruciatingly slow: No sooner would a burn get going, circumscribed as it was, than lunchtime would come and the flames would be put out. Could the North Branchers have another go tomorrow? No, they were typically told, the Forest Preserve people had other things scheduled. Consequently, says Packard, "we'd burn four or eight acres where we'd been hoping to burn thirty or a hundred."

This went on for two springs. The North Branchers, in these early years of burning, always set their fires in the spring. One reason was that the early-emerging green shoots of the choking, alien bluegrass would be destroyed, while the prairie grasses had not yet come up. Another was political: "If you burn in the fall, people look at this charred death, this Smokey the Bear stuff, all winter, whereas if you burn in the spring, it's all greened up in a couple of weeks and it looks great."

Finally, in the spring of 1982, the Forest Preserve District, with many other fish to fry and its confidence in the North Branchers growing, simply called up Packard one day and said the North Branchers could go ahead and do the burns themselves, unsupervised. "We were thrilled," says Packard. "We felt for the first time that these prairies were really ours, that we were really managing them. It was sort of like when your parents give you a car for the first time. Me? I can do that? We knew now it was really going to happen, that the burning was going to be done with a vigor that the prairie required."

On a warm, dry, windy weekday in April 1982—perfect conditions for a burn—fifteen to twenty North Branchers gathered at Miami Woods Prairie and built, in Packard's words, "a wonderful backfire and then set this glorious fire on the upwind side, and it roared down through the prairie and crashed into these big patches of brush, and whirled up into little fire tornados, and the brush was gone, and there was this white powder left."

There was one tense moment. Packard didn't have much confidence that the backfire would contain such a huge blaze; "I was pretty nervous it was going to get to the other end and jump across. The Chicago River was on the downwind side. I didn't have a lot of fear it was going to jump the river, but it could have burned up the woods, and we felt we had to keep it out of the oaks. We had promised the Forest Preserve District, Sam Gabriel, all of them, that we'd keep it out of the trees." In the back of his mind at the time was the experience of another prairie preservation group in which a blaze did jump the backfire, raced across part of a county, and burned down some farm buildings.

"Fire is not fun," Packard later wrote in an annotated scrapbook about the Miami Woods project. "A good fire is an awesome experience, perhaps an inspiring one, but if someone thinks it's fun, he [doesn't] understand it." Prairie buffs, he wrote, liked to talk about "controlled burns" and "often like to show the public photos of little ankle-high flames with a couple of fellows standing over them with lots of equipment ready to put the fire out at the slightest provocation. But a real prairie fire is out of control. The protection of things not to be burned has to be done in the planning and the backfiring before the real fire starts. A headfire in heavy fuel burns everything in its path. That apparent lack of control once the headfire is started is difficult for some people to accept. But it's what nature wants."

Moreover, he wrote, some animals are indeed killed by the fire; while burning greatly enriches the life of the prairie in the long run and most prairie animals have evolved strategies to avoid fire, an occasional rabbit, vole, or snake is burned to death.

Fears aside, the Miami backfire held. The North Branchers' first real, wild prairie fire was a success. Excited and elated, they went on to burn five other prairie remnants that same day, ending the day dirty, exhausted, and triumphant.

The effect of the burning was immediate and dramatic. The brush was decisively defeated. Large expanses of prairie that had been suppressed by brush and alien weeds like bluegrass and timothy were suddenly open, ready for restoration. The North Branchers had hoped that prairie species would come back spontaneously after the burn. In some places, for some species, that happened. In most places, for most species, it did not; the North Branchers would have to continue to rely on plantings. But in the wake of the fire, with competition by nonprairie vegetation eliminated, prairie plants that had already taken root as a result of earlier seed sowing grew bigger and proliferated. Miami Woods Prairie, the main experimental site, erupted in color. Especially spectacular were the yellow clusters of the golden Alexanders in the spring and the flat-topped white clusters of Virginia mountain-mint, the drooping yellow petals of the prairie coneflower, and the elongated clusters of the rough blazing star's bright, pink, chrysanthemumlike blooms in the summer.

The remnant prairies, now truly resurgent, were off and running.

As the prairie restoration began to take off, the human institution known as the North Branch Prairie Project was developing a strong life and character of its own—essential, its leaders believed, if the restoration effort were to succeed over the long term. As the enterprise developed a reputation and word spread, it began to attract a wide variety of capable volunteers.

On the heels of Larry and Chris Hodak, for instance, came John and Jane Balaban, the high school math teacher and the pharmacist. Like many of the North Branchers, they had had a long love affair with the outdoors. In the 1970s they had taken classes in prairies and prairie restoration at Chicago's Morton Arboretum. By 1977 they were trying to save a prairie remnant on Chicago's South Side. Seeking information, they contacted the Illinois Nature Preserves Commission and through it met Steve Packard. Later, after they had saved up enough money to buy their own house and move out of an apartment above John's parents, they settled on the North Side, in the town of Skokie. Packard soon recruited them to the North Branch project. Within a year they were already chief stewards of one of the North Branch sites, Bunker Hill Prairie.

"I didn't know anything about restoring the sites to presettlement conditions" in those early years, John Balaban recalls. "I don't think I had any idea of that." But it was clear that here was an attractive opportunity to take an ecologically degraded area and nurse it to a healthier state.

Very soon, the Balabans emerged as the project's most expert taxonomists apart from Packard. Taxonomists are specialists in the identification and classification of species. The Balabans had been delving deeply into this discipline for some years before they met Packard. A lot of people don't like to do the tedious work of "keying down" field samples by painstakingly hunting them up in the botanical literature. But the Balabans enjoyed the unending challenge of becoming acquainted with the endless diversity of the prairies. "The more you learn," says Jane, "the more impressed you are with how little you know." It wasn't long before Packard would ask the Balabans along when it was necessary to inventory a new group of plants in a newly explored patch of prairie remnant. And as the North Branch enterprise progressed, the Balabans built and maintained the project's increasingly detailed and sophisticated data base.

About the same time came Pete Baldo, a technician at Argonne National Laboratory, then in his early thirties. Attuned to nature since his days as a Boy Scout and farmer's son in California, he found most of what passed for nature in Chicago's parks "just so artificial." When a copy of a Sierra Club newsletter arrived with an insert describing the North Branch workdays, it caught his attention. One Sunday morning in the fall of 1980 he drove past a spot along the freeway where the North Branchers were picking prairie-plant seeds from the wild for planting at the restoration sites. Although he was on his way to his office for some overtime, Baldo pulled over and joined the North Branchers for a morning of prairie work before proceeding on to Argonne.

He found that first day frustrating. "Steve would give me a plant and say, 'Pick some more of these,' and I couldn't tell the plant from the others." But for Baldo it was the start of an intellectual odyssey in which he came to learn and appreciate "the amazing complexity of an ecosystem I had never really understood before; I really got into it." The experience, he says today, "opened my eyes, because even though they're not very big, the North Branch prairies are as much a natural area as any national park is."

Why people stayed with the North Branch is more important than why they showed up for the first workday, Baldo believes. In his case, it was partly because the project offered "something I could do while I was in Chicago." But beyond that, "the real reason I stayed in it was the group of people Steve attracted. Very nice people. I felt comfortable with them. Intelligent. People with technical backgrounds who had gotten interested in the prairie, mainly because of Steve." In the environmental movement, he said, "you tend to get some strident, very opinionated, very ideological people. Sometimes they tend to drive other people away. I never met any of those in the North Branch Prairie Project. I guess you could say they were fairly liberal, but they were always objective about things."

And there was Preston Spinks, union carpenter and gardener extraordinaire. He lived next to Wayside Prairie, a restoration site near Miami Woods. "I saw these people out there working on Sunday mornings, and I was curious as to what was going on, so one morning I figured, well, I'll just stop by and say hello. That happened to be the day they had their annual party." He had been pursuing his own little experiment, transplanting seedlings of osage orange, a tree native to the American Southwest, into the Forest Preserve site. "I wouldn't do that now," he says, "but at the time I thought it was a good idea."

Spinks had long since become an amateur expert in plant propagation. He once imported dahlia tubers from Holland and used advanced propagation techniques to breed prizewinning flowers for display at conservatory shows and the Illinois State Fair. At one show, his plants won 114 awards. When he saw what the North Branchers were doing, "I said, 'These guys are wonderful, but they don't know a damned thing about plants.'" Spinks was disdainful, John Balaban recalls, of the made-up term, "rootlings." Not a proper horticultural term, Spinks grumbled. "It drove him crazy," Balaban chuckles.

Spinks brought fundamental gardening knowledge to the project, and he suggested a number of changes in technique. All were eagerly accepted. One was the "wonder bar," a long pole with some spongy material attached to the end, to apply herbicides without bending over. (Use of herbicides was one compromise the North Branchers made in the interest of speeding up restoration, and Spinks showed them how to do it.) Over the years the North Branchers developed many inexpensive but successful techniques through simple trial and error. There were the screen-bottomed boxes to winnow seeds from seed heads. There was the plastic milk jug cut and modified to serve as a field seed-collector. There were a number of experiments in seed processing, some using rolling pins, coffee grinders, blenders. In one simple expedient, seed pods were placed in a plastic bag and a rolling pin was employed to crush the pods and liberate the seeds. Spinks had preached the value of the old-fashioned scythes he'd used in his youth. John Balaban found one at a garage sale and discovered that it was better than anything else for controlling certain weeds that tend to invade restoration sites.

Spinks's most spectacular achievement, perhaps, was

in growing mass quantities of hard-to-cultivate prairie plants as seed providers for the restoration effort. From the beginning, gardening was an integral part of the North Branch project. From Packard's perspective it had both a practical and a political-psychological purpose.

On the practical side, some prairie species had become so rare that it was all but impossible to collect enough seed in the wild to plant the scores of acres of ground in the restoration sites. In other cases, nature is extremely inefficient in that relatively few seeds produce viable plants, and so hundreds of thousands or even hundreds of millions of seeds are needed. Moreover, it is often difficult if not impossible to be there at the exact moment when a wild plant pops and sheds its seeds; in one's own garden, the moment is more easily captured. But the truly wonderful thing about having lots of seed, in Packard's words, is that "you then can throw it everywhere year after year. Sooner or later, when conditions are right, each species will begin to take hold in just the right place. That is, if you can throw the seed everywhere, then it can choose just the right place for itself. And the few plants that take hold will scatter more and more seed around that vicinity year after year after year." The North Branchers also found it valuable to raise and transplant young plants in the case of some species that spread by sending out rhizomes, or runners.

The political-psychological value of gardening, in Packard's view, is that it is a powerful way of fostering a bond between the volunteers and the ecosystem. People particularly loved to transplant young plants to the prairie, Packard says, "because it was much less abstract work. It was work people understood easily. It's one thing for me to say, 'Let's rake these seeds into the ground, and I have a lot of confidence they'll look great five years from now.' It is quite another to hold a precious little orphan plant in your hand, dig a hole for it, place it tenderly in the ground, and press the soil back snugly around it. You develop affection for this little plant being." While that proved an excellent technique for some species, the most effective technique for most was to plant seeds. And the backyard gardens that grow seeds for sowing also provide a powerful psychic tie to the land: The seeds that come from the wildflowers in the garden will be sprouting in the wild next year, or next, or next.

Early on, Packard and Larry Hodak were the only gardeners. The Balabans soon allowed Packard to use some of their property to expand his plantings. Packard credits Baldo with getting into gardening "in a spectacular way." He dug up his backyard and planted rows and rows of prairie clover, spiderwort, violet wood sorrel, northern dropseed, blazing-star, and the like, and he has raised huge quantities of seed over the years, turning the yard into a riot of colorful prairie patches edged by neatly mowed strips of lawn.

Baldo readily defers to Spinks as the champion gardener in the group. "Basically, Steve just gave me seeds and I planted them," Baldo says. "But Preston is a genius. There must be dozens of species of plants he propagated, possibly for the first time ever. He had gobs of hoary puccoon plants. To grow just one of those is hard. But he'd come to workdays with flats of them. Whole flats."

What was his secret? "To be absolutely honest with you," Spinks said, "I don't know. I can't tell you why it works for me and nobody else. The only thing I can say is that I tried to copy nature as much as possible." In the end, with the most difficult-to-grow plants, "you say a Hail Mary and leave it," he says.

Packard says that "when Preston was willing to take over the leadership of the gardening, we did things his way. That was how we worked. Those taking the initiative made the decisions—so long as no serious harm was being done. If someone taking initiative said, 'Packard's idea is dumb; I've got a better one,' my struggle would be to forget my ego, forget that in many cases I actually knew the situation better and in fact had a more practical approach, but instead to say, 'Yes, I'm dumb and so-and-so is better at this,' and that person would throw [himself or herself] into the project and ultimately learn more than any of us" about the particular subject.

From the start, Packard tried to foster a cooperative, collegial approach to running the project rather than a hierarchical approach. "Even though Steve was the guiding spirit," says Pete Baldo, "we all felt like we were participants in the organizing. He often deferred to our views. Most of the volunteer stuff you get involved in, some person in the agency thinks about what kind of jobs they'd like volunteers to do. Usually they're jobs they don't want to do. You don't feel like this is really your operation, that you're a part of it. You really felt like you were part of the North Branch Prairie Project."

The coherence of the North Branch group was strengthened by its continuing social life. In the early years, says John Balaban, "there was a lot more socializing and a lot less science. We had a lot of potluck suppers, we'd go down into the city and bring food and get together and talk about what happened. It was a very loose structure, just friends getting together."

Getting people involved in the project, getting them to care about it, ranked as a prime objective, coequal with the actual restoration work itself. Only in this way, the project's leaders believed, could the project be sustained over the decades necessary to see it through. "In fact," Packard said in later years, "our goal is to create something that lasts forever. Like the congregation of a church, it has to continue from generation to generation. If people forget about one of these prairies, it's gone." Sometimes, says John Balaban, the most efficient way of carrying out the work was not always the best in terms of getting people to care. "I don't think we've ever made a decision that hurt the [ecosystem] in order to get people involved," he said in retrospect, "but sometimes we've chosen the

slower path. Maybe we could have accomplished something faster if we had brought in the bulldozers or some
such thing," or brought in experts to help with the work.

Packard was clearly first among equals, but a coequal
was emerging in these early years. He was Ross Sweeny,
an engineer in his early thirties who had recently moved
to Chicago from Richmond, Virginia. He had fallen in love
with Virginia's mountains, and on his arrival in Chicago
he began to look around for outdoor activities. "If you do
that very long and get into any depth," he says, "you end
up with a prairie, and it becomes a brand-new experience.
It's so different from anything else that you become
hooked on it." One night at an Audubon Society meeting,
he asked how a person could get involved with prairie
restoration. A representative of the North Branch project
happened to be there, and Sweeny and his wife, Robbie,
signed on.

Gradually, Sweeny took over much of the organizational and administrative burden of the project, while
Packard concentrated on the science. Sweeny organized
the workdays, the operational heart of the project. He arranged for tools to get to the site. He made sure someone
was there to lead the effort. He and Packard would confer
about just what work had to be done, with Packard's ecological judgment the general guide. At seed-mixing time
in the fall, Sweeny would make sure all the equipment
and containers and seed were ready so that volunteers'
time would be used to maximum effect. He maintained
mailing lists and prepared schedules and mailed them out
and took care of paperwork. He took over responsibility
for the annual potluck supper, the one official social function of the year. He would organize attacks on special
problems. One year, for instance, he declared "the year of
the weed" and arranged for volunteers to put in extra time
pulling weeds. He was always on the phone, calling people. Like Packard, he got his hands dirty on Sunday mornings. Like all the volunteers, he worked on different sites

in different weeks, moving from one to another as the occasion demanded. And he, too, grew prairie plants in his garden.

But the clear leader in terms of the all-important ecology of restoration was, and remained, Packard. His biggest conceptual challenges still lay ahead.

Up to this point, Packard and his confreres had been thinking prairie. How to get the prairie plants established. How to generate enough seed to repopulate the open lands. The best techniques to use. But beyond the remnants of open prairie at Miami Woods, and also farther north at Somme Prairie Grove, lay thick barriers of brushy gray dogwood and buckthorn, fifty feet to a quarter of a mile wide, and beyond those, the gnarled forms of the big oaks that had once been the linchpins of the tallgrass savanna. They were not a major preoccupation initially, but now, more and more, they began to intrigue Packard. He carried in his head a vision of the presettlement landscape: rich grassland running up to, under, and through the oaks. Without that, restoration would be incomplete. At the same time, expanding the restoration effort into the oak groves would contribute to what the North Branchers saw as a unique objective: not merely to restore, maintain, and manage a given area of prairie, but to enlarge the area itself—to make a start, however small, toward reversing the ecological damage and bringing the prairies and savannas back from the brink.

And the oaks exerted a come-hither attraction. They were special—ancient, evocative of millennia past, almost sacred. In Packard's mind, there was something "druidic" about them. Everyone recognized them as the original trees of the region, and cutting them down in the interest of restoration was considered off limits. By this time, says Packard, "we sort of had the authority to do what we could get away with. There was this sort of unwritten agreement: We would do things and get approval in retrospect. If God didn't send lightning bolts down, and the scientists didn't complain, and the public didn't complain, it would be all right. But the oaks were beyond the pale."

Only once did they cut some. In this they followed Betz's preference—a preference he would later abandon in the case of oak savannas—for cutting down trees so that prairies could flourish. "Betz was saying the prairie is much too small; cut all the trees out" so that the prairie will be large enough for prairie birds to return, says Packard. So they removed a few small young oaks in the belief that if the trees were left to grow, they would kill a whole area of prairie underneath them. It was also feared that cowbirds, which frequent woodland edges and lay their eggs in the nests of other species, would be attracted by the trees and act as parasites on the bobolinks, meadowlarks, sedge wrens, upland sandpipers, and other birds that might return to nest in the adjacent open land if it ever got big enough. But even as he cut the small oaks, Packard recalls, "I felt bad, I felt nervous about it."

In Packard's mind, a more inclusive vision was beginning to compete with Betz's prairie ideal. Packard later explained: "Rather than 'restore prairie,' this impulse said, 'restore nature.' Back then there was no restoration of anything but prairie or wetland that I'd ever heard of. But this 'nature' idea was very deep and compelling. I knew that however big we might hope the prairie might grow, Sam Gabriel would never let us cut down the old oaks. On one hand I thought this was too bad—limiting recovery potential for these tiny remnants. On another level, though, I felt Gabriel was right. The oaks and the trilliums under them were part of the holy thing we were groping for."

The North Branchers resolved to eliminate the buckthorn thickets that choked the oak groves on their sites so that whatever natural relationship had once existed between the oaks and the prairie could be reestablished.

"Free the oaks," became the restorers' somewhat joking battle cry.

But how to do it?

At first they tried fire, the obvious tool, the natural remedy. The North Branchers would let their deliberately set prairie fires blast into the brush and toward the oak groves as far as they could go. But during most of those years in the early 1980s, the brush patches wouldn't burn. Ten-foot flames would roar across the open prairies and up to the edge of the brush. But in the thickets, there was no grass, the essential fuel of a prairie fire, only green wood and matted leaves. The blaze would quickly die. What brush did burn grew back quickly. Fire may have kept brush from getting a toehold under the oaks in pre-settlement times, but once established there in dense green thickets, it defied the flames.

The obvious way to speed up the process of extending the resurgent prairie back under the oaks was to go back to the laborious task of cutting brush by hand. In the first of four experiments, at Miami Woods, the North Branchers cut a thirty-by-thirty-foot opening in the brush to begin to create an open stretch extending from the prairie to the edge of the North Branch itself. They scattered a choice mixture of prairie-plant seeds on the bare, crumbly earth, raked it in, and waited for results. The first growing season, things looked terrific. Packard thought it was one of the best plantings the North Branchers had ever done. He had never seen so much grass coming up, and little baby rattlesnake-masters were sprouting all over the place. But by the second and third years, it was clear that something was wrong. The prairie plants were failing to thrive, and it didn't seem as if they would take over the spot after all.

Packard was not happy to see that three of what he at first believed to be sprouting prairie grasses were in fact unfamiliar species. He collected and pressed them for future identification and then, with a hundred other different things to do, forgot about them.

In Experiment 2, also at Miami Woods, Packard and company expanded a natural prairie opening into an oak grove by clearing away perhaps seventy-five feet of hawthorn, buckthorn, and young elms and ashes. They sowed prairie seeds in the opening and under the oaks. "And so here we had it, whole and complete, we thought," Packard remembers, "so we waited for the prairie to come up."

There wasn't much the first year. The second year, the prairie plants started to look pretty good—away from the oaks. Under them, nothing. To add insult to disappointment, Canada thistles, as pestilential a weed as exists in those parts, began taking over the ground under the oaks.

In Experiments 3 and 4, the North Branchers transferred their efforts to Somme Prairie Grove. Specifically, to the oak copse that they would one day name Vestal Grove.

They created two small openings in Vestal Grove by girdling, and thereby killing, some cherry and hickory trees. In these openings they planted prairie seed. "We came back the next summer, and the summer after that, and after that, and nothing was happening," says Packard. "It was getting briary, and the brush was growing worse."

All four experiments were failures, but interesting failures that, unknown to Packard at the time, would lead to the most interesting and satisfying experiment of all. What would happen, Packard wondered, if the restorers burned all of Vestal Grove? Its especially thick litter of dead leaves might provide enough fuel for the fire to succeed, and he had a feeling that if planting-under-the-oaks were undertaken on a larger scale, the results might be different.

The decision was therefore made to burn Vestal Grove.

4

THE SAVANNA PUZZLE

An almost impenetrable thicket of Tartarian honey-suckle and especially of buckthorn, higher than a person's head and nasty enough to rip the clothes and score the flesh of anyone trying to bull through it, had long since replaced virtually all other growth under the towering oaks of Vestal Grove. But even in that severely degraded condition, the grove's underlying beauty and potential were apparent. It was by far the largest and best grove of bur oaks to be found among the North Branch restoration sites. Sitting on the western slope of the Deerfield Moraine, it was also well drained, drier, more amenable to fire. In a few spots, conical blossoms of the woodland-and-prairie flower called the shooting star, their backswept petals resembling tiny pink shuttlecocks, held on tenaciously, a tantalizing hint of the glory that once was and might be again.

And Vestal Grove was relatively isolated. All the other North Branch sites were next to bicycle trails or picnic shelters and parking lots. But apart from teenaged partiers, few people ever came to Vestal Grove. It was bureaucratically isolated, too. The site lay in a different division of the Forest Preserve District, and its superintendent seemed indifferent. "We never met him, never saw him, he didn't care what we were doing," says Packard. "It just seemed like we could get away with it," he said of the plan to burn the grove.

Still, he was very nervous about it. Would the fire hurt the oaks? The answer was unclear at this point; so far as Packard knew, no one since the Indians had done it. While bur oaks resisted fire, would a buildup of fuel in fire's long absence create a catastrophic blaze? This would be a major test of the Forest Preserve District's de facto policy of allowing the North Branchers free rein to experiment so long as no one complained.

On an April weekday in 1984, Packard and a crew of North Branchers bit the bullet. Leaving a wall of buckthorn along Dundee Road to screen what they were doing (the screen remains in place to this day), they set their backfire, extended it around the two sides of the plot, set the headfire, and waited for the drama. They got none. Although the carpet of leaves did burn, "it was a pathetic fire, very disappointing," says Packard. "It hardly flickered. The overall feeling of the group after this day was over was that it had all been much ado about nothing. It hadn't worked."

But a few weeks later, lo and behold, most of the buckthorn and Tartarian honeysuckle had died. Aside from a few small resprouts, the grove's understory, as scientists call vegetation under trees, had been transformed from dense brush to entirely open ground. On one side of the fire line, where the screen was left in place, remained a dense buckthorn thicket; on the other side, nothing but dead skeletons. Where you could see ahead for only five or ten feet before, there was now a clear view for fifty to a hundred yards. Vestal Grove was now ready, the jubilant North Branchers believed, for a rebirth.

All that hopeful summer of 1984, an excited Steve Packard would crawl around on his hands and knees on the floor of Vestal Grove, looking for prairie plants to appear. Although the idea that humans must intervene to reestablish degraded ecosystems had firmly taken hold among the North Branchers, they preferred to wait for the plant to reappear from whatever natural seed bank had lain dormant in the soil over the years. The North Branchers' experience over the previous six or seven years had bred a strong appreciation of patience. Nature moves to the rhythm of the seasons, and the North Branchers had learned to measure progress in accumulations of seasons, over years. One year does not itself disaster portend. So when little developed at Vestal Grove that first year, Packard was not disheartened. Two or three plant species did appear, including one unusual species characteristic of what Packard would soon call "closed savanna" and later change to "woodland," the maple-leaved goosefoot, a relative of the South American grain called quinoa. But apart from that, nothing significant came up.

The second year, it became clear that things were going seriously wrong. Tiny specimens of Canada thistle, a spiny weed with adult stems about four feet tall, began appearing everywhere. Dandelions and burdocks, alien to the prairie and the savanna, were increasing exponentially. Maybe, Packard thought, there simply weren't enough viable seeds left to set off a resurgence. Or, in view of the failure of the prairie plants to grow under the oaks at both Miami Woods and Vestal Grove, maybe there was another reason.

For the North Branch enterprise as a whole, this was a time of expanding success and rising expectations. But the burning of Vestal Grove was crucial. It was the biggest experiment the North Branchers had tried. A point of no return had been reached, and the whole project was at a critical and vulnerable point. Vestal Grove itself "was either going to be something wonderful or it was going to be a disaster," Packard thought. "If someone were to show up right then, they'd see a whole lot of dead stuff and a whole lot of burdock and dandelion, and they'd say, 'What a mess this is. These people are degrading the Forest Preserve.' I dreaded some armchair ecologist coming there and saying, 'My god, the Forest Preserve District shouldn't be allowing these people to do these crazy things.' There was a great threat of failure and of bad public relations. At the same time, the potential was there. It was ready to be restored. We just had to figure out what was supposed to grow in there."

Until the North Branchers burned Vestal Grove, Packard had not gotten serious about the savannas; prairie restoration had been the name of the game. But now he began to focus on the savannas more and more. His research had earlier introduced him to the concept of savanna. In the late 1950s, Dr. John T. Curtis at the University of Wisconsin Arboretum in Madison had defined a savanna as a grassland with trees in which up to 50 percent of the area in question is covered by forest canopy. Curtis's landmark 1959 book, *The Vegetation of Wisconsin*, had applications far beyond that state. The savanna community it described in detail flourished all along the northeastern boundary of the prairie peninsula, where woodlands, prairie, and savanna had formed their ever-shifting mosaic in presettlement times. Curtis's treatment of savannas was as crucial to Packard's early understanding as it was in spurring him on in what would soon become a near-obsessional effort to investigate the faint savanna remnants of metropolitan Chicago.

Curtis's book described the savanna as a "striking" and "peculiar" combination of grassland and forest "in which the bulk of the land was occupied by grasses and a few shrubs, but which also had widely spaced tall trees, frequently of a single species at a given place."[2] He traced the origin of the term to the native Carib Indians of the

Caribbean. Savannas occur all over the world, but Curtis noted that in temperate zones, they are best developed "in the climatic belt separating the grasslands from the forests." He wrote that in Wisconsin (and by extension in northern Illinois, though he didn't say so), the savanna "constituted one of the most widespread communities in presettlement times." The most familiar and extensive type of savanna in this region was what Curtis called "oak openings." In upland areas, according to Curtis, these were typified by bur oaks and moist prairie, with grasses rather than trees dominant; and in lowlands by swamp white oak and wet-to-moist prairie, again with grasses dominant.

Citing a number of early accounts, Curtis set forth a picture of some oak openings as having been somewhat regularly spaced as in a common orchard, with the bur oaks resembling apple trees while displaying their characteristic, unmistakable gnarled-oak appearance; while others stood as dense copses surrounded by open land. They seem to have captured the esthetic fancy of early settlers. One J. W. Hoyt, writing in 1860, praised "the charming, homesteadlike expressions they give to the landscape."

Curtis concluded that the oak openings varied not only in density but also in the spatial distribution of the trees, with "extreme aggregation" the rule, the trees being arranged in "isolated patches, or groves, or as tongues, or irregular peninsulas of widely spaced trees projecting from denser forest into the open prairie." The beauty of this intermixture of trees and grassland, he wrote, "must indeed have been unique."

In setting his dividing line between forest and savanna at 50-percent canopy coverage, Curtis characterized it as "an arbitrary limit" imposed "purely for convenience." He noted an agreement among "several writers" that the oak openings resulted not from a migration of bur oaks into the prairie but rather from the reverse: an invasion of woodland by prairie species. The early writers all commented on the role of fire in creating and maintaining the openings. When new settlers stopped the fire, Curtis wrote, "a very rapid change took place in the oak openings. Within a decade, the openings became filled by saplings and brush and within twenty-five to thirty years, dense forests were present."

When fires were allowed to sweep the landscape, Curtis wrote, young oaks perished in the flames. But their roots survived to send up new shoots. Fire would destroy most trees of any age, but if a bur oak could be spared for twelve or fifteen years, it would survive future conflagrations. Because of the absence of fire, Curtis wrote, "an oak savanna with an intact ground layer is the rarest plant community in Wisconsin today."

In Illinois, too. In the late 1970s, the state of Illinois undertook a comprehensive inventory of surviving natural ecosystems and found that they covered only seven hundredths of one percent (.07 percent) of Illinois's land area. In the case of savannas, the picture was even grimmer: The inventory uncovered only a handful of very small fragments, totaling 11.2 acres, in the entire state. Packard would later conclude that most of these were so fragmented and relatively poor in species that they weren't all that helpful as guides to what the presettlement savanna ecosystem had been like.

For their purposes, the Illinois surveyors diverged from Curtis and defined savanna as a grassland in which up to 80 percent of the surface was covered by a canopy of trees. While it was "a wonderful study," Packard says, it contained a fundamental error, at least in the case of savannas: By limiting the study only to pristine ecosystems, it failed to recognize degraded and suppressed ecosystems that might be restored. "They were looking for stuff that was changeless, eternal, and most important, unaffected by people in any way," says Packard. The result was that the inventory virtually defined the fire-dependent, black-soil tallgrass savannas out of existence. In Packard's view, "they looked around for 'undisturbed' black-soil savannas and didn't find any." (There are sandy-soil savannas as well, with different species of oaks, and in some parts of the country's midsection, including Missouri and northern Indiana, they were quite extensive in presettlement times. But in northern Illinois, Wisconsin, Iowa, and parts of Indiana, they were a relatively minor player compared to the more extensive bur-oak savannas growing in the region's deep, moist loam.)

The tendency to define surviving natural areas narrowly was perhaps understandable, since neither restoration nor the understanding of natural disturbance had yet risen high on many people's priority list, or even captured their attention. "It was not something a conservationist ought to have time for; people were doing this stuff, but they were basically hobbyists and dabblers—so it was thought," says Packard. His employers up to that point saw it that way, and were leery of his spending so much time on the North Branch project.

In the summer of 1984, as Packard was crawling around in Vestal Grove looking vainly for prairie plants to pop up, savannas suddenly were propelled to the forefront of his awareness in a way that also liberated the North Branch project and at last brought it into the conservation mainstream.

A year earlier, Packard had left his job with the Natural Land Institute, where he had been part of a staff assisting the Illinois Nature Preserves Commission in setting up nature preserves, and joined the Illinois office of The Nature Conservancy full time. He was now part of a national conservation organization with enormous influence and expertise.

Formed in 1950 by a group of activist scientists who broke away from the Ecological Society of America, the United States' premier professional society of ecologists, the Conservancy by 1993 had grown into one of the largest

Somme Prairie Grove

Plant communities and quality of vegetation, 1983

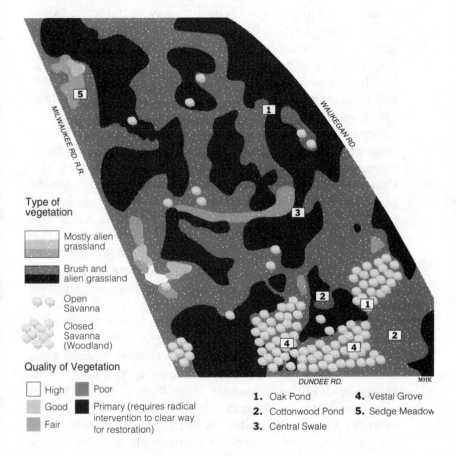

Type of vegetation

- Mostly alien grassland
- Brush and alien grassland
- Open Savanna
- Closed Savanna (Woodland)

Quality of Vegetation

- High
- Good
- Fair
- Poor
- Primary (requires radical intervention to clear way for restoration)

1. Oak Pond
2. Cottonwood Pond
3. Central Swale
4. Vestal Grove
5. Sedge Meadow

MILWAUKEE RD. R.R.

WAUKEGAN RD.

DUNDEE RD.

MHK

and most respected conservation groups anywhere. A nonprofit organization with 720,000 members that depended mostly on donations and bequests, it operated, four decades after its inception, the largest system of private nature preserves in the world: 1,300 of them, mostly in the western hemisphere. The Conservancy's basic approach is unique: it protects ecologically valuable land simply by buying it up. It has purchased more than 5.5 million acres of land, reselling 60 percent of its holdings to governments and plowing the money back into new acquisitions.

The Conservancy also works closely with federal, state, and local governments, developers, businesses, and other conservation and environmental groups to encourage environmentally friendly land use and promote effective management of nature preserves. And in one of its most important functions, it maintains in its data bank the United States' most comprehensive inventory of the state of the natural world. Public and private interests alike rely on it for information to guide them in making a wide variety of decisions about land use and conservation. The Conservancy itself uses the inventory, which is continually updated, to guide it in identifying ecosystems that are most threatened and to establish conservation priorities and strategies.

The national inventory is developed from a series of state assessments. Illinois's assessment was one of the first. Carried out independently, it was later incorporated into the Conservancy's national inventory. The man in charge of the Illinois inventory was John White, an ecologist then with the Natural Land Institute, which along with the University of Illinois performed the assessment for the state Department of Conservation. White later joined the Conservancy to help develop its inventory system and later still became an independent ecological contractor.

In June 1984, White, then with the Conservancy, sent a memo on ecological priorities to state Conservancy offices in the Midwest. He had been analyzing data from the organization's national inventory in an attempt to identify the rarest and most endangered types of ecosystems so that conservation efforts could be concentrated on them. The tallgrass savannas of the upper Midwest, he found, fit into the class of G-1, meaning that only a few, if any, prime examples of the ecosystem are known to exist globally and that it rates the highest conservation priority. The relatively endangered tallgrass prairies of northern Illinois and adjacent Iowa, with which the savannas intermingled in presettlement times, were ranked a step lower, at G-2. (In this ranking system, still used by the Conservancy, G-1 signifies "critically imperiled," G-2 "imperiled," G-3 "vulnerable," G-4 "apparently secure," and G-5 "demonstrably secure.")

"Savannas are nearly exterminated, everywhere in the Midwest," White wrote. "Remnants should be saved and restored."

Restored! Considering the source, the word electrified Packard.

"This was coming from the apostle of no-human-influence," he would say later. That is, White was part of a tradition among Midwestern ecologists and conservationists that attached primary importance to undisturbed, pristine remnants of ecosystems and tended to ignore degraded ones. "It was like Nixon going to China," Packard said. "Once that kind of person says restoration is okay, the opposition is crumbling." Even though the word *restored* "was hidden down in there, I knew how out of character that was for the Nature Conservancy and for Jack White. At that point, I said, 'Aha. This is personal fulfillment and empowerment. I'm going to be able to do what I want to do as part of the Nature Conservancy. I'm in the right place. I'm not going to be battling an insuperable tide here. I can try to bring restoration right into the mainstream of Nature Conservancy work. What's more, I'm way ahead of everybody else in the Conservancy.' It was as if, suddenly, the Pope says it's okay to do this. Or as if Mendel had gotten a memo saying that plant genetics is important, and we ought to be working on it."

With the White memo, restoration in the North Branch moved beyond the status of personal hobby, to a new plane.

But it did so just as Vestal Grove, which could turn out to be either the project's biggest triumph or its biggest fiasco, hung in a very uncertain balance. "Now it was semiofficial, and I had the backing," Packard recalls. "But Vestal Grove looked like hell."

For millions of gardeners, winter is a welcome time to study and reflect on the season past, to enjoy successes, figure out the failures, and plan for the new season. In the fall and winter of 1984–85, Packard concentrated on an ecological quest whose objective was to learn what plants would grow in Vestal Grove and the other oak groves. The quest, though no one realized it right away, marked a new phase in the North Branch project, one in which a more scientific approach would begin to take hold in earnest.

He frequented libraries, picking up all the books, articles, and miscellaneous tidbits of information he could. In an 1863 article by a naturalist named Henry Engelmann, he found confirmation of Curtis's assertion that fire was essential to the savanna ecosystem. Englemann's article reported that "barrens," as early Illinois settlers called the savannas, grew up rapidly into trees and brush following settlement and the consequent denial of fire.

But an obscure article by a scientist named Arthur G. Vestal suggested that the crucial grasses and wildflowers of the savanna, contrary to Curtis, might be neither forest nor prairie species but something different. In a 1936 article in *Transactions of the Illinois State Academy of Sciences* called "Barrens Vegetation in Illinois," Vestal, then the Illinois state botanist, wondered what the plants of the barrens had been. Surveying early accounts of the flora of the region, he concluded that after the upland oak groves had been swept by fire, they had been occupied by grassland plants. "These however failed to include some of the most characteristic prairie herbs," Vestal wrote. And he constructed a hypothetical list of what the barrens species might have been. The list was fragmentary and tentative, but it set Packard thinking.

Could it be, he wondered, that the oak groves of the North Branch had been trying to tell him something when they rejected the plantings of prairie species? Could it be that another assembly of species altogether belonged under the oaks?

In his Spartan five-room, third-floor bachelor walk-up in a modest brick apartment building in north-central Chicago, Packard keeps a little study, sometimes messy and sometimes organized, with a reproduction of Van Gogh's room at Arles on one wall and a cast-off overstuffed chair and a small bookcase full of volumes about plants on the somewhat cracked and unsteady floor. There he would settle down at night and thumb through botanical works, looking for species that, following Vestal's revelation, might grow in the oak groves. Vestal had also suggested the kind of habitat where savanna species might be found today: in forest openings and borders, cutover areas, road cuts, abandoned fields, and railroad rights-of-way in forests. They would be found there, presumably, because this was where wooded areas met open ones, creating the conditions of partial sunlight in which savanna species could grow. Looking for plants that fit this description, Packard plumbed the pages of a handy volume by H. S. Peppoon, *Flora of the Chicago Region*, published in 1927 by the Chicago Academy of Sciences. He would go to sleep at night sorting and resorting the information in his mind, trying to reconcile experience, perceptions, and the reading of plant lists.

The mother lode of information, however, turned out to be a thick, detailed, eight-hundred page compendium by Floyd Swink and Gerould Wilhelm called *Plants of the Chicago Region*, published in 1979 by Chicago's Morton Arboretum, where Swink and Wilhelm had developed reputations as first-rank taxonomists. The book is made up mostly of brief ecological notes, including typical habitats, on the region's plants. Each entry on a plant species is accompanied by a list of other species that grow in association with it, thereby making it possible to construct, though painfully and laboriously, a list of plants that grow together in a given combination of soil, moisture, and lighting conditions.

Remembering the three grasses that had popped up and flourished in the oak grove at Miami Woods while the prairie species were failing there, Packard got out the samples he had pressed and identified them in standard botanical reference works. All three turned out to be native species: wedge grass, common wood reed, and Virginia wild rye. And all seemed to fit the savanna description; wood reed, for instance, was described by Swink and Wilhelm as occurring in both moist woodlands and moist clearings. Packard studied the Swink-Wilhelm comments on these and other miscellaneous species the North Branchers had found growing on the edges of the oak groves. Soon they stopped seeming so miscellaneous. Many were listed by Swink and Wilhelm as associates of each other, or had third-party associates in common, and some were listed as growing in areas that had been burned recently.

Typically, they thrived in partial sunlight. Maybe these, rather than prairie species, were the sorts of species Vestal had speculated about; maybe these would work if planted in Vestal Grove.

So far, Packard's investigation had been somewhat random and disorganized. He now decided to go beyond flipping through the Swink-Wilhelm volume and read the entire eight hundred pages, cover to cover. Plunging into it like "an ecological mystery novel," he looked for upland plants that grew in moist soils and that frequented semi-open areas, or that lived in both woodlands and open areas, or that liked habitats with intermediate lighting. Mostly he studied the associates of each species to see if they tended to appear with the other species on his growing hypothetical list of savanna plants. He particularly looked for rare plants. He believed that in Illinois most rare plant species get that way by losing habitat. If the savanna had been home to a distinctive group of plants, maybe some of them would be rare precisely because the savannas had all but vanished. It would be all the more important to restore habitat for these species. He hoped clues to their identity would emerge from Swink's and Wilhelm's endless lists of associates.

A sample: Swink and Wilhelm listed pale Indian plantain as an uncommon plant of woodland and prairie. Among its associates they listed another rare plant, mullein foxglove, that "can be found in the tension zone of semishade between a wooded area and a recently made sunny opening."

The mullein foxglove in turn is associated with biennial gaura, a plant of "woodland borders," and tall coreopsis, a plant of "thin woods and prairie." Closing the circle, the coreopsis is also listed as an associate of Indian plantain.

Thus, a pattern begins to emerge. It unfolds further when the gaura turns out to be an associate of the coreopsis as well as of another plant, the starry campion. The campion is an associate of both the coreopsis and yet another plant, the tall bellflower.

Searching his memory, Packard remembered seeing a rare plant called glade mallow, a candidate for federal endangered species protection, growing with tall bellflower. When Packard looked up glade mallow in Swink, the associates list included tall bellflower and Virginia wild rye, one of the plants Packard found growing under oaks where he'd tried unsuccessfully to plant prairie species!

The associations could be extended a long way, and

they all describe a constellation of species—including many that are now rare—whose typical habitats cut across open and wooded areas, reflecting the light-mottled pattern that one might expect of a savanna.

Through this tedious, time-consuming process of wading through seeming acres of Latin names, Packard produced a tentative list of what he believed to be 122 likely savanna species—components, if he was right, of the vanished savanna ecosystem.

Swink and Wilhelm gave each of the plants in their compendium a numerical evaluation of ecological character. The rating scale, devised by Wilhelm, assigned each species a value from 3 to 10, depending on its rarity and its tolerance for ecological disturbance. Those on the high end of the scale are described as "conservative." They flourish only in an ecological community that is in an advanced and stable stage of succession, disappearing from the community after only a little disturbance and returning very slowly once it begins to recover. Succession is the process through which a plant community evolves to greater complexity and stability after it has been disturbed or wiped out and is recovering or reestablishing itself.

On the Wilhelm scale, a minus-3-to-0 rating applies to weedy, opportunistic species that run riot in disturbed ground and are the first to take it over. A rating of 5 applies to species that, while not necessarily uncommon, typify an advanced and complex phase of succession. A rating of 10 applies to plants that not only belong to an advanced, stable ecosystem but that also require a narrow range of ecological conditions to exist; they are picky about the niches they choose. Wilhelm also established two special ratings: a 15, for plants in the 10 category that are quite rare in the Chicago area; and a 20, for plants that are thought to be locally "threatened, endangered, or already fatally compromised."

Many of the plants on Packard's initial hypothetical list of potential savanna plants derived from the Swink-Wilhelm book had been assigned ratings of five or better; nine had a rating of 10, seven of 15, and four drew the endangered rating of 20. These last included the middling pinweed, a delicate plant with multitudes of delicate red or pink flowers; the hoary tick-trefoil, a slender plant, three to five feet high with small pink flowers and hairy stems; the great St. John's-wort, a many-branched shrub crowned by a mass of golden flowers; and buffalo clover, endangered in northeastern Illinois and rare throughout its range.

Excited by his first venture into formal science, Packard wrote up his list of 122 possible savanna species as part of a paper titled "Rediscovering the Tallgrass Savanna" and dated April 8, 1985, for publication in the academic proceedings of the Northern Illinois Prairie Workshop that June. Based on his detective work and on parallel research on midwestern savannas in general, it was intended as a wake-up call and something of a manifesto for the vanishing savanna ecosystem, and it laid down an early intellectual rationale that would undergird the effort at Vestal Grove.

The tallgrass savanna, Packard wrote, was "the least understood of the Midwest's original natural communities." While it originally dominated much of the Midwest, including northeastern Illinois, he wrote, "no healthy example remains." He went on to point out that although northeastern Illinois had the bulk of the state's nature preserves, "there is no savanna restoration effort, nor is there yet any substantial research or writing about this rare and strikingly beautiful landscape." And what was true in northeastern Illinois was also true throughout the Midwest.

Packard distinguished the tallgrass or "black-soil" savanna from the similar, but related, community of "barrens" found on relatively sterile or shallow soil in southern Illinois, and from a second related community, sand savanna, that grew up along the Lake Michigan dunes and on glacial sand deposits like those along the Kankakee River. He pointed out that sand savannas, anchored by black oak rather than bur oak, had survived comparatively well, mainly because they are less valuable as farmland and because the sandy soil was less hospitable to weeds, brush, and trees.

Packard argued for a savanna restoration effort much like the multiple efforts that the North Branchers and others were making in prairie restoration. But in the case of savannas, the paper said, "there are unique difficulties to overcome," the most serious of which was a total lack of any pristine example of natural tallgrass savanna to guide the effort. "Our benchmark prairies are narrow strips along railroad rights-of-way," Packard wrote. But "no such minirefuges were possible for the savanna" because "a thirty-three-foot strip is too small for the savanna dynamic to function."

And in a passage presaging an argument that would later raise academic eyebrows and blood pressures when Packard made it more prominently and authoritatively, he flew in the face of accepted wisdom by suggesting that the tallgrass savanna was not just a prairie with trees, but rather a distinctive ecological community of another kind altogether.

But the main feature of the paper was Packard's list of proposed savanna species. The list, he wrote, "includes only those savanna species that are not typical of mature prairie, woods, or sand savanna." In more open savanna, he suggested, typical prairie plants might make a larger showing, while forest species might be in greater evidence where trees are denser.

In the absence of a real-world example of an intact tallgrass savanna, Packard wrote, "it is impossible at the present to determine if the species presented here do in fact function as a component of the savanna. In order to find out, it may be necessary to attempt to restore missing natural conditions." This process, he wrote, "would be a profoundly interesting one to watch."

Indeed. And Vestal Grove would be the first experiment.

But now that he thought he knew what species might grow there, how could he find the plants that would provide the seeds for the experiment?

Bob Betz knew how.

5

PRAIRIE PHOENIX

From the beginning, Betz's influence pervaded the North Branch project. Packard frequently called him to ask for advice, which Betz willingly gave. It carried the weight of authority, for by this time Betz—a husky field scholar with a bushy, graying beard, a tough inner core forged on the streets of blue-collar Chicago, and the temperament of a maverick—had emerged as one of the great gurus of prairie ecology. His crowning achievement has been the dramatic restoration, still unfolding, of a 1,000-acre prairie on the grounds of the Fermi National Accelerator Laboratory just outside Chicago. While subatomic particles shoot through the circular underground tunnel of the accelerator, a prairie ecosystem is being reborn in and around the ring in what used to be cornfields, establishing Betz as a foremost pioneer in large-scale prairie restoration.

Betz, a professor at Northeastern Illinois University, followed an earlier tradition dating back to the 1930s. At the dedication of the University of Wisconsin Arboretum at Madison in 1934, Aldo Leopold proposed the reconstruction of "a sample of original Wisconsin" that would re-create what the state looked like when the first settlers arrived there in the 1840s. Over the next decades, the Madison group went some distance toward that objective. By the 1980s, the arboretum had grown to 1,200 acres on which samples of some 30 ecological communities existed in restored form, the oldest and most extensive such sample collection in the country. A 60-acre restored prairie was the centerpiece, and for some species in some seasons, it approached the ecological variety and richness of the presettlement prairie. The experiment has succeeded in providing a secure haven for scores of prairie species. But after half a century, the pioneer project offers continuing testimony to the difficulties of restoration: Even after all that time, alien weeds still crop up, and it does not yet contain a full complement of prairie species.

Growing up in the years before World War II in Bridgeport, a blue-collar Chicago neighborhood where his father delivered milk to the future mayor Richard Daley, young Bob Betz faced long odds against ever following in the tradition of the Wisconsin ecologists. Not that he lacked a basic academic cast of mind. The eldest of seven children, he was expected to do well in school, and did. He was an avid reader. Living as he did in a neighborhood with no public library, he read nearly every page of the family's encyclopedia and devoured such works as *Westward Ho,* Plutarch's *Lives* and *Ivanhoe* in a twenty-volume set of the "World's Greatest Literature." (The volumes were offered at fifty cents apiece by the *Chicago Daily News* and one came every week.) As a sixth-grader, he began to appreciate classical music on the radio and convinced his parents to let him take piano lessons at a neighborhood settlement house. They bought him an old upright. (He continued to play the classics into adulthood.)

Like most youths in similar circumstances in countless neighborhoods, he tried to fit in but found that it wasn't easy; he felt odd, out of place. He played baseball with his friends but had little interest in it. His real interests included the many plants and animals he raised—fish, cray-fish, earthworms, caterpillars, and even houseflies. He tried to grow in his backyard every type of weed he could find in the cracks of the sidewalks and alleys. Since neither he nor any of the adults he knew seemed to know the weeds' names, he made up his own. A slender youth as well as intellectual, he felt compelled to turn to bodybuild-ing to ward off harrassment by bullies. It worked.

The city itself was to young Betz not a place of excite-ment but a desolate realm of concrete and asphalt. "Is this my lot?" he would wonder. He found some comfort in the wisps of nature that existed on small neighborhood plots, islands of wildflowers, weeds, butterflies, and other in-sects that he wrongly imagined to be prairie fragments where the Indians used to roam and hunt buffalo.

As the time for college neared, he found his interests focusing on science. But in Bridgeport, as in many other neighborhoods whose residents were preoccupied with surviving the Great Depression, college was usually out of the question. Very few scholarships and aid grants were available in those days. Most youths were encouraged sim-ply to graduate from high school and get "a good-paying job." Betz's father urged his sons to aspire to skilled trades like tool-and-die making and plumbing.

Young Bob's sights were set higher, and he enrolled at the Illinois Institute of Technology with the idea of becom-ing a chemical engineer. He thought that would allow him to make a living while pursuing his scientific interests. He chose I.I.T. because it was within walking distance of his home and he wouldn't have to spend money on carfare, and because he could get into a cooperative work program to finance his schooling. He had completed only one se-mester before he was drafted into the Army in January 1943. His grades at I.I.T. were such that the Army sent him to Reed College in Portland, Oregon, for training as a meteorologist. "When I got there," he recalls, "I realized for the first time in my life that there were people like me. There was nothing wrong with me."

After Betz had been in the program for a year, the Army found it had no more need for meteorological officers. Betz was retrained as a mortarman and machine gunner and posted to Europe. He survived the war, but many of his buddies did not. Afterward, the Army sent him to the University of Basel in Switzerland for two months, where he studied zoology, mineralogy, and German. The experience convinced him to switch from engineering to biology and chemistry when he returned to I.I.T. under the G.I. Bill. He earned a degree in biology, a master's in microbiology, and a Ph.D. in biochemistry. In time he learned to read six languages and eventually turned his attention to the Algonquian language as an aid in learning more about the ecological role of the midwestern Indians. But his early professional field was biochemistry, and he seemed set for a career in it. He spent more than three years happily working on one particular enzyme.

Then all that went by the boards.

One day in 1960, Betz was asked if he would like to go along on a field trip to a surviving prairie remnant in southern Illinois. The leader of the trip was one Floyd Swink, a renowned plant taxonomist then with the Cook County Forest Preserve District. Betz knew little about prairies then. He had once been introduced to them in a botany course, but it hadn't made much of an impression. He nevertheless thought the field trip just might be interesting.

Prairies in 1960 had not made much of an impression in the world of ecology and conservation, and few people in Illinois knew or cared much about them. "But Swink knew what a prairie was, and the plants that made up a prairie community," says Betz. "He knew almost every plant that grew in the Middle West on sight, whether it was in flower or not. He could even name a plant from just half of one leaf."

Swink led his small field-trip group to a prairie remnant along some railroad tracks, where the right-of-way had protected it from destruction by farmers and developers. "For the first time in my life I saw a real prairie. I was enthralled," Betz recalls. "I had never seen any of these prairie plants before, and I said to myself, 'This is what I want to study for the rest of my life.' I was hooked on prairie." Although he would continue to teach biochemistry and other subjects, he now devoted all his research to the prairie.

Betz began scouring northeastern Illinois, looking for prairie remnants in other undisturbed areas along railroad tracks, in vacant lots, wherever they might conceivably have survived. "I got into it real deep," he recalls. "I read what little there was on prairies; it became an obsession." And he was actually finding prairie remnants. One day, he excitedly called Swink to tell him of a new find and asked him to come look at it and at some species Betz couldn't identify. Swink brought with him Ray Schulenberg, a horticulturalist from the Morton Arboretum outside Chicago, whose field was the propagation of woody plants in the greenhouse. But Schulenberg, who was familiar with Curtis's work in Wisconsin, also had a strong interest in prairies.

Betz and Schulenberg struck up a friendship and working alliance that would carry on through the years. Schulenberg's skill was as a horticulturalist, and the two began working the prairies as a team. On weekends they'd go out for a morning or an afternoon, looking for prairie remnants. Then, one day in 1962, Betz discovered his first cemetery prairie. It was to open new vistas for him. "I was walking along a railroad track in open farmland about twenty-five miles from my house," he recalls, "and I looked down the track some distance and saw to my amazement seven- and eight-foot-tall prairie dock and compass plants, both indicators of prairie. I ran down the track, and there, in a cemetery, was a whole acre covered with virgin prairie." He thought it was one of the most wonderful things he had ever seen—"a small peek into the past of what the whole countryside surrounding the cemetery must have been like."

With their new discoveries, Betz and Schulenberg began to focus on the possibility of setting up a network of small prairie preserves. "If prairies were being saved," Betz says, "they were being saved by accident. There was no organized effort to save them. It was a plant community that was just forgotten. It was wrong to let the prairie become extinct without doing anything about it. At least we'd try to save it."

The same year that Betz discovered his first cemetery prairie, Schulenberg was asked by his superiors at the Morton Arboretum to create a restored prairie on the west side of the arboretum property. He agreed enthusiastically. Gathering seeds from prairie remnants in the Chicago area, he raised some as seedlings, transplanting them in spring and early summer, and scattered the remaining seeds on the restoration site. The site at the arboretum became a showcase of painstaking, labor-intensive restoration. It was, in effect, a sort of hothouse prototype, in the friendly confines of the arboretum, of what Packard would later undertake with his volunteers in the less friendly confines of public preserves. In the first year of Schulenberg's experiment, half an acre was planted with prairie species. Teams of workers tended them intensively, tediously weeding the site so that the prairie plants wouldn't be out-competed. By the end of the second year, the emerging new plant community had become "tight" enough, ecologically speaking, so that with the help of fire, it became more difficult for weeds to invade. Eventually the project grew to about ten acres. And although early spring plants never took hold, Schulenberg and company did succeed in establishing 110 prairie species in one of the first projects to nurture such botanical variety and complexity. Soon the project had gained a reputation as an Illinois model for prairie restoration.

Betz, meanwhile, systematically set about finding more cemetery prairies and restoring degraded ones to health. Aided by county highway maps that fortuitously indicated the locations of cemeteries, he visited more than 800 of these old settler cemeteries dating back to the 1830s and 1840s. About 150 of them displayed at least vestiges of the original prairie along the edges or around tombstones. A few looked like virgin prairies. Others had been mowed continuously through the years, but some tiny prairie plants peeked out from the lawn grass. "The thought struck me that if the mowing could be discontinued and the vegetation burned, these little 'bonsai' prairie plants might recover and the prairie [might be] reconstituted," Betz said.

He convinced a number of cemetery boards of trustees to set aside their properties as "prairie preserves." Some, possibly to deflect any criticism when the mowing stopped, asked that signs be posted identifying the cemeteries as such. Betz had some made up, identifying the cemeteries as among the last remnants of the prairie that once covered Illinois, and informing visitors that they were being preserved as a memorial to the settlers buried there. It identified the preserving organization as the Prairie Preservation Society of Northeastern Illinois University. "The total membership," says Betz, "was me."

Betz began to manage the prairies seriously, weeding by hand, cutting brush, and burning the plots each spring. "I'd pull thousands of ragweed and other weeds," he says. "I'd be out there all day, shirt off, from nine in the morning till seven or eight at night, alone." He would get school kids to help with the burning; and "lo and behold, with the fires, in a year or two the prairie emerged like the phoenix." He had not planted seed one; the prairie plants had been in the ground all along, waiting for the proper conditions to flower again. When the mowing stopped and the weeds disappeared, they did.

All the while, Betz was learning about the prairie plants, not only their names, but their characteristics, their requirements, how to handle them, the positions they held in the ecological community of the prairie. He was learning from Schulenberg, too, how to grow and rear prairie seedlings, most of which had never been cultivated in a greenhouse before. He was reading voraciously, learning as much about the theory of prairie ecology as was then known. He was, in short, fast becoming a true expert on the prairie.

By the early 1970s, a number of conservation organizations had become interested in prairies and involved in their preservation, and Betz worked with many. But it soon became apparent, in Betz's words, that "if the prairies were to be saved for posterity, it had to be done on a grand scale"; that while small prairie preserves are useful, in the long run they tend to lose genetic material. This meant that the very thing that had destroyed the prairies—agricultural machinery like plows—would have to be used to build them again. The idea was to create a large-scale prairie preserve of a thousand or more acres with all the original flora and fauna. It would serve as a living gene bank for further reconstructions, yield valuable information for other restorationists, and possibly inspire county and state agencies to undertake similar large-scale projects.

One day in the summer of 1972, Betz and Swink were in the car on a field trip, and Swink mentioned that the Fermi National Accelerator Laboratory at Batavia, outside Chicago, was under construction, and that the lab's management had called the Morton Arboretum, where Swink by then had become chief taxonomist, to ask for advice on landscaping the site with conventional garden plants.

"Just in passing," Betz remembers, "I told Swink, 'Why do they want to do that? Why do they want to put in these biological monstrosities that everybody plants? Why don't they put it back into prairie, the way it was before?'"

A month of so later, Betz attended an academic conference on prairies at Kansas State University. There he heard Dr. Robert Jenkins, chief scientist of the Nature Conservancy, describe a large-scale preservation project the Conservancy was planning for the Virginia coast. Near the end of the talk, he mentioned that the Conservancy was interested in prairies, and that it would like, some day, to rebuild a large prairie in, say, Kansas or Nebraska. After the talk, Betz introduced himself to Jenkins and said that he might want to consider Illinois or Iowa for the project, since, with more abundant rainfall, that was where the "real eastern tallgrass prairie" had existed.

Jenkins seemed taken aback, Betz remembers, but the next night Betz and some others were sitting in the hotel lobby when Jenkins walked in, came over, and began talking about how he and other Conservancy people that day had visited the nearby Fort Riley military post and speculated on the possibility of managing a large prairie tract on government land. The Conservancy has subsequently done just that with a variety of ecosystem types on a number of tracts owned by the military.

"Two things jelled together," says Betz. "I said, 'Well, if you want government land to build a prairie, then there's Fermilab at Batavia, Illinois. They have almost 7,000 acres. That's the kind of place you want to build your prairie.'" Jenkins recalls that although Betz brought up the idea, "he couldn't quite believe they could get it done; I was instantly enthusiastic and was quite sure they could." Two days later in Chicago, Betz recalls, "I called Fermilab and got hold of an assistant to Dr. Robert R. Wilson, the laboratory director. It turned out that Wilson was very interested in prairies." Wilson, Betz said, knew prairies because he was from Wyoming. He was also, says Betz, a visionary who had already brought a few bison to Fermilab to start a herd. "It was like manna from heaven for us," Betz says of the collaboration with Wilson. "It was like a positron and an electron meeting in a flash of light."

The result was that Fermilab gave permission, as a first step, to create a prairie on 650 acres of land in the center of the new accelerator ring. Betz and Schulenberg set to work on the first truly large-scale experiment in prairie restoration, with a long-term goal of returning the land to presettlement conditions.

It was clear from the start that the labor-intensive methods Schulenberg had employed would not be practical for a job of this size. It would take decades, maybe a century, to complete the project that way. It was also clear that it would not be possible to weed and tend the plants once they were established; there would simply be too many of them. "They would have to live as wild plants, and they would have to cut the mustard on their own," says Betz.

To solve the problem of large-scale planting, Betz adopted the method he had envisioned from the beginning: plowing up the ground and using modern agricultural machinery to replant it.

Betz and Schulenberg decided that if the restoration was to be ecologically and genetically faithful, all the seed had to come from natural locations within a 50-mile radius of the site. Fermilab mobilized a corps of about 100 volunteers, some of them lab employees, and they began to collect seeds in the late summer and early fall of 1974. The seed was then cleaned, moistened, and stored in a refrigerator to enable it to break dormancy and germinate properly when planted. In the first week of June 1975, Fermilab employees planted 400 pounds of the stratified seeds, representing about 70 species of prairie plants, in a first, 9-acre plot inside the accelerator ring, in ground that had been plowed and disked the previous autumn. After the ground had been disked again to eliminate weed seedlings, the seeds were injected by using a Nisbet drill. This is a contraption in which seeds fall from a storage box into chutes that take them between two rotary blades that cut furrows in the soil into which the seeds go. After the blades pass, the soil on the sides of the furrow collapses and covers the seed.

Then Betz, Schulenberg, and the ground crew that planted the seeds (some were farmers) stepped back and waited.

Weeds came up. A big crop of them. Lamb's quarters. Amaranth. Giant ragweed. Thistles. Alien daisies. Dandelions. Betz, ever the optimist, was convinced that the prairie plants would eventually win out. "I always felt that the native plants were ecologically programmed to succeed in this region, and that they would eventually prevail over the weeds," Betz says, "though I had no proof."

By the end of the 1975 growing season, the weeds had produced their seeds and were dead. But below them, prairie seedlings had survived the shading of the tall weeds during that first summer of growth. They were only about an inch tall, but they had outlasted the weeds. While the annual weeds would have to start all over again from seed in 1976 and ensuing years, the little prairie plants would start growth using nutrients stored in the five-inch roots they sank that first year. Many visiting conservationists and scientists thought the project had failed, but Betz kept in mind that new prairie plants grow downward more than upward, spending most of their energy on the creation of a big, deep root system that enables them to survive fire and drought. The roots of big bluestem grass, for instance, are often deeper than the ten-foot above-ground plant is tall, enabling it to tap deep reserves of water. Prairie plants' spurt of top growth comes late in the year. The second year, they begin forming clumps and expanding. All of this is now commonly accepted prairie-ecology wisdom. But then, few people knew anything about it.

The second year proved Betz right. After a bloom of thistle and other biennial weeds that reminded him of a cotton field, the prairie plants started to appear for the first time above the weeds, and by the third year the grasses were tall and thick enough to provide enough fuel for a fire. The first fires "tipped the balance," says Betz, "and the prairie plants began to take over the whole tract. All the dandelions were running for cover. It was fascinating to watch."

With that success, expansion began. Betz and the volunteers planted eleven acres in the spring of 1976 and made a quantum leap by planting thirty acres in 1977. All the while, they were refining their methods. The Nisbet drill was superseded by a modified highway salt spreader that broadcast the seeds more efficiently. This was followed by an all-terrain spreader with huge balloon tires and ultimately by a fertilizer buggy that spreads seeds as well as it does fertilizer. Soon the site contained such an expanse of prairie vegetation that the restorationists were able to collect some species of seed from their own plots without having to depend on remnants elsewhere. In the first few years the seed was collected painstakingly by hand, but later a self-propelled combine was used to harvest thousands of pounds of seed from the Fermilab prairie.

In spite of the apparent success, many volunteers became restless and discouraged because things seemed to move so slowly. "People thought it was going to happen right quick, and then the allure goes off," says Betz. Except for a handful of stalwarts, volunteers dropped away en masse. "Everybody thought it was going to die," says Betz, "and it almost did die. Even I had originally thought that new plant species would come in faster than they did, but I knew that if I could keep it going, it would flower, and the people would come back."

About seven years after the first planting, Fermilab

held a reunion to thank those who had worked on the project over the years. It was in August, and the prairie grasses waved spectacularly thick and lush. That opened the eyes of many volunteers. They flocked back and the momentum returned.

By 1983 the workers were planting 50 to 60 acres at a crack. In 1990, 150 acres were planted. As of 1992, nearly 1,000 acres had been seeded and Fermilab had long since become the largest prairie restored from scratch in the United States, with some 125 native plant species flourishing there. "We've never lost a plot," Betz says. Even in major drought years, the deep roots of the prairie plants enabled them to survive.

With the establishment of the plants, prairie fauna began showing up. Meadowlarks, which were starting to disappear in some parts of Illinois, appeared in growing numbers. Bobolinks. Falcons. Red-tailed hawks, eight breeding pairs of them. Loggerhead shrikes. Upland sandpipers. Coyotes. Badgers. Red foxes. But pheasants and other exotic animal species have also taken to the site, and an exploding and voracious population of deer found it a cornucopia. The restorationists would love to see bison run loose on the land. But the site is still too small to support a herd, says Betz; to let bison run loose now "would wreck it."

Betz has developed definite ideas about how the resurgent prairie evolves—the process that ecologists call succession. The community develops in a precise fashion and order, he believes, beginning with what he calls a few hardy, competitive "matrix species" of plants. "You cannot put a prairie in backwards," he says. "It appears that you have to start with some basic competitive plants that prepare the way for the others." There are about two dozen of these matrix species, which is about 10 percent of the species total. Chief among the matrix plants are the two big grasses, Indian grass and big bluestem, tough and aggressive enough to drive out exotic interlopers and weeds.

He describes the matrix plants as "very good infighters." Even more important, perhaps, the matrix plants prepare the ground by helping to change the soil, adding antibiotic chemicals and organic matter that in turn nourish succeeding waves of prairie species. Soil analysis has shown that the once-depleted soil at Fermilab is taking on the overall structure of the crumbly, porous virgin prairie soil that originally made farmers' mouths water, although it still contains only half the organic carbon of virgin soil.

Once the matrix plants prepare the way, the other prairie plants "invade the matrix in steps," says Betz. "You don't get a full-blown prairie all at once." Left to its own devices, a prairie would take centuries to regenerate in a farmer's field deliberately left fallow. In the first stages of succession, short-lived weeds whose seeds have been in the soil for years would take over. In time, though, if seeds of the two big grasses were in the soil as well, or if they blew over the fallow field from adjacent prairie patches, they would crowd out the weeds and eventually dominate the field. Still later, wildflowers native to the prairie would proliferate and compete with the grasses, making them smaller and less dominant.

The objective of Betz and his associates is to speed up this process. On a sunny day in late July 1992, from the fifteen-story tower of Robert Rathbun Wilson Hall, Fermilab's futuristic-looking headquarters building, plots of emerging prairie in different phases of succession unfold toward the horizon. Examined close up, each provides a snapshot of a given phase. In one, planted in the spring of 1992, weeds like Queen Anne's lace and foxtail grass still dominate; prairie grasses lurk as tiny shoots, five inches tall, hidden by taller vegetation. Betz, warming to his task and talking nonstop with infectious enthusiasm, points them out. A sunflowerlike compass plant and yellow coneflowers, which look like small shuttlecocks, have taken root also.

In another plot, two years old, the yellow coneflowers

have taken over completely. In still another, planted in June 1986, Indian grass and big bluestem grass are undergoing their own succession duet. Indian grass dominated the site in the early years, but now big bluestem, its slender, dark bluish stems rising thickly as high as Betz's head, is crowding it out. Some of the twenty-odd other prairie plants seeded in 1986 are also showing themselves, including rattlesnake-master, wild bergamot, early goldenrod, showy tick-trefoil, and prairie dock. Betz hops from plant to plant, pointing them out eagerly, spouting Latin names as he goes. Gradually, as more species show themselves, a more complex matrix establishes itself; the ecosystem is beginning to "tighten up." To reach this stage of succession naturally would take perhaps thirty years; Betz and company achieved it in one fifth that time. Once the matrix is firmly established, still other seeds, of more conservative plants, will be planted.

The oldest plot, first planted in June 1975 in the middle of the ring of the Fermi accelerator, "is beginning to look like a prairie," says Betz. Here, neither of the two big early grasses is nearly as tall or as widespread. They are now in competition with a welter of prairie wildflowers. There are perhaps eighty-two species in the plot, and maybe 20 percent of them are in bloom in late July, including cream indigo, prairie coreopsis, nodding wild onion, and much bigger rattlesnake-masters than in the newer plots. "This is spectacular," Betz exults. "Oh, I love this." But even this plot is a long way from its mature stage. In that stage, a lower, smaller, more delicate grass called prairie dropseed will appear to keep company with flowers like prairie gentians, lilies, and orchids.

It will be decades before the Fermilab restoration reaches its prime, says Betz, and "we're running a race with time. Labs don't last forever, and who knows what will happen then?" That is why he and his colleagues hope, eventually, to restore as many acres as they can, not only prairie but savannas, woods, marshes, and open riverside meadows. A successful re-creation of a full expanse of presettlement Illinois landscape would be more likely to hold its own against future development pressures.

In the ideal vision, this restored prairie would run on its own, with fire and action by grazers like bison to keep it going.

As the 1970s gave way to the 1980s, a growing coterie of northeastern Illinois prairie people had developed around Betz and his colleagues. Swink was perhaps the godfather. Betz and Schulenberg were among the first disciples, and they were joined by people like Ron Panzer, an expert on insects, Marlin Bowles, Gerry Wilhelm, and, in time, Steve Packard. This group became the nucleus of a growing prairie preservation movement. From the start, its leaders were mavericks who often challenged conventional academic and conservation wisdom, and consequently they often found themselves cajoling, arguing, and finagling.

The argument over the burning of prairies and savannas is a case in point, an illustration of a gap that, in Betz's view, separates what he sees as ivory-tower ecological theorists from field experimentalists whose observations are rooted in reality. The trouble with many academics, he said, is that "they have not really worked with these systems on a hands-on basis. Much of the fieldwork is done by graduate students." Moreover, he said, "there is a tendency for many scientists, and other scholars as well, to refrain from questioning assumptions and theories of the scientific establishment or highly respected scientists of the past. The history of science is replete with individuals who have challenged the establishment and have been summarily rebuffed," only to be vindicated later. One well-known example is the German meteorologist Alfred L. Wegener, who first proposed the theory of continental drift, once thought heretical but now accepted as standard.

So it was with the burning of prairies. Betz and Schulenberg, neither of them with formal training as theoretical ecologists, knew from historical accounts that the Indians burned the prairies. They knew that in the absence of fire, prairie vegetation became choked by woody shrubs and trees and stifled by the remains of previous years' growth. The obvious answer: start burning the prairies again. Betz personally encountered little opposition in burning prairies he was managing or restoring. But after prairie preservation became fashionable and governments and conservation organizations began to acquire them, these agencies often turned to the scientific establishment for advice on managing them. "Invariably," Betz said, "part of their advice was: 'Don't burn.'" Where in the literature does it say it's all right? Who wrote it? If it wasn't in the scientific literature, then it shouldn't be done. So some establishment scientists argued.

Packard naturally gravitated to the prairie coterie, mavericks like himself. Soon the Betz-Packard relationship became a two-way street, with Packard now learning things, especially about the savannas, and passing them on to Betz. "We were bouncing ideas back and forth, stimulating one another," says Betz. "Some of the things he was telling me, I never knew. He built up credibility with the Forest Preserve District, and all of a sudden he begins to rise, and here comes this leader, and he's someone to be reckoned with."

But in 1985, with Vestal Grove beckoning, Packard's problem was to find the plants that would bring it fully back to life. Here, Betz's experience perhaps became most crucial. Packard looked to Betz's early success in prospecting for prairie species along railroad rights-of-way and in cemeteries. He was fully aware of how this had paved the way for Betz's success in re-creating the Fermilab prairie. Would it be possible to take a leaf from Betz's manual and use it to resurrect Vestal Grove? Yes, he concluded:

"I said, 'What Betz did for the prairie, I can do for the savanna.'"

6

WINTER OF DOUBT, GLORIOUS SPRING

But where, in the real world of metropolitan Chicago, would you actually go to find savanna species? One of the best places, it occurred to Packard, might be the roughs of golf courses. They had been put in scenic places on purpose, and bur oak groves were among the most scenic. And the roughs should be ideal, because they are basically left alone to grow as they will.

This reasoning came to little. After scouring a number of golf courses, Packard and his companions in restoration had to conclude that they didn't add up to much. Their response was to redouble their efforts. That summer of 1985, Packard, John Balaban, and Jill Riddell, a Nature Conservancy staffer, scoured the Chicago metropolitan area in search of spots where oaks coexisted with relatively open areas that might harbor some refugee savanna species. Nine times out of ten they would arrive at a site only to have their hopes dashed as yet another wall of buckthorn or rank weeds confronted them. They took to calling these botanically degraded spots "wrist-slitters," as in "I think I'll slit my wrists."

Here and there, though, they would find some of what they were looking for: pitiful little enclaves of some of the plants on Packard's hypothetical list, a few at a time, clinging to existence in more-or-less shady nooks in the area's forest preserve districts, or along horse paths, or on railroad rights-of-way. Rare savanna species would turn up especially on the edges of bridle paths in the forest preserve districts. Packard reasoned that these plants would have filled up the oak groves in earlier years, when fire kept less hardy trees from taking over and closing out the sun. With the disappearance of fire, he thought, the woods got darker and darker until the last place savanna plants could hang on was in the more open areas created by the bridle paths. He would later prove this to his own satisfaction by watching savanna species like poke milkweed, big-leaved aster, nodding fescue, and zig-zag goldenrod march back into the wooded areas once fires were reinstituted.

BIG-LEAVED ASTER

Now and again, the hunt for what Packard began calling his oddball savanna species would turn up an absolutely delightful surprise. One hot day, he was exploring a railroad right-of-way at a site called Cuba Marsh. Parts of it had been heavily treated with herbicide and hadn't looked all that promising. At first glance it seemed to be another wrist-slitter. But looking way down the tracks, Packard saw that the railroad crossed the marsh and that about halfway across, an oak-covered peninsula jutted out into the marsh. Packard thought the railroad might have kept cows off that little piece of savanna. He said to himself, "It's interesting, and it's protected, and maybe I ought to give it a try. But do I want to drag my butt all the way down there? I don't know." He did, and was handsomely rewarded. The site turned out to be one of the few real bonanzas uncovered by the North Branchers. There, on a steep slope the herbicide hadn't reached, grew thousands of representatives of dozens of species on his savanna list: Canada milk vetch, for instance, and veiny pea, violet bush clover, and lots of blooms of the snapdragonlike

CANADA
MILK-VETCH

figwort. A hummingbird, now rare in the Chicago region, was visiting them with great excitement. The hummingbird, Packard realized, lives in trees, not on prairies but not in deep woods either; it is a perfect candidate for the savanna.

On another occasion, he and his compadres were scouting out a part of the Cook County Forest Preserve District called Palos Hills, just west of Chicago. There, in a relatively open and bright stretch of mostly closed woodland, they discovered a beautiful, brilliant red but unfamiliar flower. "For a person like myself," Packard said later, "to find a new plant is a special little event. It's hard to explain. It's sort of like when a bird-watcher adds a new species to his life list; you look it up in your field guide and read everything about it, and you go home at night and look it up in your big books, and you remember everything about it. It's sort of like making a new friend; these plants are going to be with me for life; these are part of this family I'm rescuing; this is a component of this wonderful system that we hope we're going to see flourish."

The red flower turned out to be a species called the fire pink, an inhabitant of open woods and thickets, and growing right next to it was a spectacular, wide-leafed grass that was also unfamiliar to Packard. Without grasses, he knew, the prairies would not exist; flowers are not enough. Similarly, he reasoned, grasses were probably critical to the structure of the savanna ecosystem. Could this wide-leafed specimen be one of them? And could it be an associate of the fire pink? Consulting Swink and Wilhelm, he found that it was—and that the wide-leafed grass, panic grass, was on his hypothetical list of savanna plants. He thought, "Bingo, this is working." Little by little, he felt, he was finding in nature the pieces of an elegant ecological puzzle whose theoretical outlines he had already deduced.

As the pattern emerged, it took much of the sting out of bad reviews that Packard's initial savanna paper, including the hypothetical species list, had received from some scientists to whom he sent it for review and comment. He was particularly stung by the criticism of Marlin Bowles and Victoria A. Nuzzo, an ecological consultant whose own, ultimately influential paper on savannas was about to be published. Bowles and Nuzzo said the piece needed much greater technical analysis, more precision and scientific rigor. They suggested that it be offered to a general readership rather than a scientific one. And they saw danger in Packard's approach. The hypothetical species list was "likely to be treated as a recipe by some people," they wrote in a formal critique. "This could be dangerous and result in savanna restoration with species that are untested. We need to further examine our existing savannas for development of such a list."

At one point, Packard recalls, he was urged to stop working on the subject and "let someone do it who will do it right"—that is, with a proper scientific approach. "Marlin, trying to be helpful, said that it was not the right thing to read lists of associates in a book and experiment with restoration to try to figure things out" that way, Packard recalls. "Marlin insisted that what we should do was go to the best savannas there are and make species lists that should be our standard." Packard argued that the existing savanna remnants were so degraded that they offered an incomplete and unsatisfactory inventory of original savanna species and would result in an inaccurate and impoverished species list.

In Packard's eyes, Bowles and Nuzzo came to be seen as adherents of an academic perspective, shared by many botanists, that prefers to describe what is presently observable. Packard felt that approach unsuited to reconstructing a vanished ecosystem. Basically, says Packard, "what they were saying is that the way to find out what a savanna is, is to go out and find one and describe it. If it's badly degraded, that's it; that's the best there is." The approach can also lead to other errors, Packard believes. For instance, Nuzzo suggested that poke milkweed, identified by Packard as a savanna species, wasn't that at all. Rather, Nuzzo said that in her experience it appeared in grazed woodlands twenty or thirty years after grazing ceased. That may be where it was found at present, Packard conceded. But where did it grow before European settlers appeared with their cows? After all, this was a plant that had evolved over millennia. To Packard, poke milkweed in a grazed woodland was a savanna refugee hanging on as best it could in the least hostile environment it could find.

By working from his theoretical list of savanna species, he hoped to find out which other species like poke milkweed would flourish in a savanna setting by sowing them in a restored savanna plot. Their secure survival there

POKE MILKWEED

would not only constitute a major rescue effort, it would also provide the scientific proof of the pudding. But the descriptive botanists weren't ready for this kind of experimentation. Research-through-restoration—the enterprise on which Packard had embarked—was a concept whose time had not yet come.

The Bowles-Nuzzo comments were "profoundly discouraging," Packard says now. "They were patting me on the head, saying, 'You're not a scientist, and you should leave this to other people.'"

Bowles sees it somewhat differently. "What Steve had was a theoretical paper with no framework or frame of reference to it. It was simply his observations. When you're working in the field of science, you can go only so far with something like that. I think we all urged him to get more data before he published. This happens with lots of people when they publish for the first time. They get disenchanted. Only with time do people get used to peer review." Peer review is a standard test of validity in science, in which one scientist's work is subjected to critical analysis by others in the field before the work is published.

Packard indeed concedes that perhaps he was too thin-skinned at the time. But there was some balm to be found. Whatever the scientific deficiencies of his first attempt at publication, some professionals were beginning to show interest in the general thrust of his savanna work. Floyd Swink and Jack White were especially encouraging, and as they and others showed interest, new avenues began to open up for the North Branchers. Packard's list of savanna species, for instance, rang a bell with Dr. Wayne Schennum, an ecologist with the McHenry County Conservation District. He remembered a site in the wealthy suburb of Lake Forest that he had investigated in 1979. Although it included many big old oaks along with stretches of prairie and wetlands, the Illinois state inventory had rejected it as a conservation area on the ground that it was too weedy and disturbed. Schennum had nevertheless been impressed by the variety of plants that grew there. In reviewing Packard's hypothetical list, he recalled that the Lake Forest site might very well have been rich in what Packard now thought to be savanna species.

On his first visit to the site, Packard took one look and gasped. The plot was studded by oaks, some of them scattered and widely spaced, others tightly clustered: a savanna arrangement. Where the trees were farther apart, the understory was dominated by Indian grass and big bluestem. Where they were closer together, there was bottlebrush and wide-leafed panic grass, both species on the hypothetical species list. In fact, it literally swarmed with such species. Packard informed a local conservation group, Lake Forest Openlands, which got permission from the owners to burn the site. Once burned, it yielded a profusion of both prairie and savanna plants: the prairie white-fringed orchid, for example, and the endangered small yellow lady's slipper, and the equally endangered creamy vetchling, a classic savanna species. The site was named Middle Fork Savanna, after the middle fork of the North Branch. The North Branch restorationists harvested large quantities of seed there for the Vestal Grove experiment.

By the end of the 1985 growing season, the North Branchers had identified nearly two dozen sites within practical reach where seeds of plants on the hypothetical savanna list could be gathered. Not yet sure how much of the North Branchers' time and energy he dared divert to the fledgling and still uncertain savanna effort, Packard gathered most of the savanna seeds himself that first year. That fall, in Ross Sweeny's garage, a crew of North Branchers undertook the major task of combining the seeds into a mixture that could be sowed in Vestal Grove. This process begins with the assembly of hundreds of separate bags of seeds gathered from numerous sites. This wealth of germ plasm is sifted through screens to break the seed heads apart and then dumped onto big plastic sheets to make the mixes for sowing. A prairie mixture might end up as a five-bushel mound of seed and fluff to be prepared for planting by mixing with rakes and shovels.

The seeds of prairie plants are dry and easy to handle; the North Branchers would often sift them through their fingers with pleasure. Savanna seed turned out to be a different ballgame entirely, and the difference, when it became obvious, resulted in a flash of insight about the ecological character of the savanna. There was no pleasure-sifting of savanna seeds through the fingers because many of them were messy, runny, even disgusting mixtures of rotting fruits, berries, and nuts. When the North Branchers reached into the collection bags that first time, they pulled out what Packard described as "multicolored handfuls of lumpy, oozy glop,"[3] the genetic material of more than three dozen species of plants. Together, they made the point that the savanna developed in a different way

PURPLE
MILKWEED

from the prairie. While prairie seeds are dispersed predominantly by wind, many of the heavier seeds of savanna plants were probably dispersed by animals that buried nuts or carried fruits elsewhere and discarded the seeds after eating the pulp.

In Sweeny's garage, the fruits and nuts were mixed with the tidier seeds of grasses, sedges, and flowers found in semisunny areas, and with regular prairie seed, to produce two basic savanna mixes. One was made up of seeds of plants that grow where there is relatively more sunlight, like Canada rye, white false indigo, purple milkweed, violet bush clover, and large-flowered gerardia. The other contained seeds of plants that grow where there is relatively less sunlight, like wood reed, columbine, big-leafed aster, bloodroot, yellow pimpernel, and tall thistle. Many plants, like bottlebrush grass, were included in both mixes.

On November 11, 1985, Packard sowed both mixtures in Vestal Grove. Carrying a large kitchen garbage bag filled with "light" savanna mix and another filled with "dark" mix, he started at the east end of the grove. Walking due south from the grove's northern edge, he would grab a big handful of seed. Though mostly dry by now, much as a cherry would dry if left in the sun, the mixture still tended to stick together. So rather than scatter it to the wind, he would move his hand back and forth in front of him as he walked, shaking the seeds gently to separate them and letting them rain down on the black soil under the oaks. As he moved, he kept an eye aloft to determine whether the part of the tree canopy directly above covered more than half the sky or less. If more, he would sow "light" mixture; if less, "dark" mixture. If uncertain, he would sow both.

Reaching the end of the north-to-south sowing path, he would move over a bit and repeat the process, working south-to-north, back and forth, alternating directions until the entire grove was covered.

Packard did all this with no great sense of confidence; lots of experiments had failed, and it was entirely uncertain what, if anything, would come of all his efforts. Still, he couldn't wait for spring.

The winter of 1985–86 was one of intellectual doubt and discontent. Although Packard's confidence in the validity of his list of potential savanna species was steadily growing, one implied but very large criticism was tough to shake. John Curtis, the recognized pioneer authority on the midwestern savanna, had written that the oak savanna flora was essentially a mixture of prairie and forest species. Of the classic tallgrass oak savanna of southern Wisconsin and northeastern Illinois, the type of community he called "oak openings," Curtis wrote: Of the prevalent oak-opening species, "sixteen species reach equal or higher levels in the prairies, and the same number have an optimum in the southern [Wisconsin] forests. Only one . . . reaches its optimum in the oak openings. . . ."[4] To Packard, it seemed clear that Curtis did not consider the savanna a distinct floristic community in its own right, one having species that are as characteristic of the savanna as the classic prairie or forest species are characteristic of those communities. He questioned Curtis's species list as being incomplete and not reflective of the real savannas of presettlement days. Packard felt that the authority of Curtis's research was diminished by the fact that Curtis's sampling of species in the oak openings was done in the 1950s, long after burning had ceased and the original vegetation was gone. Still, Packard wrote, "it was hard to ignore the fine botanists who had done the best it was possible to do—especially since the only contrary information was our controversial 'research by restoration' effort on the North Branch."[5]

At the same time, Marlin Bowles continued to insist that Packard's hypothetical list of savanna species should be subject to proof through observation of real savannas in the wild. When Packard continued to protest that no good examples existed any longer, Bowles would say, "then find it in the literature," meaning the body of scientific literature. That seemed a daunting if not hopeless task, since, despite a wealth of literature on prairies, there seemed to be much less on the savannas—and maybe nothing at all that would validate Packard's species list.

Even if the planting at Vestal Grove succeeded, it was becoming clear that its results might not be accepted unless the validation could be produced. So Packard set out to find it, making himself a frequent presence at the University of Chicago library. He did it with misgivings: "I was really out of my element trying to do science; I had no training in it. Also, it was a big investment of time, and I was extremely busy. I was trying to save all these other places by building this constituency. I was working every night, every Saturday, every Sunday, in one way or another. I did a lot of speaking to very tiny groups at great distances. I also had a wife I wanted to spend time with, and I was worried that I was being wasteful of my time by going to the library, that this was a luxury, that it was borderline frivolous to try to be doing this science. Jack White said, 'Don't try to do academic research; you and I are better at other things.'"

On the other hand, Packard had "every confidence" that "if I could locate a species list in the literature, it was going to be the same stuff I found" by reading Swink-Wilhelm and scouring the Chicago area for remnant savanna species. "I didn't feel there was a lot of likelihood that a list would prove me wrong; if one could be found, I felt, it would prove me right. I could just see this pattern emerging. It seemed as if I had discovered this wonderful thing, that there was this rich ecosystem that was almost extinct, and probably rescuable, and that either I was going to figure out how to do this or the battered remnants were all going to die, and that if I could find the [confirming] information, then I could save these fair damsels."

So he would carve out odd bits of time to go to the library. Christmas Day, for instance. His wife Mim, a nurse, would work on such days because the hospital paid triple time; Steve would seize the opportunity to do research on a day when access to the stacks was easier.

Acting on a tip from a colleague, Max Hutchinson of the Natural Land Institute, he looked up two privately published studies by Dr. Alice L. Kibbe, a biology professor at Carthage College in Kenosha, Wisconsin. Hutchinson said he thought that Kibbe had written about savanna species. The studies happened to be in the card catalog, and he retrieved them. Throughout the two works, which had been published in 1926 and 1952, he found references to plants that grew in "barrens." The Kibbe material, while helpful, went only so far. But it opened another research avenue: Every time Kibbe cited a plant of the barrens, she would cite as the authority a Dr. S. B. Mead, who had published a series of lists of barrens plants in an obscure early Illinois publication called *The Prairie Farmer*, in 1846.

Somehow, the publication in which Mead's list appeared had been misfiled. Packard finally located it, however, and it did, indeed, contain "this enormous list of plants; I felt chills; I said, 'Okay, I think this is what I've been looking for all this time. It could have said, click, click, click, here are the species; Packard, you're wrong. That might have added to the chills.'"

Mead was a physician who, like other country doctors of his era, became a botanist as well: Wild plants were their primary pharmacy. He listed all the plants he had observed in west-central Illinois as he traveled his doctor's rounds on horseback. As one of the region's first settlers, he started his work in 1833, before most of the land had been plowed and grazed, and his plant lists—published starkly, with no accompanying text—thus reflected pre-settlement conditions. The list was something of a hodge-podge, with the plants arranged in no apparent order. The Latin names were archaic—meaningless, in many cases, to anyone armed with a present-day species list. But, miracle of miracles, each plant name was followed by a letter or two denoting the type of habitat in which the plant had been observed: *P* for prairie, *T* for timber, *S* for sand.

And *B* for barrens. Savanna!

Though his excitement was growing, Packard worried that many of the archaic scientific names listed by Mead would be undecipherable. Scientific names change from time to time as taxonomists reclassify species. Could the identity of those on Mead's list be traced to the present? Packard certainly would try. He wrote down the names of the 112 species that Mead had observed in the barrens and "ran home with them, feeling like I had this great ancient document that needed translating."

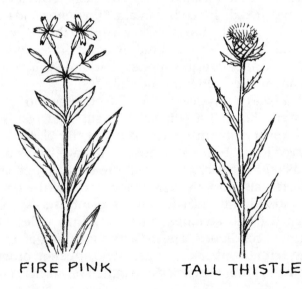

FIRE PINK   TALL THISTLE

The Swink-Wilhelm compendium of Illinois flora included the archaic names of many plants along with the current ones, and Packard eagerly dived back into the thick volume to decipher as many of Mead's listings as possible. A very old copy of *Gray's New Manual of Botany* contained others, and together the two books enabled Packard to make considerable headway. For example, Mead listed kittentails only as *Gymnandria houghtoniana*. In later taxonomies, it became *Wulfenia houghtoniana*, and later *Synthyris houghtoniana*. By 1908, in Gray's manual, it was given as *Synthyris bullii*. Today the accepted name is *Besseya bulli*, although Swink and Wilhelm call it *Wulfenia bulii*. Packard successfully traced this sort of evolution for scores of species. When stymied, he sought Floyd Swink's

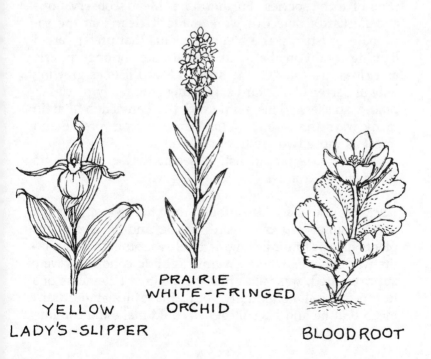

YELLOW
LADY'S-SLIPPER

PRAIRIE
WHITE-FRINGED
ORCHID

BLOODROOT

first-hand help in pinning down modern designations.

Slowly, a pattern emerged from these translations, and it confirmed Packard's earlier findings. When he would finally identify one of Mead's plants, he says, it would often turn out to be "one of my babies." Mead's list, he discovered, contained twenty-one species Mead had observed growing only on barrens, or savannas, that also appeared on Packard's hypothetical list of savanna-only species. Packard considered this a remarkable convergence, since many of the species on Mead's list—one variety of cactus, for instance—did not grow in northern Illinois; they were adapted to the climate and the different soils of central Illinois. But Mead's list did contain nineteen savanna-only species that were close relatives of savanna-only species on Packard's hypothetical list, meaning they like similar lighting conditions. If they were included, Packard's list was validated by Mead's observations to the tune of forty species. Furthermore, Mead's observations and Packard's detective work made it clear that the savanna ecosystem was a blend of plants that prefer varied lighting conditions between the extremes of open prairie and closed forest. "Of the species Mead lists as growing only in barrens," Packard said, "there are really no classic prairie species." This reinforced his conviction that in many ways the savanna is as different from prairie and forest as those two are from each other.

Mead's 138-year-old list, it seemed, was the Rosetta stone of the savanna.

Packard now had little doubt that his list of savanna plants, supported by Mead's article and by the actual plants he was finding clinging to life as refugees in out-of-the-way enclaves where savanna lighting conditions were approximated, was valid; that it constituted elements of a lost ecological community. But this affirmation didn't mean that he and his colleagues could make the community come back to life. Would the seeds he had planted in Vestal Grove, many of them now given legitimacy by Mead's article, actually grow? "I was very scared we would have a failed experiment on our hands," Packard remembers. His fear was all the sharper because the North Branchers had gone out on a limb by burning Vestal Grove. No one was burning oak groves at the time, though Betz, Wilhelm, and others were advocating it. When they proposed to the Illinois Nature Preserves Commission in December 1984 that the commission allow burning of oak groves in its dedicated preserves as being necessary to their preservation and restoration, it drew a ferocious attack from a high official of the commission. He berated Packard at some length, Packard recalls, insisting that the woods would be destroyed and houses would burn down and the commission would get sued and no one would ever again agree to serve on the commission, and accusing Packard of being the kind of person who gives conservation a bad name.

With that sort of attitude about, a failure at Vestal Grove would only invite more criticism. To have burned the grove without specific authorization, to have only briars, dandelions, and thistles come up—as had been the case until now—would provide much ammunition for the critics. When he gathered and sowed the seeds at Vestal Grove, Packard was operating on logic and faith. What if it didn't work? "We may be in a lot of trouble over this," Packard thought at the time, "and this could set us back" in the broader restoration effort.

In the spring of 1986, Vestal Grove wiped away all the fears and bestowed sweet vindication. The season, Packard wrote later, arrived with "amazing grace."[6]

Where only black dirt and weeds had been before, countless tiny cotyledons—the first, fragile, preformed leaves that burst from germinating seeds—cast a soft, green sheen across the grove's floor. Many of the species on Mead's list were now soaking up the sunlight filtering through the oaks, probably for the first time in a century and a half on that spot. Packard didn't yet know the plants well enough to recognize species by their cotyledons, but it was clear that the grove was coming alive—poof!—like magic. "I remember this tremendous sense of confirmation," Packard says. "It was as if the ecosystem patted me on the back and said, 'Okay, kid, you've done well.' I had a very strong sense that we were *there*, that this was *it*. But I was still nervous about it. What if it turns out that I'm misidentifying them and that they're in fact not the plants I think they are? And even if they are the right plants, they might be totally overwhelmed by weeds and killed off. But by that spring, we were nevertheless pretty confident we knew what we were doing."

When a resurrected ecosystem like Vestal Grove explodes into life, it does so gradually, over a period of years. There is no one day, or even any one season, when it bursts forth in complete glory. Many of the seeds sown by Packard in November 1985 did not sprout until several years later, and many have still not appeared. But there has been a steady buildup of species from that first planting, as first one wave of plants (to adopt Betz's formulation) kicked in, and then another. The first year, most of the plants that appeared turned out to be grasses. Bottlebrush grass, for instance, with its distinctive spiky head that looks as if it could indeed scrub out the inside of a jar, popped up all over the place, as did silky wild rye, Virginia wild rye, nodding fescue, woodland brome—and woodreed, *Cinna arundinacea*, Packard's old friend from the earlier days at Miami Woods and from his exhaustive analysis of the Swink-Wilhelm compendium. Nowhere in northeastern Illinois, Packard was certain, was there such a rich and abundant mixture of woodland-savanna grasses.

Wildflowers soon began to pop from the seeds as well. Packard remembers being especially struck in the earlier years by an abundance of sweet black-eyed Susans, mullein foxgloves, and yellow pimpernels, all of them ecologically finicky species that require a stable ecosystem in a relatively advanced stage of succession in which to flourish.

Together, the proliferating species were beginning to knit together a rich ground cover. In the beginning the covering was thinner, dependent as it was on the small number of seeds that had been planted compared with the lavish seed-spill that nature would provide. And provide it did. As the new plants grew, they broadcast thousands of their own seeds. After that, "there would be ground where every square inch had something coming up," Packard recalls. "We were seeing the superorganism that holds the soil together actually completing itself. It's almost like skin forming where there had been a cut or something; it closes over and becomes healthy."

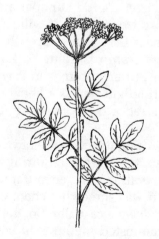

YELLOW PIMPERNEL

The return of animal life was signaled by the arrival of rose-breasted grosbeaks, classic inhabitants of open woodlands that grow next to fields. With their big, parrotlike beaks and flashy red-white-and-black plumage, they seemed to Packard "so exotic and appropriate." They thrived in the grove.

So did a number of newly appearing, uncommon butterfly species, including the Appalachian brown, a brownish, rose-cast flitter with a row of eyespots bordering the edges of its rounded wings; the brilliant orange great-spangled fritillary, a connoisseur of sweet black-eyed Susan nectar; and a variety of hairstreaks. Soon the rare Edwards's hairstreak became the commonest hairstreak butterfly in the grove. Oak thickets and dense oak stands among open woods are its habitat, and the grove was made to order. It lays its eggs on oak twigs, and the emerging caterpillars feed on oak leaves. The small adults, their warm-brown wings flecked with orange and blue, depend on nectar from the grove's flowers, and that apparently is what lured them back. "They're pugnacious little things," says Packard. "One will sit on some prominent flower or leaf and lord it over a little subopening [like] a shaft of light between two tree trunks. It will sit there and watch, and if I walk in, it flies at my face; this thing about the size of a postage stamp is going to kick my butt out of there. If another butterfly comes in it will try and scare it off, and this dogfight starts. They chase each other around, and if a lot of them get going they whirl around like a tornado."

But the most dramatic evidence of what was happening was less obvious to the eye, requiring deeper and more systematic observation. As encouraging as the grove's flowering was, it was somewhat chaotic and hard to keep track of when viewed casually. So the North Branchers adopted the time-tested methods of botanists to identify and keep close track of each species as it appeared, thrived, and stabilized, building a data base that continues to evolve and grow as the grove evolves.

Their device was that of the transect. This is nothing more than an imaginary line drawn along a compass azimuth from one end of the grove to the other, along which plants are sampled from year to year to determine how the ecological community is assembling and reassembling itself. Packard did the first transect himself, to establish a base line, before the first plants came up, when the grove was a tangle of buckthorn interrupted by black patches of soil where some of the brush had been burned. "It was a very odd feeling," he recalls. "I knew I was starting on this exciting adventure when I started that first transect." Beginning at one end of the grove, he would move along the transect, placing a sort of Hula Hoop made from hardware-store plastic tubing on the ground at five-meter intervals. Then every plant inside the hoop was identified. A plot thus delineated is called a quadrat by ecologists. Every second year at least, every quadrat has been inventoried and the results entered on a tally sheet on a clipboard and eventually in a computerized data base maintained by John Balaban at his home.

By 1991, the transect sampling had found 136 native species growing in Vestal Grove. Sixty-three of them, or 46 percent of the total, had a Wilhelm-Swink ecological-quality rating of 5 or better, indicating that they belonged to a stable ecosystem in an advanced succession phase. A handful were truly special, including the big-leafed aster and the willow aster, each with a quality rating of 10, indicating they can survive only in a specific, narrow range of ecological conditions, conditions that had now been established in Vestal Grove; Kalm's brome, with a rating of 15, indicating that it is quite rare in the Chicago area; and the beautiful, yellow-petaled, great St. John's-wort, with a rating of 20, the rarest on the list. Under the Wilhelm-Swink system, it was considered to be locally threatened or endangered. Now whole patches of it flower in July both in Vestal Grove and other sun-dappled parts of Somme Prairie Grove.

The North Branchers needed no trained ecologists to tell them how uncommon many of the plant species were. Volunteer Laurel Ross, who had come to oversee the savanna seed collection by 1992, often found only a few scattered specimens of many plant species in the continuing search of savanna remnants in metropolitan Chicago. From these, very few seeds could be collected. But by 1992, Vestal Grove and other North Branch savannas were producing more than three hundred gallons of savanna seed a year, vastly more than could be found in all the railroad rights-of-way, all the horsepath edges and forest edges, all the thousands of acres of forest preserves. Clearly, the grove had become an effective haven and breeding ground for diverse species of plants that had barely been clinging to a shrinking ecological niche for so long.

Applying a formula derived from Wilhelm's species rating system, Packard and Balaban tried to measure the long-term trend in the grove's biological richness. The formula combines two measures: the Wilhelm-Swink ecological quality index of the plants in a given quadrat and the number of species in the quadrat. According to this formula, the average index for Vestal Grove's nineteen quadrats in 1985–86 was 3.5. In 1986–87 it rose to 7.6; in 1988, to 12.1; in 1989, to 12.8; and in 1991 to 13.9. "It's a smooth curve," says Packard. "There really is no one, single time when Vestal Grove blossomed all at once. Each year it was a little better, which is what you'd expect from an ecosystem unfolding."

Exactly when the name Vestal Grove emerged is unclear. But by 1988 it had stuck, and there is no doubt about its provenance. Arthur Vestal, whose 1936 article had suggested to Packard that maybe the oak groves were neither all-forest nor all-prairie but a different kind of ecosystem altogether, "was the first person I ever read who theorized

that the savannas were something special and that someone ought to do something to try to save them," Packard
says now. "I thought that was prescient, and that it was a
noble thought." Also, Packard was taking heat, as he saw
it, from those who thought he "wasn't properly respectful
of the botanical establishment." Vestal had been a pillar
of Illinois botany, and honoring him might convey to critics that Packard did indeed respect the botanical tradition.

"Plus," he says, "it was a fun name, because it sounded
like virgins, as in vestal virgins."

PART TWO

PART TWO

7

A NATIONAL
MOVEMENT

Steve Packard and Bob Betz are not alone in their labors. The 1980s and 1990s have seen a flowering of other restoration efforts not only on the prairies and savannas of their own region, but also in other types of ecosystems across America, from the forests of northern California to the piney woods and wetlands of Florida and from the offshore islands of the Northeast to the deserts of the Southwest.

No longer content to try to hold the line in an often losing attempt to protect nature, conservationists are at last moving from the defensive to the offensive. They are striking back, and restoration is their tool. Restoration makes it possible to go beyond preserving what remains of nature to reexpand its reach.

The need is acute if conservation biologists are right. It seems possible that within the last half century humans have so transformed and degraded the biosphere—the fine weave of life, land, water, and air—that a mass extinction of plant, animal, and microbial species could take place within our children's lifetimes. There have been five big extinctions of life in the last 600 million years, usually linked to climatic change, in which 35 to 95 percent of all species then on the planet vanished. In each case, according to the fossil record, it took 10 million years or more for biological diversity to rebuild. Now the threat comes from human activity, which has come to rank with nature's largest forces as a transformer of the biosphere. As humans plant crops, build cities, cut down trees, drain wetlands, and alter the course and ecology of rivers and streams, they destroy species habitat. In time, if enough patches of a given type of habitat disappear, the species that live in it will be doomed to extinction. Pollution also plays a role, as do hunting and overexploitation of biological resources, such as overfishing that threatens marine keystone species like sharks. But habitat destruction—coupled with the introduction of exotic plants, animals, and microbes that choke out native species in what habitat remains—appears to be the main threat to biodiversity.

Scientists are uncertain how many species are being doomed by humanity's pell-mell expansion. But Dr. Edward O. Wilson of Harvard University, a leading conservation biologist, and a colleague, the late Dr. Robert MacArthur, have shown on the basis of field observations that when a patch of habitat is reduced in area by 90 percent, the number of species living in it eventually shrinks by about half. At the rate at which habitats were being destroyed in the early 1990s, especially in the tropical forests, Wilson has calculated that a quarter or more of the earth's species could be doomed to eventual extinction in the next half century. The rate of habitat destruction could increase given the swelling of human population. United Nations demographers figure that the global population, 5.7 billion in 1993, will reach 10 billion around the year 2050 before stabilizing at about 11 billion by 2200.

The world would be a poorer, less interesting place in the face of an extinction spasm, robbing humanity, as Dr.

Peter H. Raven of the Missouri Botanical Garden puts it, "of the organisms that give wonder and beauty and joy to the world." But the biodiversity question matters not just because life is valuable and beautiful in its own right, though that is reason enough. Nature is the ground from which humanity sprang, and on which its future survival depends. It is not simply that nature provides the raw materials for such necessities as food and medicine, though this is true, too. It is that biodiversity appears vital to the functioning of the global ecosystem, and any significant reduction in species, either globally or at the ecosystem level, could undermine the biosphere at large. The diversity of life, for instance, interacts with the oceans and the atmosphere to regulate climate. It is essential in creating soils and holding them in place. It removes pollution from water and maintains a microbial balance in which pathogens that might harm humans are kept under control.

Ecologists are only beginning to probe the relationship between biodiversity and the stability of ecosystems, but early evidence indicates that the richer an ecosystem is in species, the more stable it is, and the more able to withstand disturbance and natural catastrophe like disease or climatic stress. Some scientists have held that biodiversity does not matter to ecosystem stability so long as there are one or two species to carry out each important ecosystem function, like photosynthesis, pollination, plant consumption, predation, and decomposition of detritus and waste. But such data as exist support the opposite view: that biodiversity is crucial to ecosystem stability. A greater diversity of plant species, for instance, means there is a better chance that some of the species will be resistant to drought. When drought comes, field experiments have shown, these species step up their growth to make up for the biomass lost when the drought kills or stunts other species. Reduce species, the early evidence shows, and an ecosystem becomes progressively less robust and less able to withstand stress. At some point—conservation biologists do not know exactly where it is—the web of life in a given ecosystem begins to unravel as its populations of species shrink, and one by one the species disappear altogether. Those species may still exist someplace, but their absence from a particular ecosystem weakens it; and if many ecosystems are weakened in this way, the health of the biosphere at large could eventually be placed at risk. Conservationists argue that this is a chance manifestly not worth taking.

There are other, equally important levels of biodiversity besides that of the species. Ecosystems display their own widely distinctive traits, and each plays a unique role in the biosphere. On the finest level, the array of alternative genes, or alleles, embodied in individuals within the same species provide the raw material on which evolution works. Individuals with a combination of genes that enables them to adapt better to a given set of environmental conditions will survive better in those conditions. Over time, as environmental conditions change or populations of a given species move into new environments, individuals with the favorable alleles gradually replace others in the population. This leads to the emergence of new species. Thus, preserving species, both globally and at the ecosystem level, is not enough; large enough numbers of a species must also be saved so that the array of alleles can be conserved. And they must be preserved in natural ecosystems, since evolution cannot unfold very well in a frozen seed bank or a zoo.

One way or another, whether through organized control programs or the self-interest of individuals or regional population crashes as people outrun their resources in various parts of the world, human population growth will eventually be checked. The trick, many conservation biologists believe, is to preserve as many species, alleles, plant and animal communities, and ecosystems as possible until then.

That is where restoration comes in. It is both a means of preserving biodiversity until the spasm is over and of regreening the planet afterward.

"One becomes pessimistic if you think of [the biodiversity problem] in terms of years or decades," says Michael Soulé of the University of California at Santa Cruz. "But if we can protect most of the larger life forms on the planet and maintain healthy examples of most of the biological systems, the ecosystems, then I think there's hope in the long run for restoration to reanimate and revivify the planet once this [population surge] has passed."

Robert Jenkins, the former science director of the Nature Conservancy, says that "it's pretty clear that the trajectory of human proliferation at this time does not intend to leave a lot of habitat" for the rest of nature's creatures. In the meantime, he says, the task of conservationists is to create as many "lifeboats" as possible. "We have always thought that what we were doing was sustaining the materials with which the earth could one day be reclothed after the human species gets its affairs in order." But even the lifeboats—nature preserves—could be threatened. Restoration can repair them and create new ones. "I like restoration," says Jenkins. "It's the only really proactive kind of thing we do. Everything else is an orderly retreat."

Restoration could turn out to be a godsend if the threat of global warming materializes as a result of heat-trapping gases released into the atmosphere by the burning of fossil fuels like coal, oil, and natural gas. The world's organisms and ecosystems have adapted many times in the remote past to climatic changes as big or bigger than that expected to result from human activity. Those natural changes took place over hundreds or thousands of years, however; anthropogenic global warming, if it develops as many climatologists predict, will take place in mere decades, and many organisms and ecosystems would likely not be able to adapt that quickly. Significant greenhouse warming, for instance, would probably change the distribution of plants and animals as northern climes become warmer. This would mean disaster for some biodiversity preserves and the species in them and would threaten to undo decades of conservation efforts. Restoration would provide the means to reestablish ecosystems and the species they contain in new, more hospitable localities.

Restoration is coming to be viewed as so promising that in 1991, a special panel of the National Research Council recommended that the nation undertake an ambitious long-term program to restore 400,000 miles of ecologically degraded rivers and streams and 2 million acres of damaged lakes over the next two decades. In 1992, at the Earth Summit in Rio de Janeiro, the nations of the world signed a biodiversity treaty that committed them to undertake, where practicable and appropriate, a number of comprehensive conservation measures—including ecosystem restoration.

And no less an eminence than Edward Wilson has written that the rescue of the "living dead"—species doomed to extinction if left alone—"can be accomplished if natural habitats are not only preserved but enlarged, sliding the numbers of survivable species back up the logarithmic curve that connects quantity of biodiversity to amount of area.

"Here," he wrote, "is the means to end the great extinction spasm. The next century will, I believe, be the era of restoration in ecology."[7]

But what is restoration?

As conceived of by the emerging mainstream of restorationists, it does not mean what is usually called reclamation: replanting a strip-mined area with exotic vegetation, for instance. It does not include reforestation in which ecosystem values are irrelevant and whose sole purpose, as is often the case, is to plant a one-species tree "crop" for harvesting, just as if a farmer were planting his field. It does not include manipulating lakes and streams solely for human use—boating and fishing, for instance—to the exclusion of other biological and ecological values. The cosmetic planting of a few wild grasses and flowering plants simply to make things pretty and green, as real-estate developers sometimes do in an effort to enhance the esthetics of their projects or deflect criticism or both, does not constitute restoration in its new sense. Nor does revivifying lakes deadened by acid rain through the application of limestone, if that is all that's done. The lake life that existed before acidification may come back, but the ecosystem may still be degraded by silt, for instance, or exotic species.

Ecological restoration is broader and more encompassing. Its purpose, as commonly conceived by American restorationists, is to return an ecosystem as nearly as possible to the condition in which it functioned before Europeans disturbed it. The express and primary goal is to preserve and promote biological diversity and the relationships among organisms, earth, air, sunlight, and water that ecologists call "ecosystem functions." The object is not to make a detailed carbon copy of the original. That is not possible, since the set of events that led up to the point when the Europeans arrived cannot be reproduced. And even if that could be done, as will be seen later, ecosystems might not develop in precisely the same way as they did originally; the assembly of a biological community rarely if ever takes exactly the same path twice, and ecosystems may exist perfectly well in alternative states.

The purpose is, rather, to re-create as nearly as possible the essentials of the ecosystem's structure, including as many original species of plants, animals, and microbes as possible, and enable them to interact as they once did. In this way ecosystem stability can be maintained, evolutionary processes can continue, new species can eventually emerge, and biodiversity can continue to be maintained into the future.

Restoration is generally viewed as a deliberate effort to

compensate for humans' destructive influence. This seems not only logical and practical, but also just: Humans have disrupted the system, so humans should fix it. In fact, according to the emerging restorationist philosophy, only humans *can* fix it. To pretend otherwise, on the grounds that people should let "nature" take its own course, is seen by restorationists—and increasingly by conservationists generally—as naively delusional. If allowed to guide policy, according to the new conservationists, a laissez-faire approach to conservation will guarantee failure.

The line between restoration and other, less-than-optimal kinds of rehabilitation is not always hard and fast. Restoring trout streams, for example, as has been widely done in the United States, happily restores the entire stream habitat, to the delight not only of fishermen but conservationists as well. But the trout themselves are frequently exotic species from abroad or from some other region of North America, and so the restored ecosystem, while close to its natural conditions, is in some considerable measure inauthentic.

That may be acceptable, depending on how badly an ecosystem has been degraded. "In general, the better the condition of a site, the more 'natural' it is, the more effort the restorationist will want to invest in 'purity' . . . and in excluding exotics," Dr. Daniel Janzen, an ace restorationist from the University of Pennsylvania who works in the dry tropical forests of Costa Rica, wrote in 1992.[8] Janzen likened the enterprise to restoring a building: "Enormous care might be put into restoring a slightly damaged thirteenth century cathedral to its Medieval condition. However, if the cathedral has been reduced to rubble, and most of the bricks were long ago removed for paving stones, the ensuing discussion among the architects and others planning its restoration will be quite different. They might even wind up with electric lights and a loudspeaker system built into the pulpit." In time, when restorationists are more secure in their art and more confident of their scientific ground, they might want to include compatible exotics in the restoration mix in selected cases. But Janzen raises the prospect that exotics could "merrily leave the restoration area" and become established elsewhere as pests. Most restorationists now are having enough trouble keeping escaped exotics from choking out native species to even consider such a risky step as introducing exotics on purpose.

Even with the least degraded ecosystems, conditions may have changed so much in the last three centuries that returning to presettlement conditions would be impossible even if presettlement assemblies of flora and fauna were re-created exactly. The ideal is surely unattainable if only because the landscape is now so fragmented by human activity that the ecosystems most in need of restoration cannot be integrated with it. Unless they are, the system is unlikely to be self-regulating and self-sustaining. For example, it is clearly impractical to introduce wolves and cougars back into places like the Chicago suburbs to control the deer population. And if the deer population gets out of control, the deer may destroy the entire restoration project. For another example, exotic plant species have become so firmly and irrevocably established outside nature preserves and restoration sites that they constantly invade the sites.

The experience of the Hutcheson Memorial Forest at Rutgers University is highly illuminating in this regard. In 1955, an apparently virgin patch of mature forest was set aside there on the assumption that protecting the tract but otherwise leaving it alone would be an effective conservation strategy. Thirty years later, Norway maple, Japanese honeysuckle, and the Chinese tree of heaven—exotics, all—had become abundant in the forest. Many native wildflowers had become rare. Oaks, the ecological backbone of the forest, were no longer regenerating. Ecologists now believe that the eastern oaks, just like the bur oaks at Vestal Grove, require periodic fires to keep maples, in this case sugar maples, from crowding them out. The oaks withstand fire, the maples do not. Absent fire, the maples increasingly take over. Hutcheson Forest is now largely a product of changes wrought as a result of European settlement; its natural evolutionary course has been deflected.

To prevent this and similar distorting factors from degrading restoration sites all over again, most restored ecosystems—and other nature preserves as well—are going to have to be managed and manipulated by humans indefinitely, in the view of Dr. John Cairns, Jr., of Virginia Polytechnic Institute, the chairman of the National Research Council study on restoring lakes, streams, and wetlands. Human intervention might be less crucial if the population explosion subsides and very large areas can be restored and preserved. Even then, humans' worldwide and apparently irreversible transplantation of plants and animals, with the consequent crowding out of many native species by a handful of exotics for which there are no effective controls in the new land, might still make management necessary. People, having altered the global ecosystem so extensively, may already have no choice but to manage it. In any case, the sight of cadres of restorationists, conservationists, and their volunteer troops digging, chopping, cutting, burning, planting, and taking constant inventories of species is likely to become increasingly familiar.

Restoration projects typically face formidable investigational, conceptual, and political obstacles that can make or break the venture even before the field-workers get their hands dirty and their brows sweaty. Figuring out what the predisturbance ecosystem was like, as Packard found, can be a knotty challenge; yet this kind of investigative ecology may be essential to many projects. Deciding on a specific objective is critical. Getting the science right can be intimidating. Securing community approval and support, given traditional attitudes about nature and conservation, can be ticklish. Dealing with politicians, bureaucracies, and entrenched interests tests both patience and political skill. Failure is always a possibility. Temporary and partial setbacks abound. Sometimes failure is abject, especially when restorationists have not done their homework or adopted the right goals or are not sufficiently committed or just do not know what they are doing.

Some projects present greater obstacles than others. As will be seen, for instance, ecosystem basics like water flows and water tables have been so altered in many wetlands that only partial restoration is possible. On the other hand, some forests tend to regenerate well given a relatively small push. And in cases where the goal is profit rather than protection of species, as when developers are allowed to destroy wild habitat on the condition that they restore other habitat destroyed earlier, unsatisfactory results often ensue.

Nevertheless, a movement has been born. And despite all the obstacles, despite the sure limitations on success, it has raised hopes that restoration can be a powerful strategy for preserving biodiversity and the natural functioning of the biosphere.

Nobody knows exactly how many projects have been undertaken. But there are certainly hundreds and possibly thousands, according to Dr. William R. Jordan, III, the editor of *Restoration & Management Notes*, a journal whose pages and whose base at the University of Wisconsin has served as a clearinghouse for ideas about restoration. The movement is particularly strong in the Midwest, California, and Florida, where, in all three cases, The Nature Conservancy has taken a leading role. Riverine ecosystems in Arizona and Ohio, pine forests in Texas, salt marshes in Washington State—all are restoration targets. From the Pacific Northwest to Long Island, people are burning and cutting exotic plant species so that stifled ecosystems can breathe again. Restorationists are simultaneously at work in other countries, too. From the Caledonian forests of

Scotland to the forests of South India, people are beginning to restore some of the world's wildlands. In Costa
Rica, both coral reefs and tropical forests are being
regenerated.

Discussion of such efforts lies beyond the scope of a
work dealing with the restoration movement in the United
States. But one—Dan Janzen's reforestation effort in Costa
Rica—demands special mention because it is so ambitious,
so promising as a model for the developing world, and so
often held up by American restorationists as an example
of what is possible on a large scale.

Janzen's project involves a 425-square-mile tract of dry
tropical forest in northwestern Costa Rica called the Guanacaste Conservation Area. Dry tropical forests, which ac-
counted for 60 percent of all tropical forests before
Europeans spread around the globe, are green and lush
in the rainy season. But they turn brown and crackly in
the dry season, which makes them easily cleared by fire.
The early Spanish immediately did this, converting the
forests to pastures and farms that exist to this day. Now
less than 2 percent of the original 200,000-plus square
miles of Mesoamerican dry tropical forests survives.
What's left continues to decay ecologically, and Janzen says
that in the areas of most rapid decay, perhaps half the
remaining species could disappear in the next twenty
years.

"We got it just in time," he says.

The Guanacaste tract, named after the region's distinctive guanacaste tree, contains perhaps 300,000 living species, probably as many as occur in all of North America.
Probably only one species, the scarlet macaw, has been
driven to extinction by the destruction of the forests, but
many species are drastically reduced in numbers. A lot
"are hanging on in little populations," says Janzen.

A simple idea underlies the Guanacaste project: Stop
the burning and let the forest come back naturally—the
exact reverse of what one does in restoring a savanna or

prairie. Many forests not dependent on fire tend to rees-tablish themselves if left alone, as has been amply demon-strated in many industrialized countries where farming has ceased and succession has been allowed to start up again. The northeastern United States is a prime example.

The Guanacaste strategy was to buy up pastureland around existing islands of relatively undisturbed forest. These undisturbed forests would gradually expand to the abandoned pastures as wind and animals carried seeds out of the forest. Nineteen species of forest trees, includ-ing the mahogany, have seeds light enough to be dis-persed by wind. Some two hundred other species have seeds too heavy for this. The guanacaste tree, for one, produces a fruit about the size of a human hand. Inside it are large oval seeds too heavy to be carried by the wind. Instead, horses and cows allowed to graze the pasture eat them, and they are deposited, intact, when the animals defecate in the pastures. Young guanacaste trees sprout rapidly from the deposits. After six years or so, the tree's growth suddenly spurts. Fifteen years after it sprouted, the tree's trunk is as thick as a man's waist and growing about half an inch in diameter a year. To people who say that horses and cows are not natural, that they were put there by humans, Janzen responds that horses and other grazing animals were an integral part of the forest ecosys-tem until human hunters extinguished them about ten thousand years ago. (Today's horses are the descendants of those introduced by Europeans.)

Once trees begin to rise in the now-fireless open areas, according to Janzen, other animals begin to respond. Birds rest in the tree branches, and when they take off, their dung deposits seeds of yet other tree species. "There's a constant rain of these bird-dispersed seeds coming down under that horse-dispersed tree," says Janzen, and in due course several species of trees will have combined to form an island of forest in the middle of the pasture. Peccaries (wild pigs) and coyotes also disperse seeds in this manner.

But the "real champion seed disperser" is the agouti, a cat-sized rodent that buries acorns and other nuts all over the place just like North American squirrels. The nuts are too big and hard to go through the gut of just any animal today. Ancient ground sloths ate and distributed the hard seeds before humans extinguished the sloths, but today the distributive function has been taken over by the agouti. It is the agoutis, says Janzen, that "finally give you back an intact forest."

In the Guanacaste Conservation Area today, there are no more big, open areas of pasture. The former grazing lands are covered with small trees, an incipient forest. In twenty or thirty years, Janzen believes, the forest will no longer be flammable and the fire-control program can end. But it may take centuries, he says, for the original forest to come all the way back.

The same promise and the same limitations are on display in a sampling of the United States' more illuminating restoration projects, as of 1993, described in the next chapter. Most are in early stages. None have yet to flower fully. But together they suggest the breadth and variety of the nascent movement in America.

8

RESTORATION
SMORGASBORD

When the California gold rush began in 1849, the banks of the Sacramento River—California's largest, draining a third of the state—were a dense, ecologically complex tangle of trees, shrubs, and vines harboring more living species than any other forest ecosystem in the state. The canopy was dominated by cottonwood and oak, with a subcanopy of box elder, Oregon ash, and elderberry. Chains of grapevine, pipevine, and Virginia's bower draped the trees, and a thick understory characterized by mugwort, native sedges, and native grasses carpeted the forest floor. Willow, sycamore, alder, buttonbush, and wild rose grew along backwater sloughs and gravel bars. The forest abounded with Columbia mule deer, gray foxes, river otters, porcupines, and ring-tailed cats. Yellow-billed cuckoos, blue grosbeaks, yellow-breasted chats, willow flycatchers, Bell's vireos, and yellow warblers flitted through the branches.

All except the last three species still live in the valley, but on disconnected blocks of land whose fragmentation and small scale cannot assure the presence of all species indefinitely. It is a measure of the forests' waning ecological vitality that the yellow-billed cuckoo is listed by the state of California as endangered, and the valley elderberry longhorn beetle, which lives inside the elderberry shrubs' stems and roots, is listed as threatened. Before the gold rush of 1849, 800,000 acres of riparian forests and woodlands grew along the Sacramento. Miners, finding that they could make a more reliable living farming the rich alluvial soil that supported the forests, were the first to clear them. Today less than 20,000 acres, or 2 percent, remain. Dams, the diversion of water from the river, and the pumping of ground water for irrigation, coupled with the cutting of trees, have resulted in the near-collapse of the riparian ecosystem.

Even before the disastrous Midwestern floods of 1993, more and more farmers were concluding that floodplains —like chaparral ecosystems where houses burn down, beach communities at the mercy of oceanic storms, and a number of other places highly vulnerable to nature's ravages—were not meant for human occupation. The point was periodically driven home to the Sacramento Valley farmers by devastating floods that brought economic disaster. In 1986, floodwaters killed thousands of acres of almond trees and damaged prune orchards. Afterward, farmers had to bear ruinous costs to remove layers of sand and silt deposited by the flood. In 1987, Congress offered the farmers a way out by establishing the Sacramento River National Wildlife Refuge for the protection and restoration of riparian forests. Under that law, the U.S. Fish and Wildlife Service has purchased land to protect existing blocks of forest, as well as flood-prone orchard lands suitable for restoration. Farmers have used their money from the sale of the floodlands to develop new orchards on higher ground. Other state and federal agencies have also bought up blocks for preservation and restoration, and the Nature Conservancy has stepped in to do the restoration.

The Conservancy had already undertaken similar projects on the Kern and Cosumnes rivers, two of the several forest, grassland, saltbush plain, coastal dune, and desert oasis undertakings that make California a leader in the nascent restoration movement. Building on their earlier experience, Conservancy workers headed by Dr. F. Thomas Griggs, an ecologist working out of Hamilton City on the Sacramento, in 1989 launched a two-part strategy aimed at long-term protection of what remains of the riparian ecosystem's biological diversity. One part of the strategy aims at preserving the remaining blocks of forest along the river. The other part aims at enlarging the acreage of those blocks through restoration, and then connecting the blocks by restoring corridors between them. The idea is to create, in effect, a larger preserve whose scale makes it ecologically viable enough to secure the future of the native species. Over the next two decades, the Conservancy hopes to restore between 11,000 and 15,000 acres along a 100-mile stretch of the Sacramento between Red Bluff and Colusa. The ultimate goal is to withdraw all human intervention from this enlarged and reconnected ecosystem and let it function on its own.

Recognizing that it cannot do the job alone, the Conservancy has sought help. First, money. While the federal legislation provided funds for land acquisition, it put up none for restoration. So the Conservancy and the Fish and Wildlife Service joined in a creative financial arrangement: The farmer who previously owned the property leases it back; the rent he pays covers the costs of restoration. He is allowed to replant what land is not yet being restored, which helps his cash flow, and any work he does for The Conservancy is deducted from the rent.

But the arrangement also seeks to go a step further and tap the farmer's skills. "I've worked with a lot of farmers and cattlemen," says Tom Griggs, "and my belief is that farmers are practicing ecologists. They go out daily and make decisions on the basis of soil, weed competition, climate, and so on, and they know how to take care of large acreages. They already have the eye of an ecologist; it's just that their goal is to maximize production, and ours is to get native trees established and functioning as a community." Plus, they are in command of modern agricultural technology that might be enlisted in the restoration cause.

The relationship between farmers and restoration ecologists is being tested in the centerpiece of the young project, a 700-acre tract of flood-prone farmland at Kopta Slough on the Sacramento near the town of Corning. The tract is adjacent to a 200-acre block of forest, and restoring the entire 700 acres, as planned, would create a large preserve. In at least three other areas, the Conservancy plans to restore even bigger blocks of 2,000 to 3,000 acres.

The basic plan in Kopta Slough has been to use standard agricultural practices to plant trees on a large scale. The technique involves running a big farm implement called a ripping tooth through the soil to gouge out a thirty-inch trench. The plantings go in the trench: acorns in November and December, stem cuttings in January and February, and rooted seedlings raised in a greenhouse in February and March. A local farmer does the soil ripping. Volunteers do the planting and raise the greenhouse seedlings. (More about the volunteers later.) The farmer uses existing irrigation facilities to water the young trees until they become established.

In 1989, the first year of the Kopta Slough effort, the volunteers planted seventeen acres in cottonwood and sandbar willow. At the end of that growing season, the roots of some cottonwoods were exposed with a backhoe. They had grown far enough to reach the water table more than sixteen feet beneath the surface; after two years they no longer needed to be irrigated.

In 1990, the volunteers planted fifty acres in cottonwood, valley oak, sycamore, box elder, elderberry, and three species of willow. Backhoe excavations after two years revealed that the cottonwoods, now more than twenty feet tall, had sunk their roots to the water table again, and that elderberry, arroyo willow, sycamore, and valley oak had pushed their roots down seven feet and more.

In 1991, seventy-three more acres of trees were planted, this time in conjunction with kidney beans. The main reason for the mixing of trees and crops was to take advantage of summer irrigation by crop sprinklers. But 80 percent of the trees died because the crop was planted too late and the irrigation was delayed. The survivors did well, however, and by the end of their first season had grown to six to ten feet. In 1992, Griggs and company replanted the failed areas and experimented with planting trees in an alfalfa field.

Mixing trees and crops may seem like a step backward, but it has the advantage of cutting costs while protecting the trees as they get established. Once the trees are planted according to a schedule determined by Conservancy staff members, the farmer irrigates them along with the alfalfa crop, and he mows the alfalfa several times during the season. The mowing keeps both alfalfa and weeds from competing with the young trees. The farmer keeps the alfalfa. Without the farmer's efforts, the restorationists would have to foot the bill for irrigation and weed control. With them, it comes free.

The restorationists put this arrangement into practice at Kopta Slough in 1993, with the volunteers planting acorns, in rows alongside the alfalfa, on one hundred acres. After an agriculture-to-forest transition of four or five years, it is hoped, the trees will be well enough established so that natural ecological processes take over and the restorationists and the farmer walk away—the restorationists to move on to another tract and the farmer to go about his business on other land outside the floodplain. In time, Griggs believes, natural succession will dissolve the straight-line pattern of the trees, and they will be naturally distributed.

After four years of activity at Kopta Slough, the forest was clearly coming back. Some cottonwoods planted in 1989 topped thirty feet and were eight inches in diameter at chest height. Some oaks, which grow more slowly and were planted a year later than the earliest cottonwoods, had reached ten feet. Nature is uneven, of course, and some trees did not do as well.

But it seemed as if the conditions for a resumption of natural forest processes were being established.

An old saw says that the people of Martha's Vineyard consider any resident not born on the island an off-islander. Tom Chase, whose ancestors arrived in 1642, would exclude even himself, since the original residents were there ten thousand years ago. And for millennia, those Indians, like their counterparts in the Midwest, lived as an integral part of an ecosystem that had co-evolved with them. Before Europeans arrived, the south-central part of the island consisted of an assembly of open, mostly treeless habitats—heathland, coastal prairie and savanna, maritime shrubland and frost bottoms (slight depressions where cold air settles, frost-killing all vegetation but scrub oaks)—knit together in a seamless ecosystem sprouting from sandy soils deposited by the leading edge of the last glacier. Given a distinct character by a combination of drought, salt, wind, late-season frosts, acidic soil, and above all fire, the coastal sandplains were home to some typical prairie species but also some species of their own, like sandplain blue-eyed grass and the Nantucket shadbush, a small shrub with white flowers. Heath hens and hawks abounded. The American burying beetle and butterflies like the regal fritillary were two of an uncountable host of invertebrates that lived there. The purseweb spider, which spends its whole life in a silken tube in the ground safe from the fires that periodically sweep the plains, was another.

It took nearly three hundred years, but Europeans and

their descendants all but destroyed this teeming ecosystem. Like the midwestern prairies, the sandplains depended on fire; without it, they would be invaded by shrubs and trees, and their open character would be lost. That is exactly what happened. Like the Indians of the Midwest, those on the Vineyard had not only permitted fire, they had used it to manage the landscape and its wildlife. This changed when English settlers came with their crops and sheep and flammable buildings. They used fire to clear fields for planting, but suppressed it once that was done. Huckleberry and shrubby scrub oak—some of the oaks today are fifteen to twenty feet tall—led a takeover of the land by woodland species.

In the early twentieth century, conservationists became alarmed by the decline of the heath hen, an eastern race of the prairie chicken. The state of Massachusetts purchased some land and put together a preserve where the hen could be protected. And then, in those days before ecologists understood very much about what made the island ecosystem tick, they proceeded in well-intentioned ignorance to dismantle most of what was left of it. They stepped up fire suppression, believing that it was inimical to the heath hen. In fact, the birds fattened on the armies of insects that appeared in the wake of a fire, and the fire cleared away thick brush that otherwise hindered the birds' mobility. The early conservationists shot cats that preyed on the heath hens. But they also shot hawks, a keystone predator essential to the ecosystem's functioning. They grew corn to feed the heath hens, but the stored corn attracted rats that ran free in the absence of predators and ate the heath hens' eggs. And as often happens when fire is suppressed, the occasional accidental fire had so much fuel and raged so hotly that it destroyed many nests and eggs that would have survived the more modest blazes of presettlement times.

Today, 5,000 acres of sandplain habitat have been preserved by the state or private conservation groups. But the ecosystem, a degraded shadow of its former self, is one of the most threatened on earth. Uncounted species, including the regal fritillary and the burying beetle, have disappeared from the island. And the heath hen is extinct. Period. Another Vineyard resident told Tom Chase of a day in 1936 when he and his father came upon the last surviving heath hen, a male, drumming his wings, calling for a mate that would never come.

Chase now is the regional ecologist for the Trustees of Reservations, a Massachusetts conservation organization founded in 1891. One day in December 1991, Chase and representatives of other Vineyard conservation groups met to try to figure out what to do about the sad state of the sandplains. Individually, those who attended had thought a lot about restoration and the use of fire to bring back ecosystems that depended on it. Some work with fire ecology had been done on neighboring Nantucket, and the Vineyard people were familiar with it, and through the emerging literature on restoration they were conversant with the work of the Chicago group, including Steve Packard. But at the 1991 meeting, Chase recalls, "it suddenly just clicked. We all realized that [restoration] was all we could do, since there isn't much land left to be acquired on the Vineyard, and the only hope was to make the best of what we had." The group realized "that this was the right thing to do, and the time was now."

The Martha's Vineyard Sandplain Restoration Project, or Sandplain Group as it came to be called, was governed by six voting members from conservation organizations and the state department of environmental management. It was understood from the start that it would be necessary to reintroduce fire to the sandplains. But the group feared that public opposition might pose a problem. It was not that islanders would necessarily raise an alarm. "We found that with very few exceptions the islanders understood," says Chase. Many old-timers remembered the burning of land for such agricultural purposes as improving blueberry crops, and "it seemed that the island intuitively appreciated the role of fire."

But could the same be said of off-island environmentalists who might see the burning as unwarranted destruction of nature? "We live in a time of deforestation, when people think all tree-killing is bad, and here we were, killing trees, telling them it was good!" To head off any difficulty, the group undertook a public-relations campaign as one of its first acts. The heads of major state conservation organizations were asked to write letters of support that could be used to deflect challenges. The group emphasized other benefits besides the primary one—preservation of species—that restoration might bring: Safety, since controlled burning would lessen the danger of unplanned and uncontrolled fires by reducing accumulated dead vegetation that would provide fuel. Public health, since fire would destroy brush that harbors the deer mouse and deer tick, the host and vector of Lyme disease, and would also kill ticks directly. Water conservation, since the fire would kill trees that in the summer absorb and evaporate vast amounts of rainwater that would otherwise seep into the ground and recharge the Vineyard's aquifer. And public enjoyment, since restoration of the sandplains would allow the return of game animals like rabbits and quail that once lived there.

The group advertised in *The Vineyard Gazette* for volunteers to help conduct the prescribed burns. It secured foundation grants totaling $8,000 to buy fireproof suits and firefighting and communications equipment. Thirty-six volunteers came forward, and in March 1992 they attended training lectures, demonstrations, and outdoor practice sessions. A few weeks later the group conducted its first three burns. The results were encouraging. Brush and trees were reduced, and native wildflowers increased. The burning, Chase said, has returned nutrients to the soil, has favored many species of plants by eliminating a long-built-up layer of thatch and dead vegetation, has allowed seeds long sequestered under the debris to sprout, and has encouraged perennials to grow more vigorously and produce more seed.

Eventually, the Sandplain Group hopes to restore at least 1,000 acres, the minimum deemed necessary to reestablish a functioning ecosystem. In 1993, the group was moving on to the collecting of native plants and their seeds for replanting; working with private landowners to develop "micro-refuges" that might be connected with the public lands and with each other by restored corridors; mapping the biological landscape to see what species remain there (the short-eared owl, the upland sandpiper, and many other birds no longer breed on Martha's Vineyard but might do so again if sufficient habitat can be restored); trying to figure out how often each diverse part of the ecosystem should be burned; and attempting to unravel the system's complex interrelationships.

It is exciting, says Tom Chase, but also more complicated than he expected. "Nothing is as simple as you think."

They call it the Garden of Eden, a thirty-five-mile strip of bluffs and ravines along the Apalachicola River in the panhandle of Florida. The Apalachicola is the only Florida river with headwaters in the Appalachians. Its shaded ravines and cool tributaries provided an ideal refuge for northern species of plants and animals driven south by the glaciers, and many of these ancient species still live there. Perhaps a hundred are rare, including the torreya tree, one of the rarest conifers in the world. In the uplands, a distinctive longleaf pine ecosystem once flourished, the evolutionary descendant of vegetation that covered these highlands as far back as the late Miocene period, some 12 million to 15 million years ago. When Europeans arrived in the American Southeast, the longleaf pines dominated the landscape in a broad arc sweeping along the coast and reaching inland to the piedmont from southern Virginia through the Carolinas to Georgia and Florida and westward to east Texas. Estimates of its presettlement extent range from 60 million to 90 million acres, making it one of the most extensive ecosystems—landscape is perhaps a better term—in the country. Along with the prairie-savanna landscape, the longleaf pine forests were one of the largest ecological provinces in the country. It may also have been the largest expanse dominated by any one tree species. With sixty or seventy species of herbaceous plants per square meter under the pines, it was one of the most biologically diverse as well.

The system owed its ecological character not only to the longleaf pine, but also to wiregrass, a tough under-story plant that grows in clumps of long, narrow leaves that curl in so much that they look tubular. These leaves provide fuel for low-intensity fires that sweep the ecosys-tem from time to time, killing the shoots of hardwood trees like turkey oak, bluejack oak, and sand live oak that otherwise would compete with the longleaf pines. The young pines themselves, which look much like wiregrass, put most of their energy into producing roots, just like a midwestern prairie grass or wildflower. And like those grasses, they quickly regrow their top shoots following a fire. After a few seasons, a young pine undergoes a growth spurt that puts its canopy out of the reach of the ground fires, and from then on, its bark thick enough to withstand the "cool fires," it is secure. The fires also fostered one of the planet's richest concentrations of understory plants as well as an abundance of distinctive animals. One of these was the gopher tortoise, a keystone species in whose bur-rows live more than 350 species of small vertebrates and invertebrates.

Today, as a result of clearing and logging, only 2 per-cent of the original longleaf-pine, wiregrass landscape re-mains. Much of what is gone was replaced by hardwoods or introduced species of commercially valuable "planta-tion" pines. As with the midwestern savannas and the Martha's Vineyard sandplains, a lot of what remains of the longleaf-pine system is severely degraded by fire suppression. And like the savannas and sandplains, the pines are now one of the world's most threatened ecosystems.

In the Garden of Eden, The Nature Conservancy in the 1980s bought up about 6,300 acres of land as a protected preserve. The deep ravines remain largely intact, but in the flat, sandy upland areas of the preserve, a longleaf-pine, wiregrass forest was mostly destroyed in the 1950s. Lumber companies clearcut the pines and bulldozed "waste" branches and ground vegetation, including wiregrass, into long windrows. Then they planted commercially profitable slash pines, in plantation rows, and suppressed fire. The slash pines did not do well in the sandy soil.

"We bought the place only for the ravines, but the uplands came with them," said Greg Seamon, the Conservancy staffer in charge of the site. "At the time we looked on them as a burden, but eventually we came to understand that management of the uplands influences the ravines." For instance, the highly prized torreya evergreen of the ravines, considered globally endangered because it grows in just five places, has been suffering from a blight. Laboratory experiments indicate that smoke can suppress the blight. If fires were restored to the uplands, the smoke could settle into the ravines and might slow the blight. Fire would also eliminate hardwoods at the top of the ravines that shut off light, thus benefiting a number of ravine species including the torreya. For this and other reasons, the Conservancy started cutting the artificially introduced slash pines, replanting longleaf pines, and reintroducing fire.

In 1984, contract laborers and volunteers planted the first 300,000 young longleafs. The basic technique was to use what is called a dibble, simply a bar with a T-shaped handle on the top and a hole in the bottom, to punch holes in the ground. One person pokes the holes, then two others follow behind inserting a young tree in each.

The trees are planted in a random pattern. At first, they were put in the ground bare-rooted. But only about 10 percent survived, so the restorationists switched to "containerized" trees whose roots are encased in a soil plug containing potting soil and fertilizer. This eliminates the problem of arranging the roots properly in the hole. The second and succeeding rounds of planting, beginning in 1988, produced survival rates of 68 to 82 percent. By the end of the winter planting season of 1991–92, nearly 800,000 trees had been put in the ground, with an overall survival rate of 59 percent—70 percent if the 1984 bare-root planting is excluded. By the end of March 1993, 50,000 more were planted by a growing force of volunteers that gradually displaced all the contract workers. As of mid-1993, 2,100 acres had been planted in trees. Eight volunteers can easily plant 5,000 a day, and the reforestation in 1993 was proceeding apace.

So far, so good. But the early effort to reintroduce fire to retard and eventually kill the slash pines went less than well. The flames sputtered out after a bit. Why? Not enough wiregrass remained to produce fuel, and what had survived languished in what Seamon calls "small, spindly clumps" in the shade of shrubs and hardwoods. The restorationists seemed stymied for a time, since the conventional scientific wisdom held that wiregrass did not bloom and did not set seed, and therefore could not be restored once extirpated. Ron Myers, director of the Conservancy's national fire management and research program, and Paula Seamon, who is the program's technical assistant and also Greg Seamon's wife, demonstrated that the conventional wisdom was false. In tests conducted out of the Conservancy's office at Tall Timbers Research Station in Tallahassee, they confirmed what other experimenters had also found: that wiregrass does indeed flower—profusely—and produces seed if it is burned during the growing season rather than in the winter, as had previously been done.

They discovered further that the seed can be harvested if the plants are caught at precisely the right time, after the seed matures but before it drops from the stem and is lost. In northern Florida, the seed matures in late fall or early winter. To gauge when to harvest, Paula Seamon and Myers collect small samples of seeds starting in late October. The seeds are placed on moist filter paper in petri dishes. If ready for harvest, they will germinate in five to ten days. The process is repeated until this happens. Then the harvest begins. The seed is gathered by running the fingers up the flowering stalk with the seed collecting between the fingertips. Wiregrass is grown from the seeds in a nursery at Tall Timbers, then transplanted to the field, by hand, using either a dibble or a trowel.

This is slow work, and at a rate of three to five acres a year it will take a long time to restore wiregrass to 2,600 acres. The restorationists are now trying to figure out how to speed things up. Using combines and fertilizer spreaders to harvest and broadcast seed, as Bob Betz does at Fermilab, would not work at the Apalachicola bluffs because there are trees in the way. There are lots of unanswered questions, and years of hard work lie ahead.

As Greg Seamon says, "This is all new. . . . We're bumbling along on the cutting edge, [but] we're convinced that we're headed in the right direction."

Deserts, contrary to their image as sterile voids, are complex biotic communities just like forests or prairies. The flat Sonoran expanse between Phoenix and Tucson, for instance, once was home to a rich array of life. Its signature plant was a shrub called the saltbush. Coyotes prowled there among barrel and queen-of-the-night cacti. Harris's hawks teamed up in cooperative relays to run jackrabbits literally to death. Burrowing owls hollowed out tunnels to protect their families from the 100-degree heat. Kit foxes, sidewinders, kangaroo rats, javelinas, ground squirrels, and lizards, predator and prey, flourished among the saltbush, creosote bush, wolfberry, ironwood, mesquite, and the night-blooming cereus—a natural community exquisitely adapted to heat and aridity.

In the 1930s, farmers discovered that when irrigated, these lands were even better at producing cotton, pecans, and melons than the moister soils farther east. So they plowed them up, and for years the desert was green with crops. Then the economics of agriculture turned sour, and farmland was increasingly abandoned starting in the 1950s. Arizona's pioneering Groundwater Management Act of 1980 took some land out of agriculture as a water-conservation measure. Later, growing municipalities increasingly strapped for water bought up other farmland for its water rights, creating what came to be called "water farms." As a result of all these factors, at least 160,000 acres in Arizona's five southern counties have been retired permanently from agriculture.

But nature has had a hard, almost impossible time reclaiming most of this territory in the way forests reclaimed vast tracts of the country's northeastern quadrant starting in the mid-nineteenth century. As farmers left their lands in the Northeast to move on to what they saw as greener pastures in the West or to become urban dwellers, croplands were abandoned wholesale. Areas that had been cleared of forest to create farms gradually returned to forest. In the Middle Atlantic region, for instance, forest cover is estimated to have doubled, from 20 percent to 40 percent of its presettlement extent, in the last century. And although numerous exotic species now mix with a predominantly native vegetation and some species like the chestnut tree have disappeared, much of the landscape has substantially recovered its former character.

But that kind of natural recovery is not much happening in the saltbush scrublands, nor is it likely to in the foreseeable future, says Dr. Laura L. Jackson, a research ecologist who until the summer of 1993 worked at the Desert Botanical Garden in Phoenix. Frequently, there is no nearby source of native seeds from which to repopulate the desert in the way that seeds of trees bordering abandoned fields in the East repopulated them. Even if an occasional seed does settle in, it finds a dry, barren surface as hard as a highway. If it should somehow find a hospitable cranny, the chances are only one in ten that it will be in a year when enough rain falls for the seed to sprout. And if it sprouts, the heat may kill it anyway. Weeds are all that grow there naturally, and even they burn out and die in the summer, leaving the ground bare and cracked.

Why didn't Jackson pick a harder place to try to restore? "I couldn't get to the moon," she says. And indeed, the abandoned fields look like a moonscape in aerial photos.

Starting almost from bare ground, Jackson in the early 1990s undertook what was surely one of the most difficult restoration efforts to date. She worked at the most basic experimental level, trying to learn if plants that are the backbone of the largely eradicated ecosystem can in fact be reestablished and, if so, at what rates and against what obstacles. In her first experiment in 1990, under a grant from the Jesse Smith Noyes Foundation, she planted the dominant perennials of the original ecosystem—creosote bush, desert saltbush, linear-leaved saltbush, mesquite, wolfberry, and globemallow—on two three-acre plots barren of vegetation and animal life. Both plots had been abandoned as agricultural land in the 1950s, and now they were the kind of land of which a wag once said, "The rabbits have to pack a lunch to cross it."

The seeds for planting were donated by local seed companies or collected by Desert Botanical Garden volunteers. The plantings relied solely on available rainfall for water, but the restorationists helped the process along by creating two-foot-wide, one-foot-high ridges, or berms, to serve as minidikes to hold rainwater. The berms were constructed about fifty feet apart, paralleling each other along the contour lines of the mildly graded but essentially flat land. The plantings were made in the water-catchment areas created by the berms. Stiff-tined rippers pulled by tractors roughed up the soil to a depth of four to six inches, creating a seed bed about eight feet wide on the uphill side of each berm.

Seeds of the native perennials were broadcast in the winter rainy season of early 1991. Half of each plot was designated at random and sown with both the dominant perennials and native annual grasses. Half the seedbeds were covered with wheat-straw mulch to hold in water. The results gave "reason to be humble," Jackson later reported.[9]

The water catchments worked well; had they not, Jackson concluded, there would have been little chance of any seedlings becoming established. That first year turned out to be a relatively wet one, and two species of saltbush established themselves on both mulched and unmulched sites. But few other species came up. Moreover, only the most vigorous plants were expected to survive spring and fall droughts. As it turned out, Jackson said, desert saltbush "looked great in all plots—too thick, really." Narrowleafed saltbush waned and by 1993 had nearly died out. Globemallow did well in the spring of 1993, and Jackson found one creosote bush, about a foot high.

In subsequent experiments, new plots were planted, and this time they were irrigated during the dry season to see what effect that might have. "One thing we did learn was that the weeds don't seem to suppress the native plant that much," said Jackson. "You do get more weeds, but also more saltbush. Also, mesquite comes up really well, but it gets nailed by rabbits fast." The experimenters found also, for example, that planting the species of plants that germinate in winter and summer together, once a year, did not work. Planting in winter meant that only the winter plants came up; planting in the summer meant that only the summer plants came up. It was discovered further that applying mulch in the winter, when it was wetter, encouraged weeds; perhaps mulching's greatest utility was in the dry summer.

As humbling as the results were, the experiments nevertheless held out hope that given the right set of circumstances, much can be accomplished in restoring the saltbush desert to something resembling its former self. Jackson saw two possible strategies. In one, catchments and mulching would be used, and seedbeds would be planted repeatedly until a good rainy year comes along. This "lazy but patient" method, as Dr. Jackson calls it, mimics natural succession but helps it along by promoting better water infiltration and by making sure that when a good rain year comes, seeds are there waiting. This strategy would demand a long-term commitment, and although the cost of seeds would be high, there would be no irrigation costs, and no especially large capital expenditure would be required.

By contrast, what Jackson calls the "hardworking but impatient" approach would be capital-intensive at the start, since it would rely on irrigation, transplantation, and weed control. While this approach produces faster results, she says, it may be more wasteful in the long run.

Much research about the obstacles and requirements of desert restoration remains to be done, but Jackson hopes to have some answers ready when opportunities for large-scale restoration present themselves. Those opportunities may come as a result of Arizona's venture in water farming. Tens of thousands of acres of farmland have been purchased by cities and industries as water sources. The pumping of water from the aquifer beneath these lands will have no deleterious effect on the surface vegetation, since the aquifer is too deep for even the longest plant roots to reach. But if nothing is done with the land, it will become a weedy eyesore, the object of criticisms—already heard—that water farms are ugly and that the abandoned farmland sometimes becomes a mini-dust

bowl, producing dust storms that pose a serious highway hazard.

Sensitivity to these issues may prompt some municipalities to want to give something back to the community, and the city of Mesa donated forty acres, plus
the water to irrigate it, for further restoration experiments. The Arizona Game and Fish Heritage Fund and
the Marshall Fund of Arizona provided funds for the
experiments.

As part of the research, three hundred square miles of
abandoned farms in Pinal County were being mapped to
identify restoration priorities. Low priority would go, for
instance, to fields improving on their own. High priority
would go to fields showing poor recovery and those adjacent to remnants of intact scrubland habitat. Some tracts
next to cities might also receive high priority because they
are more accessible and therefore might be more attractive
to volunteers.

Jackson left the Desert Botanical Garden in the summer
of 1993 to join the department of biology at the University
of Northern Iowa in Cedar Falls, but she was still involved
in the experiment from afar. The plots will be monitored
to see whether any plants in the restored area spread naturally into unplanted areas. "This will tell whether it is
feasible to plant a small patch of desert species to act as a
seed source for the surrounding area over the long term,"
says Jackson. "If this is the case, then it would be a relatively inexpensive strategy that would indeed be lazy but
patient. The area is so huge, there is no way we could
restore all of it by brute force. There are going to have to
be small pockets [of restored vegetation] that spread out
and colonize new areas on their own. We're waiting and
seeing what happens now; if that planting just sits there
and does nothing for ten or twenty years, then we haven't
accomplished a thing."

She has no rosy illusions, and her judgment on the

experiment so far is testimony to the difficulties and limitations of restoration in many instances.

Even if everything works as hoped, "I couldn't restore the desert to the way it was in 1935. The shallow groundwater is gone forever, and the land has been leveled and the river flow channelized. With the original hydrology and topography gone, and the soils damaged by tillage and irrigation, I can only introduce native species and see what happens.

"There is no 'triumph' in this any more than there is triumph in putting a dressing on an amputated leg."

Perhaps the most widespread restoration activity in the United States involves wetlands. It is an enterprise full of great promise. It is also probably the most controversial, the most politically charged, the most rife with failure, the most vulnerable to incompetence, the most susceptible to profit-driven distortion, and in some ways the most difficult of restoration pursuits. The restorationist must deal not only with the vagaries of vegetation, but also with the tricky but inescapable matter of water, where it goes and how it behaves. Success, where it has come, has been partial so far.

A number of projects across the country nevertheless give tantalizing hints of what may be feasible.

In the New Jersey Meadowlands—within sight of the Empire State Building and the World Trade Center to the east and Giants Stadium to the west—restorationists have established a tiny beachhead in a broad-front effort to bring back the nation's wetlands. The Meadowlands rest in the basin of a lake formed when the last glacier pulled back from what is today the New York City metropolitan area, and a century ago they comprised a boggy area dominated by cedar and tamarack, interspersed with brackish marshes as tidal waters mixed with fresh water from the Hackensack River. Then, starting in 1914, the whole area was ditched and diked for mosquito control, and the river upstream was dammed in 1922 to create Oradell Reservoir. The drastic changes in water flow, or hydrology, transformed the area's ecology. The common reed—ecologists call it the crabgrass of the wetlands—took over, crowding out other vegetation like salt hay and salt grass, choking the ground with dead detritus that decomposed only slowly, and growing so dense that waterbirds could not land or take off among the stalks. Ecologically speaking, the Meadowlands became largely a wasteland.

Today, on a 158-acre tract owned by Hartz Mountain Industries, something reminiscent of the original marsh has been carved out of the expanse of reeds growing as tall as a house. In this one enclave the reeds are gone, replaced by newly planted marsh cordgrass, a smaller, thinner stalk that decomposes more quickly than the reeds, thereby helping recycle nutrients. Cordgrass is ubiquitous in undisturbed salt marshes on the East Coast. With its appearance in the Meadowlands, other native species like fleabane, rushes, and sedges have reappeared naturally on the site. Fish, zooplankton, and bottom-dwelling organisms have returned to the waters, as have many species of waterfowl. All this, right in the middle of metropolitan New York.

A thousand miles to the south, in the nation's most ambitious wetlands restoration project, federal and state agencies have begun a long-term effort to reverse the decline of the Everglades, one of the world's premier ecosystems. To the casual eye, the 'glades look robust. Lush waves of sawgrass march off into the distance. Up close, the shallow water of the big marsh teems with life, from floating clumps of algae that form the basis of the Everglades food web to the alligators and predatory wading birds that crown it. The wading birds tell a disturbing tale, however. Their breeding numbers have plunged by 90 percent from natural levels. This is a direct measure of the ecosystem's health; the decline of the birds is a sign that the fish and other aquatic creatures on which they feed have also declined. Thirty-three species of Everglades animals were listed by the federal government as endangered or threatened as of 1993.

The Everglades has come to this state because twentieth-century humans, in their drive to turn south Florida into cities, suburbs, and farms, have reduced the swamp by half, to about 2,000 square miles, and have diverted too much water from what remains. Relatively little can be done to re-expand the size of the Everglades, but some of the same federal and state agencies that presided over the decline of the ecosystem have joined forces to try to re-establish the natural flows and rhythms of the Everglades' water—that is, its natural hydrology. Scientists believe that if this can be done, more than enough biota survive to repopulate the marsh once hydrological conditions are right again. The result would be a healthier though still relatively small Everglades.

The task requires rearranging and partly undoing one of the most ambitious public works in American history, the network of canals and levees that have become a fixture of life in south Florida. Carol Browner, the head of the Environmental Protection Agency in the Clinton administration and a native of south Florida involved in Everglades restoration as both a federal and state official, says she was ten years old before she realized that rivers didn't have cement bottoms.

Scientists believe that except in periods of drought, most of the Everglades was originally flooded year-round. A slight north-to-south slope in the mostly flat terrain allowed a broad sheet of water, seldom more than three feet deep, to flow from Lake Okeechobee to Florida Bay, where it helped support the bay's part freshwater, part saltwater ecosystem. The water moved quite slowly, with a single drop taking a year to make the trip. The marsh became what Dr. Crawford S. Holling, an ecologist at the University of Florida, calls a "soup of organic production" consisting of algae, aquatic insects, snails, crayfish, turtles, and a variety of other aquatic organisms. These supported the higher forms, the alligators and wading birds, and ultimately the Florida panthers that stalked parts of the 'glades.

The drainage and tapping of Everglades water for human use have drastically reduced production of aquatic life. Levees dammed Lake Okeechobee, preventing the year-round sheet flow from being replenished from the Kissimmee River watershed north of the lake, and divided the remaining 'glades into a series of four big pools: Everglades National Park on the south, and three water conservation areas adjacent to it on the north, the northernmost of which contains the Loxahatchee National Wildlife Refuge. Canals diverted water from these big pools into municipal supplies, onto farmland, and, for flood control, into the Atlantic Ocean and Gulf of Mexico. As a result, wet-season water levels are lower than they used to be in most of the Everglades, and wide stretches are now dry during most of the year.

The restoration object is to enable water to flow more freely between the four pools. This will require breaching some levees and constructing new pumping stations in some places, and officials of the U.S. Army Corps of Engineers in 1994 were working out a plan to deliver more water to the ecosystem at the proper times.

It will take decades to complete the replumbing, and no one is really sure to what degree it will restore ecological health to the Everglades. But at least one indication of the crucial role of hydrology has already become manifest. In the upper end of the 'glades, in the Loxahatchee refuge, officials have already restored year-round flooding to parts of the ecosystem where the snail kite once flourished. The kite is a hawklike bird of prey that subsists solely on the apple snail. The snails require a certain water level, and when it dropped they disappeared, and the kites with them. When it came back up again, both the snails and the kites began returning.

In the plains states, wetlands are composed of millions of prairie potholes—small, shallow, marshy ponds created by depressions left when the glaciers retreated. Among other things, these potholes provided crucial habitat for waterfowl. Starting in the mid-nineteenth century, European settlers began draining them to facilitate farming, and by the 1970s an estimated 20 million acres of pothole wetlands had been reduced by half. This proportion roughly mirrors the state of wetlands nationally: An estimated 200 million acres existed in what are now the contiguous forty-eight states when European settlers arrived, most of them in the Southeast, the Northeastern coastal states, and the upper Midwest. The Environmental Protection Agency estimates that nearly half those wetlands are gone. How fast they are disappearing now is a matter of dispute, but federal estimates place the loss at between 200,000 and 400,000 acres a year.

On the northern plains and prairies, the loss of prairie potholes has been devastating to certain species of ducks, according to Dr. Joseph S. Larson, a wetlands expert at the University of Massachusetts. They provide the nesting ground for perhaps 80 percent of the ducks in North America, he said. And with the draining of so many potholes, some species like the canvasback and the redhead are in serious decline.

Now pothole restoration efforts are proliferating. Typically, they rely on the very simple expedient of blocking drainage ditches and tiles. Other wetlands across the country are being similarly reconverted. In some instances, the U.S. Fish and Wildlife Service enters into agreements with farmers under which the service acquires the right to restore and maintain the wetlands, and the property owner acquires hunting and fishing rights on the restored tract. Hundreds of thousands of acres of wetlands across the country have now been restored through cooperation between farmers and federal agencies. For the most part these projects—nearly 10,000 of them in 1993, on plots averaging a little more than twenty acres in size—involve that simple expedient of reflooding wetlands that had been drained by farmers and letting nature take its course.

But wetlands restoration has achieved its most notable success, perhaps, along the Atlantic coast. The most knowledge and experience have been gained there, according to an authoritative 1990 study of the status of the science of wetlands creation and restoration commissioned by the Environmental Protection Agency.

The godfather of coastal restoration is Dr. Ed Garbisch, a onetime chemistry professor who twenty years ago founded one of the first restoration companies, a nonprofit outfit based in Saint Michaels, Maryland, called Environmental Concern Inc. With more than 350 at least partly successful wetlands projects to his credit, Garbisch has been in business long enough to have made and learned from mistakes, and to have built up a body of practical knowledge about how wetlands work. One of his projects is the Jersey Meadowlands restoration effort.

Garbisch maintains a rich nursery of wetlands plants at his Saint Michael's headquarters on a finger of Chesapeake Bay, from which he draws the propagules for replanting wetlands up and down the coast, as well as inland in some cases. While knowing and being able to propagate the right plants is obviously critical, wetlands go one step beyond terrestrial restoration projects in their level of difficulty. That, of course, has to do with water and its depth, flow, and seasonal variations.

If the water is too deep or too shallow or is not there at the right time or is too salty or not salty enough, the project will surely fail. In some cases, it is relatively easy to get the hydrology right, as in unplugging a farm drain; or restoring an estuarine marsh, where tides make water levels predictable; or even, despite the enormity of the task, re-plumbing the Everglades. In forested wetlands and bogs, though, water fluctuations are much more subtle and difficult to detect. And in wetlands that depend on underground aquifers for their water, it may be impossible to determine them.

In many cases, irreversibly altered hydrology limits what is possible in wetlands restoration. Take the Meadowlands project, for instance. For all its success in restoring marsh plants, beating back reeds, and attracting wildlife again, it falls short of true restoration, according to the National Research Council's 1991 study of restoration in aquatic ecosystems. A major reason, according to the study, is that the Oradell Dam has so altered the hydrology and water salinity of the area that full restoration of original vegetation is impossible. Furthermore, the study said, the project has had "virtually no impact" on the regionwide ecological degradation of the Meadowlands because of "intractable conditions" imposed by damming and ditching of Meadowland marshes and the blockage of the Hackensack River.

That doesn't mean the project wasn't worth doing; it simply means that in this and many other cases, it may be necessary to settle for half a loaf or less. Ed Garbisch is a relative optimist who believes that many kinds of wetlands can be restored to their essential functions. Others, like Dr. Joy B. Zedler, a wetlands ecologist at California State University in San Diego, doubt that the original functions of many wetlands can be brought back, at least in California, where more than 90 percent of the state's original wetlands have been lost.

"I know of no one who has proved scientifically and unequivocally that they have created or restored a fully functioning ecosystem," says Dr. Mary E. Kentula, the leader of the Environmental Protection Agency's Wetlands Research Project based at Corvallis, Oregon. She was co-editor, along with Dr. Jon A. Kusler, executive director of the Association of State Wetlands Managers, of the E.P.A. state-of-the-science study on wetlands restoration. On the other hand, Kentula says, "in some parts of the country, things look very hopeful." Kusler says that "we have relatively high success rates in creating some wetlands functions in some contexts and abysmally low success rates in others."

How success is defined is important. If it is defined as returning a wetland to its pristine condition, then success in most cases will never come. But if it is defined as restoring a few limited functions, like the provision of a critical wildlife habitat or filtering pollutants out of water that flows into and then out of the wetland, then success is more attainable. Wetlands fulfill a number of other functions, too, including flood control, providing breeding grounds for commercial fisheries, and protecting shorelines from erosion. Bringing back any one of these lost functions might justify a particular restoration project, many wetlands restorationists feel.

Many hands-on practitioners say that wetlands restoration may work best when motivated by conservation concerns and carried out by people committed over the long haul to managing the recovering ecosystem. State wetlands managers and conservationists tend to display that commitment more than do developers, who, in Kusler's view, have the understandable urge to "get in and get out." It is here—when profit intervenes—that wetlands restoration has generated political heat.

The flashpoint is the practice of so-called "mitigation," in which developers are allowed by governments to drain and destroy wetlands and replace them with, say, shopping centers and housing developments if they compensate by creating new wetlands or restoring previously lost ones elsewhere. The creation of wetlands where none existed before, as might be expected, stirs skepticism. If land were suitable for a wetland, nature would probably have put one there in the first place, and for this reason Kusler and others are "not real excited," as he puts it, about creating new wetlands to compensate for the destruction of existing ones.

Restoration of previously lost wetlands is more feasible, but only if the restorationists know what they are doing. That is often not the case, and as a result the early experience with mitigation is one of frequent failure. As inexpert, inexperienced people have gotten into the act, says Ed Garbisch, their efforts are giving restoration a bad name. A number of studies made by and for federal and state governments tend to back him up. Kentula cites a number of these, by consultants and academics in Florida, Connecticut, and Oregon, which found that many projects were improperly designed and undertaken with no clear goals. Flawed hydrology, in particular, was found to be widespread. Many projects were dominated by deep, open water rather than by the shallower water with vegetation that defines a wetland. Typically, Kentula said, the studies found steep-sided ponds with up to 90 percent open water and 10 percent vegetation. In a natural wetland, the proportions would be roughly reversed. A 1991 study for the South Florida Water Management District found that many projects were constructed where surrounding land uses like parking lots and housing might prevent the wetlands from fulfilling their functions. More than half the forty projects examined had hydrological flaws; in one, for example, water was kept from the wetland by controls designed to protect a nearby housing development. Many of the projects were found to be colonized by undesirable plants. But no corrective action had been taken, and often the situation was not even being monitored.

"There are no wetlands police; the development industry knows that," says Robin Lewis, a private wetlands restorationist in Tampa. The National Research Council panel noted that "within the mitigation context, proponents of new developments are extremely eager to believe that habitat functions can be moved about at will. It is not surprising that entrepreneurs promise the desired success and that considerable effort is made to promote completed projects as successful." The funding needed to examine how restored sites function, not just what they look like, is nearly always missing, the panel said, concluding: "Project proponents do not want to know, and regulatory agencies cannot afford to find out."

Overall, however, the panel found enough promise in wetlands restoration to recommend that the United States undertake an ambitious, long-term effort to restore wetlands, lakes, rivers, and streams. As an initial target, it recommended a net gain of 10 million acres of wetlands, or a recovery of about 10 percent of the loss to date, by the year 2010.

But it emphatically said that wetlands restoration should not be used as a way to offset or justify the destruction of other wetlands. Restoration at this stage of the game, the panel said, is still too much trial and error and not enough science.

In the two years after the panel made its report, a shift in thinking about some aspects of wetlands restoration seemed to be taking place. First, said Kusler, there was a growing recognition that in many cases it is biting off too much to try to restore plant communities and deal with hydrology at the same time. Perhaps, the new thinking says, effort should be put into getting the hydrology right and then let nature do the rest.

Second, there was a growing realization that wetlands cannot be treated in isolation from the rest of the landscape. They are part of a broader watershed ecosystem and often occur in the context of a forest or a prairie or a savanna. It is this broader landscape, according to the emerging new thinking, that must be the target of restoration efforts.

In the summer of 1993, the Clinton administration put its imprimatur on a combination of mitigation and watershed approaches. It endorsed the concept of "mitigation banking," in which a developer who wishes to compensate for destroying a wetland is required to restore another one somewhere else—*before* his project is permitted to go ahead. The idea is to assemble a number of such restored tracts in the same watershed to create a large, contiguous tract of wetlands. While small fragmented plots of restored wetlands cannot effectively reestablish lost ecological functions, according to this thinking, a consolidation of many tracts may do so, to the benefit of the whole watershed.

At this writing, it is too soon to assess how the idea might work out in practice.

The same may be true for restoration in general. But if restorationists' ultimate impact on the land is still unclear, the impact of the land on restorationists is not.

9

REEMBRACING NATURE

Volunteers are the backbone, heart, and soul of the restoration movement. And whatever the eventual result of their labors may be, working to revive moribund ecosystems is transforming and strengthening their relationship with the rest of nature in ways that other encounters like outdoor recreation, farming, gardening, and bird-watching cannot. The resulting bond infuses the movement with a remarkable vitality and passion, gives it a certain tensile strength, and bids to extend its influence beyond the restoration enterprise itself to the larger human culture.

Restoration is gardening in a sense, and also agriculture, but with a big difference: Its purpose is not to shape nature to one's esthetic taste or to make a living, but rather to enable nature to take its own course. It seeks not to control and modify natural processes, but free them. It places humans not above the rest of nature, but in it, and not just as an admirer but as a participant.

"Whereas agriculture manipulates nature analytically,

arbitrarily and for gain, restoration manipulates it constructively, for its own sake and on its own terms," Bill Jordan wrote in 1990.[10] Restoration, he wrote, "gives us business to transact in the natural world, liberating us from the passive role of observers." Whatever the results of restoration, he went on, "whatever the precise nature or quality of its product, restoration represents a deliberate participation in the ecology of the community or ecosystem under restoration. It raises a whole series of questions about the system for which the restorationist has to find answers." In seeking these answers, the restorationist necessarily becomes both more knowledgeable about the natural world and more intimate with it. Over and over again, volunteers find that far from dulling the mystery and romance of the enterprise, increasing familiarity only deepens the mystery, heightens the fascination, and creates a strengthening bond with the land.

It is hard to know the degree to which ancient peoples saw the rest of nature as threat or as ally, or themselves as an integral part of nature or separate from it. But in modern times, certainly, humans have increasingly perceived themselves primarily in relation to the artificial cultural constructs of the urban world. The relative glories and flaws of industrial civilization can be endlessly analyzed and debated, but it undeniably does have the frequent effect of cutting people off from the natural realm in which their species—a species not really so far removed from its primitive origins—evolved, and on which the species still depends, despite humans' technological brilliance, for ultimate survival. The restoration and management of ecosystems, perhaps more than any other activity, is a powerful means of reconnecting, and in a way that makes nature itself the primary concern rather than what humans can extract from it. A reconnection of this sort provides a powerful incentive to preserve and rebuild the natural world.

It is likely that not many volunteers see it in all these

dimensions at the outset. People become volunteers for lots of individual reasons, and they come from all sorts of backgrounds and represent many stages of life. The North Branch group includes people whose children have left for college, college graduates who have recently established themselves and are looking for leisure activities, single people with extra time, mothers with children in school, couples looking for a common activity to share, people in conservation organizations, local citizens interested in preserving what remains of nature in their backyards, workers in jobs that give them free time at unusual hours, college and high school students who sometimes get extra credit, and youth groups like the Boy Scouts and Girl Scouts.

Some volunteer merely because it fulfills a need to contribute to the community; many other activities would serve as well. "I think all of us need very much to feel that we're doing something worthwhile and that we have something to offer," says Jane Balaban. Retired people are especially drawn to volunteer restoration work because it helps fill their days. "At this point in our lives, older people who have an interest after they retire just have a wonderful time," said Josie Bruno, a member of Tom Chase's volunteer group on Martha's Vineyard. Over the years Mrs. Bruno had developed an interest in wildflowers during family trips to the Vineyard. After moving there permanently from New York City in the early 1980s, she said, "I knew very well I needed an interest to keep me going, so this interest in wildflowers developed more into conservation, into native plants, into learning about them." A Vineyard neighbor, Carol Knapp, joined a wildflower group led by Mrs. Bruno. "We became known as people who knew species," Mrs. Knapp says, and when the sandplain restoration group got going, it was natural for them to join it. Ed, Mrs. Knapp's husband, a retired chemist, came along. "For me," he said, "this was an opportunity to learn something entirely new." The learning and the activity never end. "It's a lot of fun to get into something and go further and further," said Mrs. Bruno.

Walt Fauerso, a leader of a group of retirees working at Kopta Slough in California, describes his motivation as "a gentle defiance—we defy our aches and pains, we defy the aging process, and we're going to keep going as long as we can." But another reason, he says, is "the joy at getting back to the earth," a joy that is all the stronger because the trees he is planting are "in a reserve where we know the trees will never be cut down" and will cast their seeds and regenerate the forest in perpetuity. "So in a symbolic way," he said, "we create our own immortality. That, I think, is the ultimate thing that brings us back to the earth and fields—a feeling of worthiness and doing something that in a way is eternal."

Mark Homrighausen, a student and carpenter in the San Francisco Bay area, had been involved in environmental activities for some years. "But that sort of work is often pretty bureaucratic," he said. "You're involved with the courts, and you're pretty removed from the outdoors." So he and his wife, Janet, signed up with the Cosumnes River restoration project, one of the Nature Conservancy's early volunteer efforts in California. "I sort of expected the Volvo set to be out there, but basically no one's in the Volvo set," he said. "There are people driving delivery trucks, to Ph.D.'s, to carpenters, and all are dedicated." He talks of the excitement of being "part of a big picture to restore a major piece of lovely lost habitat" and of "the satisfaction of doing the hands-on work—when you think about it, a lot of what we do is what a migrant worker would do, digging in the dirt, putting plants in the dirt, getting muddy."

The hunger to belong to a community is also a powerful motivator. Working with other people in a joint outdoor venture harks back to the days of community barnraising, says Jane Balaban, but that sort of thing has largely been lost in modern life. Walt Fauerso described the feeling: "You get to be almost like one big family," laughing and joking, sharing hardships like the time when members of the group found themselves planting a hillside at 6,500 feet in four inches of snow, "sliding around, taking medication for their blood pressure." Sometimes there is family tragedy. Cliff Reese, a member of the group who was about eighty years old, literally died in action, from a heart attack. "He just simply rolled over and died," Fauerso recalled. "He was on his hands and knees planting acorns with a trowel. He never uttered a sound." His widow, Jessie, missed a few trips but rejoined the group. "We were all calling and checking on her and telling her it was time to get on the bus and head back to the field," says Fauerso, "and it's rewarding to see she was enjoying our friendship. We're able to laugh and joke and talk about Cliff and all he did. He was the world's biggest joke teller."

woah

But the overriding reason why people volunteer is the yearning to get closer to nature, according to a study by Lynne M. Westphal, a social scientist with the U.S. Forest Service in Chicago. She studied members of a volunteer urban forestry program, and while the study subjects were tree planters, Westphal believes the results can be extrapolated to restoration volunteers generally. She asked why the trees were important to the volunteers. The top reason was they bring nature closer. Other values in the top five were "provide shade, are pleasing to the eye, provide environmental benefits, and provide spiritual values." Purely utilitarian values, like reducing noise and raising property values, ranked at or near the bottom of a list of some two dozen values. Gender, education level, income, ethnicity, and where someone grew up did not seem to have a bearing on the ranking. Renters, however, were found more likely than homeowners to rank "bring nature closer" as an important value, while younger people were more likely to choose "provides spiritual values." It might be, Westphal speculated, that younger people interpret "spiritual" more broadly, while older people equate it with reli-

not purely utilitarian

gion. One volunteer said that for her, "bring nature closer" and "provide spiritual values" meant the same thing.

The strongly held deeper values at the top of the list are in fact "very much interlinked," Westphal said. Planting trees was seen as not only important in its own right but also as a means of "getting out and doing something very practical to help the environment," she said, and as a way of "being able to move outside the human-built environment and get back to nature in some way, which in turn links into the spiritual values. I think that these all weave in and out of each other."

Perhaps significantly for the savanna restorationists, the survey found that oaks were particularly prized, as were what are clearly savanna settings. One volunteer commented:

> . . . shade envelops you, it's like "ooh," it's comforting, when it's really hot out, to be able to sit in shade. I think it refreshes your soul, besides your body. . . . The picture in my mind right now is this huge oak, and you're in the middle of this meadow on a hot summer day, and there's something very protective, very enveloping, comforting, very homey about being in that shade.

Often, the impulse that impels a person to volunteer dates to childhood. In his book *Biophilia*, Edward Wilson describes the phenomenon more generally: "You start by loving a subject. Birds, probability theory, explosives, stars, differential equations, storm fronts, sign language, swallowtail butterflies—the odds are that the obsession will have begun in childhood. The subject will be your lodestar and give sanctuary in the shifting mental universe."[11]

Cindy Hildebrand, a volunteer at an extensive prairie restoration project at Iowa's Walnut Creek National Wildlife Refuge, is a case in point. "I was one of those chil-

dren," she says, "like a lot of kids, who was interested in insects and birds, in particular." She would frequent the nearest vacant lot, wading into waist-high weeds with caterpillars and bugs and butterflies. When she moved from Michigan to Iowa in 1977 as an adult, she "felt this immediate kinship with the tallgrass prairie." She began collecting seeds from prairie remnants about to be destroyed by development and in the process gained some expertise in prairie plants. "The imminent presence of bulldozers sharpens identification skills," she says. By 1993 the forty-year-old wife of a mathematician at Iowa State University had worked at restoring local prairie remnants, pulling weeds and cutting brush, and "dancing seed into the ground" at Walnut Creek. Besides working in the field, she had become a volunteer state-level lobbyist on legislation affecting natural areas.

In reconnecting with nature later in life, "we get a glimmer of what we felt when we were children, the joy of wonder at the trees, the sky, the animals," says Walt Fauerso.

As restoration forces one to learn more about what ecosystems contain and how they function, and as the scientific impulse joins the poetic, feelings for nature become stronger still. Wilson's thesis in *Biophilia* is that humans have an "urge to affiliate with other forms of life" that is to some degree innate. This urge, Wilson wrote, exists because the world's other living things form "the matrix in which the human mind originated and is permanently rooted." Biophilia "unfolds in the predictable fantasies and responses of individuals from early childhood onward," and these processes "appear to be part of the programs of the brain."Wilson acknowledges that this hypothesis is only beginning to be tested, but insists that the processes, characterized by "the quickness and decisiveness with which we learn particular things about certain kinds of plants and animals," are "too consistent to be dismissed as the result of purely historical events working on a mental blank slate."[12]

The biophilia hypothesis holds that evolution has endowed humans with a genetically based predisposition to affiliate with other living things that may be as important to human well-being as forming relationships with other people. Like other genetic predispositions, adherents of the hypothesis believe, the degree to which it develops depends on early childhood influences—in this case, the extent to which children are exposed to nature.

Savannas and savannalike settings, if Wilson is right, may exercise an extra-strong attraction because, in Africa, they were where humans evolved. Citing three scientists, Gordon Orians, Yi-Fu Tuan, and the late René Dubos, he argues that people are predisposed to life on the savanna. The three scientists pointed out that people go to some lengths to create savanna environments—parks, gardens, cemeteries, even shopping malls—that provide open but not barren space. "Given a completely free choice," Wilson contends, "people gravitate statistically toward a savanna-like environment."[13]

The wonder that nature inspires in humans can only be enhanced by knowledge, Wilson believes: "Because species diversity was created prior to humanity, and because we evolved within it, we have never fathomed its limits. As a consequence, the living world is the natural domain of the most restless and paradoxical part of the human spirit. Our sense of wonder grows exponentially: the greater the knowledge, the deeper the mystery, and the more we seek knowledge to create new mystery." And so, he writes, "to the extent that each person can feel like a naturalist, the old excitement of the untrammeled world will be regained."[14]

The biggest thing restoration work has done for Cindy Hildebrand, she says, "is establish a sense of connection" with the rest of nature. But, she says, "it is difficult to establish a connection if you don't know what you're looking at. The land expresses itself through the plants and animals on it. It's as hard to establish a connection with the land if you don't understand how the land is expressing itself as it is to establish a connection with a person if you don't know how he's expressing himself." By learning the flora and fauna, she says, "suddenly I have relationships with other living things in the same way I have relationships with people, and it makes life a lot richer."

Robert Lonsdorf, who in 1993 was the chief steward at Miami Woods prairie and savanna on the North Branch and who was especially engrossed in doing butterfly counts there, says restoration work "has filled a very deep need in me to give myself a sense of place and a better understanding of just how complex the natural world really is." Of the plants and animals, he says "it's been a real pleasure getting to know them in a personal way— bur oaks, for instance—and generally feeling more plugged into life on earth. I've restored myself, in a sense, to the natural world. Emotionally it's been very fulfilling." He sees the life forms he deals with "almost as artworks, and natural communities as a sort of group art." There is an ethical dimension to it, an esthetic dimension, a scientific dimension, and a recreational dimension, he says. "But at a certain level it becomes inexplicable. It becomes something you like to do because you like to do it; it has meaning because it has meaning." On a practical political level, he says, this creates "a political constituency that natural areas desperately need when madcap development, road-building, and other schemes rear up, as they continually do. It is the beginning of the restoration of our culture to nature, with all that that can imply."

In her study of tree planters, Lynne Westphal found that the planting "helps provide a sense of place in the cycle of nature and life, and helps to form bonds between people and place. This is crucial and potent, and should not be written off simply as 'liking trees.'"

With connectedness to nature here and now can also come a deeper perception: a recognition and appreciation of where one stands in relation to the long sweep of the

earth's history, from the first assembly of atoms and mole-
cules that became the planet and later created the first
living things down through the very recent ice ages to the
present. If one studies enough, geologic time shrinks. A
century seems only a month, a millennium only a year.
And the individual perceives himself or herself not as an
insignificant wisp—the evolution of the human brain, and
the special, idiosyncratic perceptions it produces are too
marvelous to think that—but not as a dominator set above
or apart from nature, either. But one does locate oneself
in the long, endlessly kaleidoscopic drama of evolution,
in the cosmos itself. If there is spirituality in restoration—
or in the study of nature and nature's forces generally—it
surely lies here.

Working as a restorationist "very much puts things in
perspective," says Jane Balaban. "A lot of what we do and
how we live today inflates man in an unnatural way. We
loom very tall on the landscape, and in my way of thinking
that's not right. I think we are part of and very much
dependent on the rest of the world, and all elements of
that community." The restoration experience enables you
"to see yourself as part of this whole fabric."

On an emotional level, she says, "there's no time when
I feel more alive than when I'm outside in a natural area."
Confessing that this can be "hard to explain without
sounding hokey," she notes that she does not warm to a
tendency among some restorationists to create restoration
rituals. Some rituals have evolved organically and seem
natural and functional—group seed sorting, for instance,
or the workday picnic, or the celebration following a successful prescribed burn. Bill Jordan, among others, con-
ceives of restoration as offering a way of celebrating
humans' place on the landscape and their relationship to
it. But Jane Balaban is wary of "people who go out and
play around with rituals. I'm not one of those. I'm more
practical. It's not enough to go wander and dream."

Nevertheless, "When I walk out in the woods, particularly if it's a woods I know, I find I'm reaching out, just to put my hand on a tree, or stroke a flowering grass. There's a very physical pleasure in being there, and being part of that, touching, feeling, smelling, whatever."

Volunteers, of course, develop their attachments and their insights to varying degrees. Some never develop them very far and drop out. Others, at the opposite end of the scale, couple their volunteer activities to allied professional ones. Karen Holland, a North Branch volunteer, organizes and coordinates restoration activities in the Great Lakes Basin for the Environmental Protection Agency. Robert Lonsdorf works for a conservation group called the Openlands Project, where his job involves the creation of linear "greenways" in the Chicago area. And Susanne Masi, a mother of two grown sons who became a North Branch volunteer in 1988, earned a degree in environmental studies to go with her bachelor's in philosophy and went to work at the Chicago Botanic Garden as a taxonomy technician dealing with native plants.

Masi's psychological-philosophical-intellectual odyssey did not reconnect her with nature—she had been connected since childhood—but her work on the North Branch deepened and expanded the attachment. As a girl, she avidly explored the woods and streams when her father, an accountant who had wanted to be a forester, took her along fishing. "My great fantasy as a kid," she recalled "was to live, Hobbit-like, in a cozy cabin in the deep woods."

As an adult she became more focused, starting with bird-watching. The Chicago-area woods and prairies she visited made nature seem very local and specific. Later, while traveling and camping with her young family, "the world of nature just came pouring in on me. So much to learn, so much to see. . . . I took along wildflower books and bird books and rock books. Mainly I started out by wanting to identify things, to name them. I had little concept of ecosystem at first, although I was aware of it as the backdrop for the different kinds of organisms I was identifying."

She felt a need to integrate this search for knowledge into her whole life, so she went to work for the Openlands Project and returned to school to earn a master's degree in environmental studies, studying under Bob Betz among others, and linked up with one of the Chicago area's most dynamic preservation groups, the Save the Prairie Society. She learned the difference between native prairie plants and exotics: "They weren't all wildflowers! Some belonged and some didn't. And different ones belonged in different types of places. This was a key for me, a direct realization of the concept of ecosystem. This gave me a way to learn, a way to grasp better what I already loved so well. . . ."

Masi offers her own experience as evidence that Wilson is correct when he says that the more knowledge one has about nature, the more mysterious and intriguing it becomes:

I have repeatedly found that understanding enriches my appreciation, doesn't reduce it. There's always plenty of mystery, plenty I won't understand about the complex interconnections of these systems. There is always something unpredictable and new, and you can't recognize this unless you know something about it. Simultaneously, we must understand these systems as scientists, appreciate them as poets, and care for them as managers of the land.

She learned about the North Branch project through the Nature Conservancy, of which she was a member, and went on a tour that Steve Packard was giving at Somme Prairie Grove in 1987. "On a warm, humid August day, surrounded by mosquitoes, he talked about savanna and disappearing oak systems and hugged a bur oak," she wrote. "I was hooked by his vision." She also toured

Bunker Bill Prairie with John Balaban, who she thought had a "solid, competent, no-nonsense understanding of plants and restoration." A year later she joined the North Branch project.

Masi, who considers herself a Wordsworthian romantic in seeing humankind and nature as a unity, said she was "profoundly affected" by Wilson's concept of biophilia: "We are, whether we admit it or not, genetically, evolutionarily, connected with the life on earth. . . . It is a connection we miss and seek. Many are aware of this in a vague way—they talk about the environment, see TV shows on rain forest and wild animals. But they don't know how to access it.

"Through restoration work we have found a way to participate in this natural world."

But Jerry Sullivan, a writer as well as a former North Branch restorationist, may offer the most original insight:

"What's happening here is that we Europeans are finally becoming Americans. We are developing an intimate relationship with this continent, and the landscapes of this continent, and we're doing it using the science of ecology, a product of our own culture, as an entryway rather than dressing up like Indians and pretending we're something we're not."

Lol

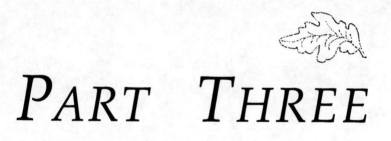

PART THREE

PART THREE

10

Crises,
Resolution, and
Expansion

Awakening and galvanizing people's latent passion to connect with nature is easier than building and maintaining institutions through which that passion can be harnessed to a long-term restoration program. Sometimes the attempt leaves blood on the floor, as Steve Packard and the North Branchers discovered.

Packard, it seems clear, was the first to tackle the problem of restoring the almost extinct, classic tallgrass savanna. But equally important, and more so in some ways, he also created from scratch a network of volunteers that became nothing less than the model for a new kind of organized environmental activism that, largely but not entirely through the widespread and potent influence of The Nature Conservancy, is starting to take root across the country. The volunteer organization not only provides highly motivated workers in numbers no public or private agency depending on hired employees could possibly hope to match, it is also evolving into a constituency—

a political and philosophical subculture, even—of some consequence. By 1993 it had enough weight, at any rate, to allow the restoration enterprise to hold its own in the broad political arena where its sometimes unconventional ideas and activities had to win acceptance.

The volunteer organization enables scientific acumen and insight to combine with constructive grassroots conservation action in a way not quite seen before. It played a role in transforming the Conservancy's philosophy and mission in the 1980s. It gave powerful expression to the growing conviction among conservationists that active human intervention on a wide scale is necessary to repair the ecological damage other humans have caused. And as the Conservancy's new "Volunteer Stewardship Network" expanded in Illinois under Packard's leadership and its basic approach was adopted in other parts of the country, Packard's stock rose—but not without some pain, political uproar, hard feelings, and two crises that could have brought Packard down, and perhaps the whole operation with him.

From the beginning, Packard had seen the North Branch operation as a possible model for similar ones elsewhere in the Chicago area. Ross Sweeny, the emerging coleader of the North Branch group, agreed. By this time the group was strong enough and had enough energy to spare. Both Larry Hodak and Pete Baldo peeled off from the North Branchers to help another group of volunteers get started on restoration activities at another site, called Wolf Road Prairie, in western Cook County, an eighty-acre site that included twenty-five acres of high-quality prairie remnant. Packard himself organized a project in southern Cook County and another at Bluff Spring Fen in Elgin, a ninety-acre site containing fens, prairie, and savanna that were home to several species of endangered orchids.

Sometime soon after Packard joined The Nature Conservancy in 1983, the director of the Illinois chapter, Ralph Brown, encouraged him to expand the network under a

$15,000, three-year grant from a philanthropy called the Chicago Community Trust. Volunteer stewardship was then a controversial proposition within the Conservancy. "The organization thought it was a stupid idea," Brown said in 1993, a decade after the event. Although the Conservancy's traditional strategy had been to protect valuable habitat by buying it up, it was beginning to take a more active role in managing ecosystems as well. But it was doing so with its own professional staff, not grassroots activists. Partly, Brown was interested in developing a volunteer network so that he wouldn't have to spend money hiring professional stewards and could spend it instead acquiring land. Partly he saw it as a way to bring new members and money into the Conservancy. Packard remembers that during his first year with the Conservancy, he described his work to a group of Conservancy staff members from around the Midwest. A number of other people gave presentations, too, and when they did, Packard says, "There would be applause, sometimes on the polite side." Dead silence greeted Packard's enthusiastic report; "People thought I was going in the wrong direction."

So it was not surprising that eyebrows were raised when the proposal was made to start a volunteer stewardship network under Conservancy auspices. "We had to get approval all the way to the top level in Washington to start something like this," Packard said. It was nevertheless approved on a trial basis with the understanding that regular reports would be made and that after three years a judgment would be made on whether the experiment was working. Under the terms of the grant, six volunteer groups would be formed each year for three years.

"I often don't pay much attention to the fine print," Packard says. "I suppose I looked at the grant proposal and said that's fine, but we're not going to do it that way. I got into trouble later when the director discovered I wasn't following the official plan, and the foundation was not happy." What Packard wanted to do was start fifty to seventy-five groups all at the same time and let them grow "organically," on their own steam. Some would work, some would fail, and some would succeed after floundering around for a while. But the ones that did work would be legitimate grassroots organizations drawing their sustenance and energy from genuine local initiative without being burdened by deadlines and requirements imposed from above. Packard had once seen another 1960s type of organizer like himself try to work according to dates and timetables, and it had stultified and ultimately wrecked the effort.

Packard launched the network with a publicity barrage asserting that the state's publicly owned natural areas were in trouble and asking for volunteers to help save them. Specifically, he asked for people to serve as stewards who would visit a site at least four times a year and write a report on it each time. The hope was that these people would develop affection for the site and do more than write reports. Maps were published showing the location of some two hundred sites in the Chicago area. A few dozen people responded, and Packard began to organize the network. He would reply to each of their quarterly reports in writing, and if a particular report indicated promise, he would visit the site with the steward with the aim of promoting further stewardship activity.

One important tactic was to encourage the fledgling stewards to attend a North Branch workday to get the feel of things, to see the possibilities, and to understand that it was not a simple or trivial idea, but a potentially fulfilling and important one. "There's a certain tone of voice at the workdays, a certain type of conversation that tends to go on," Packard says, "that springs from the kind of teaching and support that veterans give to new people; a kind of sympathetic sharing of information about techniques, coupled with a sort of unforced appreciation of the surroundings. People might stop and be quiet to listen to a bird sing, or to watch a flock of sandhill cranes fly by. In the early days, workdays went on until late, and people might watch the moon, or Venus, and talk about the day and about what had been learned, about the ecology of the site, about nature. The workdays [also] had a planned dramatic quality. For instance, we'd purposefully cut brush in such a way that there would be the most striking visual impact at the end of the day. Visitors would be amazed."

Ross Sweeny and other North Branchers became involved in developing the stewardship network along with Packard, but there was an ambivalence, a feeling among some North Branchers that despite Packard's attempt to cast the group as the "big sibling" of the network, somehow the expansion would sap the group's energy and divert effort from the North Branch, which everyone considered the first priority.

Many of the seeds of volunteerism planted by Packard did, as he anticipated, fail to take root. In many cases things never progressed beyond a single person showing up at a site a few times a year and picking up trash. Occasionally even that level of involvement prevented woods from being cut that shouldn't have been, or off-road vehicles from destroying plants and compacting soil. But at more than fifty sites, the volunteer effort was becoming solidly planted, gaining participants, forming a social unit that carried the effort on from year to year and took substantial management responsibility for the sites, as the North Branchers had for theirs. In some localities, groups were ultimately recognized officially and given institutional status by the public-agency owners of the land. In one county, for instance, the Forest Preserve District appointed the volunteers as an advisory council for natural areas management.

In late 1983 or early 1984, Ralph Brown was succeeded as the Illinois Conservancy's state director by banker and state Conservancy board member John Alexander. The

Conservancy's regional office in Minneapolis wanted Alexander's assessment of whether the experimental program should continue. Alexander, lining up with those in the Conservancy who thought this was the wrong direction in which to go, opposed the Volunteer Stewardship Network. "He claimed it was an utter failure," says Packard. "He argued that all these volunteer groups would have come together and started taking care of all these places on their own. And in fact, if you had asked the volunteers if this was something that just happened or something The Nature Conservancy created, they'd say, 'It just happened, and we did it ourselves.' And they did do it themselves. But at the same time, the Conservancy was providing crucial ingredients without which it wouldn't have happened at all. And it didn't happen anywhere else. It happened here."

Compounding things, Packard and Alexander didn't get along. According to Wendy Paulson, a member of the board of trustees of the Illinois Conservancy who had known Packard for some time, "those two didn't come close to seeing eye to eye."

Alexander says it was both a personality conflict and a communications problem. "I think the essence of it was my inability to understand or Steve's inability to explain to me exactly what it was he was doing," Alexander said from the vantage point of 1993. The volunteer network's successful course in the intervening decade, Alexander said, shows that "while perhaps I couldn't understand what he was doing, he did understand what he was doing."

John Humke, then the Conservancy's regional director and in 1993 its national director of federal agency liaison, says Packard's disinclination to be bridled may have been one factor in the tense situation. "I'm a great fan of Steve's," he said, "but there was a perception back then that while Steve was a very creative person, he was not a very manageable person, though I've seen a lot of growth in Steve Packard over the years."

The situation reached a crisis from Packard's viewpoint when, he says, Alexander informed him that he didn't think it was appropriate for Packard to continue to work for the Conservancy: "He didn't think what I was doing was what The Nature Conservancy should be doing." Alexander says he never tried to fire Packard; that his departure "would only have come about if Steve had decided to quit."

Hiring Packard had been one of Ralph Brown's last acts before he moved voluntarily back to California, his home state. "The best hire I ever made" as a conservationist, he later called it. Just before departing, he told Packard: "It's up to you to stick it out here. You're working for one of the most well-endowed conservation organizations in the world, and don't blow it." Now the conflict over the Volunteer Stewardship Network had become a supreme test of whether Packard would rise to Brown's challenge.

Paulson, who along with other board members was strongly committed to the Volunteer Stewardship Network, felt Alexander was "clearly in the wrong," and went to the board chairman about the matter—as did Packard, at the possible risk of being fired. The board supported the Volunteer Stewardship Network and Packard. Thwarted, Alexander decided to fire the sole person who assisted Packard with the Volunteer Stewardship Network. Humke, who had had several conversations with the Illinois board chairman about the situation, intervened at this point. Ordinarily he left personnel matters to state directors. But as the crisis continued in Chicago, he said, "what I began to realize was that Steve Packard is a real genius, an incredibly creative and visionary person. We could not afford to lose him. Though he was a bit of a square peg in a round hole, we don't want all round pegs."

Humke "in essence called and said, 'Things don't seem to be going as well as we hoped, and maybe it's time for a change,'" Alexander recalled. Alexander says he agreed, and resigned.

Packard emerged from the showdown in a solid position to advance his ideas within the Conservancy. By sticking with Packard, "we had confirmed he was an important player making an important contribution," says Humke, and the fight "gave him more visibility than he had had." It also gave his approach to restoration and volunteer stewardship greater prominence and credibility.

Unknown to Packard at the time, others influential in the Conservancy were also beginning to think along new lines. The conviction was growing that simply purchasing land was not enough. You could never buy up enough land to preserve biodiversity adequately. It was necessary to work with broader landscapes, with "bioregions," as they were coming to be called, and with private and public landowners. This inevitably required becoming politically engaged—something the Conservancy had always shunned. Packard expresses activism's previous lack of appeal this way: "Most of grassroots environmental advocacy work had gotten a bad name because it was so confrontational, so adversarial, and very often was more self-expression than accomplishment. It was sort of self-centered: 'I want to see myself chained to a tree.' Which is not to say that the courageous people who did some of the early theatrical environmental activities weren't doing something good. In many cases that was the right thing to do. But you can only go so far that way. Once the issue has been raised you need to use other techniques, and we were developing them. The question is how the public in a democratic country can take part in biodiversity conservation in cooperation with government. There's this mentality in the United States that democracy is wonderful but politics is dirty. You can't have democracy without politics. So we decided that our job was to figure out how to do wholesome, ethical, effective environmental politics."

Even though the Conservancy philosophy was undergoing a metamorphosis, and even though Packard had survived the showdown with Alexander, Packard still felt that he was "an oddball and would have to fight for continuation of this kind of stuff." Then one day Russ Van Herik, who had succeeded Humke as the Conservancy's regional director, phoned and asked if Packard would be willing to help write up a nomination for the Illinois chapter to receive the Conservancy's annual chapter award for best stewardship program. Packard pleaded that he was too busy, but Van Herik pressed him, pointing out that only a few in the Conservancy were talking about volunteer stewardship, public lands, and political constituencies, that the future of the organization was involved, and that if the Illinois chapter were to get the award, it would send a message. Packard complied, and sure enough Illinois won the award. The message was sent: What's going on in Illinois is good, and it would be wise to learn more about it.

But even as the Volunteer Stewardship Network was developing, big trouble was brewing for its prototype, the North Branch. It would shake the North Branch operation to its foundations and reveal the risks and perils of any grassroots volunteer operation. As is not uncommon in such organizations, a bitter schism developed. Precisely how the swirl of personalities, emotions, philosophy, territoriality, ego, and ambition interacted to bring about the crisis may be impossible to sort out. But at least some of the elements can be identified.

On one level, it was a fight over how the North Branch was to be run, and by whom; on another, a struggle over Packard himself.

At the project's outset, Packard had pretty much assumed all responsibility and direction. But soon a form of governance became established that Packard fervently believed was critical to the long-term success of the enterprise. He had long been convinced that the way in which ideas were generated and decisions were made was essential to the flowering of the project. He maintains that although he directed the project and made the most important decisions in the early years, he was also alert to any volunteers who showed leadership tendencies, and that he went out of his way to cultivate them and encourage their ideas. If someone had an idea that seemed constructive, that person would be urged to put it into practice—even if Packard himself would do it differently— if it furthered or didn't conflict with the group's central purpose. He was convinced that, in the long run, the enterprise would be better served because more people would feel they had a personal stake in it and because a unity of purpose would develop among as many of the volunteers as possible.

At the same time, he believed that a volunteer restoration effort ultimately thrives on internally generated creativity and dedication. The idea was to give volunteers the freedom of thought and action to enable them to become independent, thinking citizen-scientists whose growing knowledge and insights expand and enrich the group's understanding of how prairies and savannas work and how they best can be restored. That does not mean things are out of control or that anarchy prevails; individual initiatives must further, or at least not impede, progress toward the common goal. If people aren't on the team, then they do not earn the confidence inherent in this participatory approach.

As the project matured, a small group of dedicated leaders emerged from this way of operating. They made their decisions by consensus, before a workday started, or at lunch, or sitting in a circle on the prairie, or over the phone. Although the leaders decided how the work was to proceed, adjustments could be proposed by any participant. The group's considerable cohesion was based on personal trust and dedication among the leaders.

This collegial style of government and shared sense of community and purpose was one of the things that convinced Karen Holland, among others, to commit to the

North Branch. On her first workday in 1989, she worked in a swamp white oak savanna at Sauganash Prairie Grove, one of the North Branch sites, with "zillions of mosquitos who all loved me. I used tons of mosquito repellant, but it all sweated off, and I thought, 'This is insane. I can't believe people come back here every Sunday.'" But afterward, everyone stood back and talked, and Larry Hodak, the site steward, described what was going to be done over the next couple of years, and everyone could see what had been done that day. "There was a great sense of accomplishment and a strong sense of community," Holland says, "so I came back every time. People were continually asking questions about how we can do better. They would come up and ask your opinion. Considering I knew absolutely nothing at first, I was pretty impressed by that. I was also impressed with the process of how decisions were made in the group—again, more questions, getting as much input from as many people as possible and working toward solutions. People built on each other's ideas, and no one seemed to mind if their idea didn't come out on top. It was gradually incorporated into a bigger idea or more sensible idea . . . that was devoid of ego, almost. It had to do with the best thing we could do for the environment, not who came up with the idea."

As the North Branch project expanded, its governance became more decentralized, with volunteer groups operating with a great deal of autonomy at individual sites. But at the top, the enterprise grew beyond its ability to nourish the personal ties that had been at its core. At the same time, Packard was spending more and more time trying to develop the Volunteer Stewardship Network and devoting less energy to the North Branch. He also pulled back to concentrate on the ecology of the Somme site because Vestal Grove, the crown jewel, was there. At the same time, his wife, Mim, was dying of brain cancer. Because of all this, Packard's effectiveness within the North Branch was at a low ebb as the internal tensions built in late 1990 and early 1991. Sweeny took over as principal leader. But the extra responsibility and stress, combined with pressures at work and at home, soon forced Sweeny to agree to bequeath the leadership to a steering committee headed by a new leader, Bev Hansen.

As Packard saw it, Sweeny and Hansen operated not so much in a consensual way as in a more traditionally hierarchical fashion. "I'm not sure I'd describe it that way, but I can understand why other people would," says Sweeny, who explains that he had been trying to "diversify the leadership"; to create "more niches where tasks could be defined for people, where they could be comfortable in doing it, and yet where they could be part of a single structure going somewhere"; and to devise "some kind of a coordinating group to provide the glue that made things stick together."

Packard's personality and character were another major factor in the dispute. Like many strong leaders with a creative cast of mind, he has long tended to provoke both admiration and anger.

Many longtime associates and admirers see him as a warm friend and an approachable leader whose intelligence, vision, and ability to articulate that vision readily inspire volunteer newcomers. If the positive part of Packard's self-appraisal is right, the vision is rooted in an ability to see patterns: ecological patterns, organizational patterns, political patterns. It comes especially from perceptions of the ecological landscape itself, what it has been, what it can become, and how. More often than not, Packard says, that is what he would think about at night, in bed: "It has tremendous beauty to me. Some people get joy from solving a crossword puzzle. Some people enjoy making a work of art or playing a good game of chess. I love the beauty and elegance of trying to figure out what's going to make these species thrive in an ecosystem." He also has an obvious ability to communicate the vision through writing and speaking. "He's so charismatic, the way he speaks, the way he holds himself," says one of the earliest North Branch volunteers, Chris Hodak. "There's a certain poetry and romance about what he does and the way he presents himself."

Often in the early days, the Hodaks, Packard, and Mim spent a lot of time together. "We had a lot of fun as couples, just doing nonprairie stuff," said Chris. "After a field trip we'd all relax together and drink beer." Packard, she said, "is fun to be with" and "he has this amazing history." Occasionally, she remembers, he would dangle little snippets of the history in front of them. Once, on the way home from an Indian restaurant, "he pulled out this harmonica and started playing this amazing blues. I had no idea." Another time he talked about working with Jane Fonda in the movement. "He would drop these little things that would leave your mouth hanging open."

Packard's vision and the ability to communicate it and to build strong ties to people cut two ways. He has such confidence in the vision, some associates say, that he can be irritatingly stubborn in its defense. "He's as stubborn as I am," says Holland, who quickly emerged as a North Branch leader. "We've gotten into some terrible fights because we're stubborn. But if you back away and allow him to think he's totally right, that doesn't solve anything. If you have a point and make it well, he'll listen and will incorporate it. On the other hand, he expects you to do the same with his ideas. The one problem is that he's extremely articulate, and he expects you to do the same. . . . You can say something and mean well and understand what you're saying, and he will bring up a dozen questions and he makes you answer them, and sometimes [this] makes people angry. He may point out flaws in your argument you didn't want to see, and that can rile people."

His eagerness to learn new things also cuts two ways. "What do you think?" (actually, "Wa-da-ya think?") has been a trademark line, the sign of an attitude indispensable both for understanding nature and stimulating new ideas and insights. But he is admittedly impatient with old arguments and general assertions unsupported by data, and says he tends to brush them off and move on to other ideas and the people who advance them. This, he says, may cause some people to consider him closed-minded. And in making choices in the real world of conservation, he says, "you have to ask a lot of experts and then make a decision. When five experts say burn and two say don't burn, and you decide to burn, the five don't say much, while the two say I'm arrogant and don't listen. In many cases, the right thing to do is spend a lot of energy mollifying the two. But these days I have such broad responsibilities that I have forty-two experts saying yes and sixteen saying no, and I either have to cut way back on what I'm doing or absorb the criticism."

He pleads guilty to some insensitivity. "Some of it," he says, "is left over from the sixties, when we prized criticism and we said it's a favor when someone tells you what you're doing wrong. I think I'm much more inclined to tell people something critical to their faces rather than to tell it to ten people behind their backs, but to many people I think it seems I'm just critical, or bossy." And although he displays great patience when it comes to long-term organizational work and the unfolding of ecosystems, he admits to some impatience with people in everyday dealings. "I will sometimes say sharp things to people in an impatient tone of voice, and that's bad," he said.

Another problem was that as the Volunteer Stewardship Network grew, Packard had less time to give to close friends and associates—"my tribe"—whose friendship he had prized and cultivated over the years. "I do seem to become fast, intimate friends with people and then seem to abandon them when I must focus on subsequent projects," he said. He believes this was a factor in his increasingly sour relationship with Sweeny, to whom he had been close for many years.

Still another criticism leveled at Packard was that he

got too much credit for the project's successes. Packard believes this to be true sometimes: "People know my name and somehow assume that I'm responsible for everything good. I don't run around claiming credit. In fact, I spend a lot more time trying to get credit given to other people. But the end result still, often, is that many people don't get the credit they deserve. They resent it. . . . I don't blame them. I've felt the same way about other people. It's destructive to both sides. I wish I knew what to do about it."

In any case, Sweeny says, he became convinced that Packard was not "Mr. Perfect." Not least among Sweeny's complaints was that although Packard may have encouraged consensus-building and individual initiative within the goals of the organization, he was in firm control of the group's central purpose: "It's defined as Steve defines it." In his eyes, Packard made all the big decisions in concert with a group that Packard called "the smart people" or "the people who know things." This, to Sweeny, meant people who were "right thinkers in terms of what the savannas are all about." Sweeny also believed that the organization's governance by consensus was largely illusory, that Packard was able to impose his will. He explained it this way: "During a meeting, you let a lot of people get out there and vent their ideas, and get all these ideas together. And by the middle or three quarters of the way through the meeting, you have a very confused state of things, and a discouraged group of people who can see nothing happening. And then Steve will step in with his personality and strong sense of direction and tell people what's right. And either you don't want to go against the guy who tells you what's right, so you don't say anything, especially if you're not very knowledgeable about ecological things, or you're just very relieved someone has come up and said something. So suddenly you're doing it Steve's way. It's an excellent technique for getting things done and making group decisions. You can say that's consensus, but where does that leave all the other opinions?"

Packard says that "it's true that a person good at summarizing has extra influence. It's not true that people shut up if they disagree. Most summarized decisions get changed a bit or a lot." Moreover, as the organization grew and his responsibilities multiplied, Packard was not at a lot of meetings. And besides, he says, Sweeny and others often offered summaries.

In any event, says Jane Balaban, the Sweeny-Hansen group "felt Steve had more power than he should have. Steve is a persuasive person, and they felt he could influence people to do whatever he wanted them to do. I think it's pretty clear that's not the case, but I think they felt that."

Packard, on the other hand, believed the Sweeny-Hansen group was frustrating and blocking out from leadership roles many of the finest products of the search for citizen-scientist leaders, like the Balabans and Holland and other, more recent volunteers including Robert Lonsdorf, Laurel Ross, and Susanne Masi, people whose main interest was the ecology rather than the organization as such. "The group rose or fell with their dedication and creativity," says Packard. "Many of them didn't want to come to meetings, which seemed like a political annoyance, like the opposite of what the North Branch stood for." In trying to keep control of the operation in its own hands, he asserts, the Sweeny-Hansen group was fighting off the initiatives of these emerging but frustrated leaders.

Sweeny and his allies set out to create what they felt was a more democratic organization "where Steve would not make all the decisions." In the resulting discussions over what should replace the old structure and who should make what decisions, Sweeny and his allies wanted an organization independent of The Nature Conservancy. He feared that the North Branch was in danger of losing its autonomy. "We felt independent of the Conservancy," Sweeny said later, "and basically that means independent of Steve." Getting the Conservancy out of the picture, he said, would also mean ousting Packard.

In December 1990, what Jane Balaban would later describe as a power struggle, pure and simple, broke out into the open. Early that month, shortly after Mim's death, the new steering committee met at Packard's home to transact a number of items of business. "Somehow I knew there was something planned, plotted for this meeting," Packard recalls, "and I remember being really scared during the meeting. There was this crescendo of whispered implications." One person told Packard that some things were going to be said that might not be easy for him to take but that they were nothing personal and that things would be better for him in the long run.

Near the end of the meeting, the group took up a proposal, innocuous on its face, on the governance of the North Branch Prairie Project Educational Fund, an ancillary organization of the North Branch project. The Sweeny group proposed that the educational fund be run by a five-person board whose principal officers would be Sweeny, Hansen, and one of their allies. Packard would also be a board member, but a minority member in the context of the developing struggle. The Sweeny-Hansen group, according to Packard, argued that the educational fund's governing corporation had, in fact, become the governing body of the North Branch project itself. Packard's clear impression was that the intent of the Sweeny-Hansen group "was to establish a new kind of authority structure and that to do so they would try to drive me out." Holland, who was not particularly close to Packard, and who was at the meeting by virtue of her position as editor of the group's newsletter, smelled a rat. She narrowed her eyes, looked around the room, and said, as she and Packard remember it, "Something is going on here that I don't like."

It brought people up short. If Holland hadn't spoken

up, Packard believes, Sweeny and Hansen "might well have forced me out, and things would have happened differently."

At one point in the meeting, according to Sweeny, Packard accused him and his allies of trying to take over the North Branch operation. Now an all-out campaign began over who was to control it, determine its style of leadership, its philosophy, its purpose, its future direction. Packard feared that if the Sweeny group won, decisions "would be made by people who went to steering committee meetings and not so much by people who cared about the species and the ecology." The question, he felt, was whether the North Branch "was going to be something that is a big-free-generous-spirit sort of thing or was it going to ossify into rules and voting and politics."

The issue was formally cast in terms of the kind of organizational structure the North Branch should have. The Sweeny faction favored independent incorporation of the organization along traditional lines, with a corporate structure, officers, elections, and bylaws, and with no ties to The Nature Conservancy. An opposing group that rallied around Packard favored a loose but more formal affiliation with the Conservancy that would in effect preserve the North Branch's autonomy, lack of bureaucracy, and a consensus style of governing while reaping the benefits of guaranteed financial support and greater power in dealing with government. To Packard's opponents, this meant making the North Branch merely an appendage of the Conservancy. It would also, obviously, make it even more difficult to escape Packard's influence.

"Ross was very upset by the idea we might affiliate with The Nature Conservancy," says Jane Balaban. "He was afraid we might lose our identity and individuality and get sucked up into this bureaucracy."

One thing Packard especially didn't want, in Sweeny's view, was an organization whose leadership might change from time to time and frustrate Packard's ability to do things the way he wanted.

As the dispute ripened, some of Packard's opponents mounted a campaign against him that attempted to spotlight what they saw as his personal faults. Wendy Paulson, in her capacity as a Conservancy board member, was the recipient of telephone calls from North Branch people voicing some of the criticism. Paulson, who tried to listen sympathetically and neutralize the strong feelings while not getting involved, believes that one factor in the dispute "was probably concern that [Packard] was taking all the glory and credit."

Ecology-oriented field workers who had shied away from meetings and politics and organizational concerns came into the picture now that a crisis was afoot. One was Larry Hodak, who had cut back drastically on his North Branch activities to spend more weekends at home after the birth of his and Chris's daughters, Eleanor and Hannah. "To this day," he says, "I don't know all the details, I don't know the reasons there were such hard personal feelings about this. My best guess is that Steve sort of felt control slipping away and tried to grab it back . . . , and it really upset people who had devoted tremendous amounts of time and energy to it and felt strongly about it. I think they were upset at Steve for trying to take it back."

In Jane Balaban's view, both Packard and Sweeny "started saying they needed other people to take leadership," and meant it, "but I think both had a lot of trouble giving that up. For ten years they made all the decisions; they were the controlling force of the group. . . . I don't think Ross wanted to give up control just to have Steve take it over."

On a number of occasions, Packard says, he offered to try to work things out because the situation was hurting the group. Sweeny refused to talk about it "until this is all over." He says he declined because he felt the issue should be settled not by three people but by the group at large, in the open.

The showdown came at an all-day meeting of thirty-two key North Branchers on April 27, 1991. Packard and his allies felt the vote could go either way. Some, like Larry Hodak, didn't decide until the last day. He went with Packard. The die was cast on a nonbinding straw vote in which fifteen people voted to affiliate with the Conservancy, thirteen voted for a traditional corporate structure, and two voted for both. Sweeny was astonished that his side didn't win more votes. "You could have knocked me over with a feather," he said later. While the vote was nonbinding, Sweeny decided at that point that "I'm not going to fight this battle anymore."

Holland believes that "the effort to oust Steve did [the Sweeny-Hansen group] in. That made people angry just because it was ridiculous and unfair. How could you do that to the founder? This is a volunteer organization. How can you kick people out?"

If the other side had won, Packard says, the group might simply have split. "I think we were not prepared to give up the sites," says Packard. "The other people might have ended up with rights to the name and the mailing lists."

One by one, Sweeny and the key members of his faction left the North Branch. It was like a family splitting up. "Ross really did put his whole heart and soul into it," says Jane Balaban. "In a very real sense the North Branch is family to him."

Sweeny speaks bitterly of Packard. A number of North Branchers, he says, have become so "infatuated" with Packard, intellectually speaking, that they are like "groupies." He said he believes that some have taken leading roles because it fosters their careers in other conservation-oriented organizations, while some have left because of disagreements with Packard. Few people, he said, are now likely to criticize Packard because they, too, are reaping benefits from the project's success, and Packard has become such a mover and shaker that it is "dangerous" to criticize him.

The Schism, as Packard calls it, is a horrible memory to North Branchers who went through it. "I still get a knot in my stomach," Jane Balaban says about looking back over the minutes she took of the crucial meetings. "What a negative, unproductive, unpleasant energy sink that was!"

Afterward, decision by consensus continued to be the preferred mode of governance—perhaps to a fault; sometimes in making a decision, says Jane Balaban, who supports the concept, "we discuss it to death." And even though Packard espouses the consensus approach in theory, she says, "I don't think he always follows that in practice."

When all was said and done, the North Branch project emerged from its troubles with its health and vitality intact and the enthusiasm and commitment of its volunteers undiminished. And in common with their counterparts in other regions of the country, they continued to develop an ever-stronger bond to the landscape and the natural world at large.

"All of us are infatuated with the idea of restoration," Ross Sweeny said in the wake of the Schism. "There's no doubt about that." He has since become a restoration volunteer with a Sierra Club project in the Chicago area.

Despite his bitterness, he says that Packard "deserves a tremendous amount of credit." What Madison and Jefferson and Hamilton were to the United States, he says, Packard is to the North Branch project. As for the project itself, he says, "I'm sure it's cooking along just fine. There's little doubt it's been a spectacular success, and I think it will continue to be a success."

But the Schism provided a cautionary tale, a warning to other volunteer groups of the dangers that can threaten a restoration project. Most of all, it may have spared other groups in the spreading Volunteer Stewardship Network from going through a similar testing phase; they are able to pick up and use processes developed the hard way by the North Branchers.

With the resolution of the crisis, the North Branch resumed its role as the model for a volunteer restoration effort that, having begun so modestly in 1977, was flowering and broadcasting its own seeds across the country as never before.

The Volunteer Stewardship Network, with the North Branch as its flagship, had by 1993 grown to include more than 5,000 volunteers on 202 Illinois restoration sites encompassing more than 27,000 acres of the tallgrass savanna-prairie-woodland mosaic. Most sites were on public lands, though some were on private property where conservation easements had been granted. Of the total, 3,100 volunteers and nearly 17,000 acres were in the six counties of the Chicago region. At 41 of the 142 Chicago-area sites, encompassing more than 2,700 acres, sustained restoration work was being performed on the savanna part of the mosaic. The volunteers were responsible for managing millions of dollars' worth of public lands and had transformed the management of those lands.

The volunteer network itself was divided into twenty-five regions. In most cases a region was coterminous with a county, except for Cook County, which had four. The North Branch, as the largest project in Cook County and a model for the others, was a region in itself. It had six regional leaders, all volunteers: a regional ecologist; a regional steward, or overall coordinator of restoration and management; a coordinator of volunteer recruiting and training; an administrator; a publicist; and an editor. Packard, in addition to his paid position of science and stewardship director of the Illinois Nature Conservancy, continued to serve as the volunteer regional ecologist of the North Branch. Jane Balaban and Robert Lonsdorf shared the role of chief steward. Joanne Softcheck was the coordinator of volunteer recruiting and training. Karen Holland edited *Prairie Projections*, the North Branch newsletter. All continued to perform the physical work of brush cutting, weeding, seed gathering, and planting that restores a degraded ecosystem's health.

The organizational backbone of the network was its stewards, individual volunteers responsible for managing a specific piece of land. Many lived near the sites they managed. They drew up the management plan for the site, organized the work there, and were responsible to the landowner for what went on. "The land work is his or her own," said Laurel Ross, who in 1993 coordinated the network in Northern Illinois in her paid job as a Conservancy field representative and was a North Branch volunteer as well. The steward recruited and trained co-stewards, other volunteers who oversaw specific functions: weed control, for example, or the monitoring of butterfly and plant populations, or record keeping.

Ross oversaw a number of often elaborate and sophisticated support operations designed to help volunteers do their work more effectively. There was an apprentice stewardship program for the training of volunteers who aspire to be site managers, or stewards. Usually they were self-selected and then appointed if they showed sufficient skill. They attended courses at Chicago area institutions, but the main training came from other stewards. "To be an apprentice," Ross said, "you have to find a mentor who agrees to work with you; you have to look over the stewards and find one who has the time and interest to help you."

Once the training was completed, the steward had at his or her disposal the accumulated knowledge of the North Branchers and their sister organizations. Many of the basics, from politics to planting, were captured in an inch-thick *Steward's Handbook* published by the Conservancy. Some chapter and section titles: Surveillance and

Reporting. Relationships with Landowners and Public Agencies. Building a Relationship with Owners. Ten Easy Steps to Better Negotiating. Recruiting Volunteers. Who Volunteers? Match the Person with the Needed Skills. What Motivates Volunteers? The New Volunteer. Organizing Volunteer Workdays. Safety Concerns. Handling Visitors. Handling Trespassers, Misuse and Abuse. Relations with Neighbors of Natural Areas. Getting Publicity for Natural Areas. Weed/Exotic Plant Control. Brush Control. Seed Collecting and Dispersal.

Some sample excerpts from the handbook offer revealing glimpses into the politics and practicalities of restoration ecology, especially in an urban or suburban setting:

> Your success as a steward depends on your ability to build a rapport with people at the agency which owns your site. . . . Think about *their* position. Some agency employees have little knowledge or interest in the fact that they're responsible for rare or important ecosystems. Others may be committed indeed, and even have succeeded in getting resources so their areas need minimal assistance. But the most common situation is in between—staff people feel a certain amount of guilt that their agency isn't doing more, but they're sensitive about people pointing out problems which could imply the staff isn't doing its job. They also worry that volunteers will cause friction with another level in the bureaucracy or create new demands for time in already busy schedules.

> Look for allies. If the preserve-owning agency can't find time to pull the auto wreck out of the marsh, perhaps the local Sierra Club—or the local drag-racing association, for that matter—may agree to help. There are dividends in having many

members of the community involved with the preserve. . . .

Your contact with visitors may range from chance encounters to leading scheduled group tours. Regardless of the extent, your reception to visitors can color their attitudes about the site and conservation efforts in general. When you meet visitors, let them know what you're doing and why. . . . Emphasize what makes the preserve unique, whether it's a fen, wetland, or savanna, and define terms as necessary. . . . Perhaps one of the most personal rewards from your efforts may be capturing the attention of someone who shows up for the following workday and becomes a volunteer, or who, years later, comes to the preserve's defense when a controversy develops over prescribed burning, deer control, or a proposal for some inappropriate use. . . .

Children can be inspiring and enthusiastic visitors. . . . But children can be destructive and difficult to control. A flowery weed field is a good place to introduce groups of children to nature. Rather than having to say "no, no, no" all the time, you can free them to run around, touch and pick and collect, and catch frogs or crickets. . . .

It's valuable to get to know owners of homes, businesses, or property that border the preserve. Let them know what you're doing and why. . . . Be sensitive about burns. Burns can be a frightening prospect to a homeowner whose property isn't far from a planned burn area. . . . Clear the air about burns. Once a burn is held in an area, residents' fears will be quelled, and they'll likely see little problem with future prescribed burnings.

The volunteer network was also conducting certification classes for the leaders of prescribed burns, was publishing some specialized manuals (a butterfly monitoring handbook, for example), and was conducting ad hoc classes on aspects of restoration requested by volunteer leaders.

One sunny Saturday morning in early August 1992, for instance, volunteers attended a class at the North Branch herbarium on plant identification, a critical volunteer skill, learning to recognize two dozen or so species of dried plants. In the afternoon, the class gathered at Bunker Hill prairie and woodland, where Laurel Ross and the Balabans had gone in advance and identified the same plants, growing live in colorful midsummer array, and flagged them with unmarked tape. Using notes taken in the morning session, the class members were asked to identify dozens of live plants, from Kalm's brome to blazing star to switchgrass to northern dropseed grass ("People say it smells like hot wax, or buttered popcorn, or sex," said Laurel Ross). At the end of this treasure hunt, where the trail ended in a pleasantly sun-dappled woodland clearing, the group spread a blanket and relaxed with cheese, crackers, and cold drinks.

To generate seeds for restoration, the volunteer network also recruited and operated, through the North Branch project, a corps of more than one hundred volunteer gardeners, expanding Packard's and Hodak's original enterprise far beyond what could have been envisioned in 1977.

By 1993, the volunteer network was regarded as a shining example of how to mobilize citizens in the cause of conservation. "It's unbelievable," said Dr. Alan W. Haney, a savanna ecologist at the University of Wisconsin at Stevens Point. "You couldn't pay people" to commit themselves the way the Illinois volunteers have. John C. Sawhill, the president of The Nature Conservancy, said of Packard:

"The thing he's done that's just phenomenal is energize volunteers. The volunteer network he's built in Illinois is a model for the rest of the organization." And for restorationists outside the Conservancy as well.

The model caught on first, as might be expected, in California. Not long after the crisis in which John Alexander attempted to scuttle the Illinois Volunteer Stewardship Network, Packard was invited to give a three-minute presentation to the Conservancy's national board of governors. He showed before-and-after slides of degraded land that had been turned into "Conservancy-quality" property. Just as important, he showed pictures of people—volunteers—working on the land. Packard also told of volunteers who, having "taken the Conservancy into their hearts through the volunteer process," made contributions of $50,000 or $100,000. For some Conservancy officials, he says, "that was the only thing they heard."

The talk apparently made an impression on Steve Johnson, a Conservancy official in California. "The next time I turned around there was this beautiful volunteer newsletter" and "great reports of volunteer triumphs coming out of California," said Packard. "I said to him, 'Congratulations. You've got a great program out there. And he gave me a funny look and said, 'It's just copied after your speech.'" Johnson remembers it the same way, but isn't clear whether the speech that inspired him was the one Packard made before the national board or another one he made about the same time at a restoration conference in Berkeley.

Actually, the California volunteer network had strong local antecedents. Will Murray, the California Conservancy's membership director, was a firm advocate of the idea, and when the first volunteers were recruited in 1987, the Californians drew heavily on the experience of the Sacramento Tree Foundation, which had mobilized volunteers to plant urban trees. When the California Conservancy dedicated its Cosumnes River restoration project in the San Francisco Bay area, a precursor of Tom Griggs's project at Kopta Slough, it advertised and sent out personal invitations asking people to volunteer to plant trees at Cosumnes. Bruce Handley, who was in charge of building the volunteer team, remembers the first day they went to work there. About 220 people showed up to plant 1,800 valley oaks on 12 acres of land in January 1988. "Tom Griggs and I were standing there amazed. It looked like a swarm of locusts. We said, 'My god, look at what's happening.' It took two and a half hours. We thought it would be six or seven hours' work."

Most volunteers, about 60 percent, showed up only once, though some would return from time to time to revisit "their" trees. But what the Californians took to calling their "hard corps" remained, and by 1993 the Habitat Restoration Team, as it was called, consisted of a statewide network of more than 4,000 volunteers, from toddlers to octogenarians. "We encourage people to make it a family affair," says Handley. The toddlers may not be able to do heavy work, but they get to drop the acorn in the hole. A number of corporations recruited volunteer contingents. The Chevron Retirees Association provided a group of some one hundred volunteers—Walt Fauerso's group. In buses provided by Chevron, they trooped up to Kopta Slough, where they made up Griggs's planting crew. Later they branched out to other projects as well.

Californians who want to volunteer can call up a special telephone number. When they do, they hear something like this: "This is The Nature Conservancy's restoration team hot line. For Northern California information, press 2. For Southern California information, press 3. For membership information, press 6." Upon pressing 2 the caller is offered, for example, an array of specifics according to restoration site. Following the procedure on a given day in early 1993 yielded the following information: "This is the Cosumnes River restoration volunteer hot line. Our next volunteer workday is Saturday,

March 6. This will be a planting day and will start at ten A.M. We will have a potluck. We will provide the chicken and utensils." It went on to advise dressing in layered clothing, bringing a bag lunch and canteen of water, as well as gardening gloves, sturdy shoes, and a change of shoes and socks—"It can get quite muddy out there." After advising that the following workday would be on March 20, the voice on the recording gave directions ("Take the I-5 freeway south out of Sacramento . . .") and asked the potential volunteer to leave a name and the workday for which he or she was volunteering.

The California network originally operated statewide, with volunteers from an overall pool spreading their efforts among a number of widely scattered projects. In 1993, Handley said, the Californians were reorganizing the volunteer program so that specific groups of volunteers would focus permanently on specific watersheds. "So we're coming back to embrace Steve Packard's concept" of local people who develop a long-term relationship with a particular site or ecosystem, said Handley. As for Packard's larger contribution, Handley had this to say: "I think he showed that community volunteers can perform large-scale stewardship, and that is the model he created, to show us in the Nature Conservancy it's a do-able situation. And that's been real reinforcing. His work's kind of continuing to pioneer. Every time I hear about it, they're doing something new."

Other Conservancy restorationists have studied the Illinois operation as well. One is Greg Seamon, who says that in attempting to restore the longleaf pine-wiregrass ecosystem in Florida, "we wouldn't be able to accomplish what we have" without volunteers. In Florida in 1992, 198 volunteers put in 1,267 hours on prescribed burning, seed collection, and planting in the longleaf pine project. Seamon says that the Florida volunteers have not yet become the cohesive social and political unit that those in Illinois have. One reason may simply be that this is easier to achieve in an urban area. But Seamon has discovered another productive wrinkle. Some of the best volunteers turned out to be northern college students on spring break. Some, Seamon said in early 1993, "were so psyched by it that they're coming back this year."

Illinois, California, and Florida have perhaps the strongest programs, but Conservancy volunteers by 1993 were popping up elsewhere, too. In Arizona's Hassayampa River restoration program, volunteers go into high gear every fall in what they called the "tammy whacker season." "Tammy" stands for tamarisk, an invasive cedar tree that must be rooted out if restoration is to succeed. In Idaho, volunteers have been mobilized to replant streamside shrubs and trees in the Silver Creek watershed. One volunteer, an eighteen-year-old high school graduate from Massachusetts named Patrick Oliver, rode the bus from Boston to Twin Falls just to work as a Silver Creek volunteer.

Russ Van Herik, the former regional director of The Nature Conservancy, sees this blossoming of volunteer activity not as "something a small group of people is trying to make a lot of people get interested in," but rather as "a natural organic upwelling that we're charged with helping facilitate and foster." Packard and others, he said, did not create the movement but are merely "a small group of people trying desperately to respond to the technical demands being placed on us by an upswelling of demand, and not just in Illinois. We're seeing it everywhere."

Time was, he said, when ecological preservation, to say nothing of restoration, was seen as the preserve of "small groups of quasi-fanatics," in the same league with "people interested in postage stamps from the Malagasy Republic or skydiving." Now that has changed. "It's not a fad. It's not a hobby. It's now considered appropriate and normal. What you used to do is mow the lawn. Now what you do is tend the landscape in your area." The big question, he said, is "whether those of us who are charged with organizing a public response to ecological restoration are capable and competent enough to provide enough outlets" for the new impulse.

Packard, he said, realized that "ecological restoration has more to do with readjusting the relationship of people to the landscape than with the botanical relationships that take place."

11

PROVOKING THE PROFESSORS

But at bottom, the expanding citizen restoration movement was of course about botany—or, more broadly, ecology. And as restoration projects proliferated, a tension, sometimes creative and sometimes not, developed and strengthened between academic ecologists—keepers of the flame who had always been the source of received wisdom about ecology—and the green-thumbed, nonprofessional practitioners like Steve Packard, who had always been the recipients of that wisdom but who now were turning up knowledge and insights about the ecosystems they nurture that the academics didn't have. The professors typically reacted in one of two ways: by resisting and belittling the scientific offerings of the restorationists or by seeking to learn from what the restorationists were turning up and to integrate it with their own work.

One man in particular, Bill Jordan, set out to encourage the ferment and to turn it in a positive direction. As he saw it, restoration could become a powerful new learning tool for ecologists, whose improved ideas could in turn benefit restoration. To this end he began to promote intellectual contact and exchange of ideas between field restorationists and academics.

About the time Packard was doing his first small experiments on the North Branch, in 1977, William R. Jordan, III, was in his early thirties and looking for a job. He had grown up in Madison, Wisconsin, the son of an English teacher and a forester in the conservationist traditions of Gifford Pinchot and Aldo Leopold. It was a conservation-minded family, and a literary-minded one as well; Jordan's mother, he recalls, "kept insisting that we take an interest in people, in literature, in human experience." Following one branch of this intellectual inheritance, he earned a Ph.D. in botany at the University of Wisconsin in Madison, but found that botany was not for him. Following the other branch, he got a journalism degree and tried to be a journalist for a while but discovered that was not for him either. He applied for and won a newly created position of education coordinator at the university arboretum in Madison, onetime stronghold of Leopold and Curtis, pioneers of prairie restoration and prairie-savanna ecology. In casting about for features that set the arboretum apart, he eventually settled on its restoration activities; in time he would be describing the arboretum as the Kitty Hawk of the restoration movement. This led him in due course to articulate and promote the concept of ecological restoration, a mission for which his botany and journalism backgrounds happily had prepared him.

His forum was a small scientific journal that he founded in 1981, called *Restoration & Management Notes*. At first, lacking a scientific constituency, Jordan had to extract articles for his journal by what he calls "a kind of main force." Partly to create a constituency, he floated the idea for a society of restorationists, but it went nowhere at first. Too many scientific societies already, he was told. In the spring of 1987, however, a group of California restorationists invited him to San Diego for a conference on plant revegetation. At that meeting, the Californians and Jordan agreed to set up a "Society for Ecological Restoration and Management" as an organization where hands-in-the-dirt restorationists—conservation land managers and the like—and academic ecologists could come together and exchange ideas. About 400 people attended the organization's founding conference in 1989, and its membership by 1993, by which time its name had become simply, "Society for Ecological Restoration," had grown to about 1,800. *Restoration & Management Notes*, published by the University of Wisconsin Press, served as its journal, and its office was established at the arboretum. Contributions to the journal picked up, and both it and the society quickly became major information and idea exchanges. (In 1993, a second publication, *Restoration Ecology*, became the society's official scientific journal, although the more informal *Restoration & Management Notes* continued to flourish.) Jordan himself had emerged by the late 1980s as the restoration movement's chief idea broker and philosopher.

One of the major ideas he helped develop, along with such people as Dr. Michael E. Gilpin of the University of California at San Diego and Dr. John D. Aber in Madison, was that of restoration as an important new tool in basic ecological research. This may sound like a somewhat straightforward and prosaic proposition, but in fact it is profoundly revolutionary. Always, in the past, the flow of information and expertise had gone one way—from the academic scientists to land managers, restorationists, and other practitioners in the field. The academics did the talking and the green-thumbers did the listening. That is, of course, necessary up to a point. Steve Packard, for instance, could have gone nowhere without the accumulated scientific wisdom of Curtis and other members of the University of Wisconsin in Madison—as he is the first to recognize.

But ecology is a young, somewhat unformed science,

uncommonly full of uncertainty and a long way from providing the confidence and reliability that physics, say, imparts to bridge builders or that anatomy and physiology give to surgeons. Theoretical ecology, in the view of Jordan and a number of ecologists themselves, needs large doses of out-in-nature reality if it is to continue to grow and develop and ultimately go beyond mere description to provide the kind of confident predictive power that the hard sciences have long since achieved. Older sciences achieved it, Jordan is fond of pointing out, partly by integrating the hands-on experience of craftsmen into its procedures and experiments. Charles Darwin, for example, depended on people like "beekeepers, pigeon fanciers, and petunia growers, that kind of thing." And in fact, ecology may owe a debt to the practical, everyday labors of farmers, who, as Tom Griggs noted, deal routinely with such ecological concepts as competition and nutrient cycling.

Similarly, Jordan believes, restoration practice has much to offer ecological theory, which then might be made more predictive and, in turn, of more help to restorationists. Anthony Bradshaw, a British ecologist, sees restoration as the "acid test" of ecological theory. Bradshaw was a contributor to a 1987 book edited by Jordan, Gilpin, and Aber that brings together many essays on the role of restoration as a research tool. Its theme is that restoration is uniquely positioned to shed light on ecological questions, and to raise new ones, because it forces the restorationist to find out how an ecosystem really works. In the lead essay of their book, Jordan and company put it this way: "The idea here is simply that one of the most valuable and powerful ways of studying something is to attempt to reassemble it, to repair it, and to adjust it so that it works properly."[15]

Academic ecology has long since begun to move beyond description to experimentation in an attempt to elucidate how ecosystems work. But its experiments are for the most part limited to small segments of reality and do not come to grips with what is perhaps most important about ecology: how nature operates in the round, in all its diversity, in the totality of its relationships, in the sweep of history, and across broad spatial scales. These are precisely the dimensions most important not only to conservationists and especially to restorationists, but also to a basic understanding of ecosystems.

But ecologists, following the reductionist strategy so prevalent in science generally, have perhaps naturally tended to chop nature up into isolated, bite-sized fragments that miss the interrelatedness that is the essence of ecology. "Very little ecology deals with any processes that last more than a few years, involve more than a handful of species, and cover an area of more than a few hectares," Dr. Stuart L. Pimm, a theoretical ecologist at the University of Tennessee, wrote in 1991.[16] And the basic ecologists, those whose research is aimed at answering fundamental questions rather than looking for knowledge that can be applied immediately, may in general have the most restricted perspective. "In my experience," writes Dr. D. W. Schindler, a Canadian ecologist, "the best applied ecology programs ask broader, not narrower questions than basic research. I can think of far more cases where fundamental questions in ecology have been addressed by applied studies than I can of useful applied applications of basic research."[17]

Restoration ecologists, who according to Pimm find themselves "at the very applied end of the discipline," are precisely the people pursuing longer, broader issues. That, he says, may require less reliance on the traditional experimental approach in which nature is strictly manipulated and controls are established so that there is something with which experimental actions can be compared. The sweep of ecological relationships is inherently uncontainable in a laboratory. "We have to be more creative in the kinds of ways we test ideas," says Pimm.

*   *   *

If Steve Packard hadn't appeared when he did, Bill Jordan would have had to invent him. And if it hadn't been for Jordan, Packard's work and ideas might not so quickly have burst into such contentious prominence among scientists and conservationists, or tweaked so many nerves, or stimulated so much discussion, or become so instrumental in putting savanna restoration on the map. For there is little doubt that Packard boosted the whole savanna question to a new level of visibility, interest, and excitement among scientists and conservationists. He "raised the stakes and the temperature, and creative juices from a lot of different people began flowing," says Steve Apfelbaum, an independent ecologist who has long been associated, sometimes tensely, with Packard.

Bill Jordan had visited the Miami Woods Prairie with Packard in 1987, and they subsequently encountered each other again at a prairie conference that year. At the conference, the two talked about restoration as the acid test of ecology, and Packard told Jordan of his savanna work: of how the prairie plants wouldn't grow under the oaks, of the search for species that would grow there, and of the success in Vestal Grove. Jordan said, "Wait a minute. You've got a new idea of the flora because of your work with restoration? Holy smokes!"

It was just the sort of example of restoration-as-research Jordan was looking for. There were other examples, perhaps the clearest and earliest being the discovery through restoration work in the 1930s at the Wisconsin arboretum that fire was ecologically vital to prairies. But here was a gold-plated, live contemporary case in which restoration had not only uncovered a hidden ecosystem but was disputing the conventional wisdom about the plants that had made it up! The result was an article by Packard describing what had taken place at Vestal Grove and its environs, published in the Summer 1988 issue of *Restoration & Management Notes*. In it, Packard wasted no time challenging the standard academic view of savannas as nothing more than a prairie with trees. That concept, he wrote, is "profoundly misleading," and this time he offered the fruits of the North Branch experience at Vestal Grove as evidence:

> In contrast with the results of earlier studies, savannas *do* include a considerable number of distinctive species—that is, species that predominate in savannas but not in prairies or oak forests. It has become clear that a complement of these herbaceous species must be present if the savanna is to function healthily. . . . A number of rare plants and animals depend on savanna conditions. The long-term future of such species may well depend on our willingness and ability to restore what probably would be the first community to be saved principally through restoration. . . .

For the scientists, Packard offered a caveat:

> People who would like good solid data before they'll believe the sorts of material in this article will have to wait a few years. Most of our techniques take two to four growing seasons to produce good results. We learned by a trial-and-error process using hundreds of varying uncontrolled restoration experiments. If we had proceeded more systematically, we would by now either have spent a small fortune, or, using those resources available to us, we would only now be getting the results of the first few experiments, all of which were failures. But using craft and intuition we have developed techniques that seem to work. Forthcoming papers will provide more detailed data and documentation. This article is written for those who are interested in the impressions and insights gained from ten years of practical work.[18]

There it was: A nonprofessional, untrained in formal ecology, not a member of the academic priesthood, had taken the broader view, and at the very least had come up with a new hypothesis about the structure of a major slice of American nature. Crude and uncontrolled though the experiments were, they rested on a decade of toil in the empirical vineyards. That gave Packard's thesis a measure of authority, and it delighted Jordan's sense of what he calls "the bottom-up part of the development of ideas." To him, what Packard did in one way evoked the Wright brothers. "I love the Wright brothers," he says. "They were craftsmen who did what the scientists knew could not be done. I love the idea of Wilbur Wright struggling with the forces of the wind, and so forth, and coming to understand them better than anyone else did because he was there. There's a sort of intellectual egalitarianism about that."

At the heart of the debate set off by Packard's article was a mystery: What is a savanna? Mysteries always intrigue scientists; it is why many of them do what they do. "It's fun to try to work with something we know so little about, and it's a challenge for that reason," Dr. Evelyn Howell, a conservation biologist at the University of Wisconsin, says of the savanna question. And in science, just as night follows day, argument follows mystery.

Marlin Bowles, who had previously criticized Packard's approach as dangerous and based on insufficient data and scientific rigor, now—without necessarily buying the substance of Packard's argument about the nature of the savanna—saw the work as something to be taken seriously. By turning up Mead's list of barrens plants, Bowles felt, Packard had begun to put together a basis for comparing a restored savanna with the presettlement original. The Mead list, Bowles said, "legitimized what he was doing."

After Packard's article appeared, Dr. Andre F. Clewell, a consulting ecologist and professional restorationist from Florida who would later become president of the Society for Ecological Restoration, wrote that he was disposed to favor Packard's thesis that the savanna flora had elements distinct from those of prairie and forest. Clewell had found the same thing in a pine-oak-hickory community that had much in common with the Illinois savanna.[19]

Perhaps the strongest support, apart from some of Packard's allies in the Chicago group, came from Stuart Pimm, the theoretical ecologist. Pimm subscribes to a school of thought which holds that stable plant and animal communities fit together in special ways rather than occurring haphazardly on the landscape. He sees Packard's success at Vestal Grove as support for this view: "It didn't work until he got everything just right." And if the special-fit theory is right, it suggests that Packard's analysis of what the savanna community is like, at least as it is expressed at Vestal Grove and its environs, is right as well. Packard's article, Pimm says, "was written in complete isolation from any theory we developed. And yet it matches the theoretical intuition almost perfectly—that if you don't have all the pieces, you will wander around and not have a persistent stable state" in the ecosystem.

Packard's work, Pimm believes, also underscores the importance of history in the assembly of an ecosystem, a factor he says is often overlooked. "If you look at most ecology," he says, "it's almost the ecology of a universe that could have been created yesterday." But ecosystems are a product of their history, and "if you play the tape again you may get an entirely different evolution." That is, an ecosystem might shape up differently even if it started over again with the same materials. Computer modeling at the University of Tennessee suggests that an ecosystem can arrive at "alternative stable states" depending on the order in which species colonize it. The implications for restoration are obvious: It may never be possible to restore a community to its presettlement condition because the presettlement assembly sequences cannot be known, much less duplicated; even the most meticulous restoration effort can result in a variety of outcomes, any one of which is "natural" and "legitimate." But if a serious attempt is made to discover the presettlement floristic makeup of an ecosystem as Packard did, says Pimm, it may be possible to get reasonably close to the original.

This would still fulfill restoration's primary purpose, because many species and much genetic information would be preserved in a functioning arrangement where plants and animals can resume their evolutionary course in a way truer to their history than would otherwise be the case. As we have seen, it is not possible or necessary to make a carbon copy of the original ecosystem in order to preserve species and enable evolution to take its course and produce more species. "Just because you don't get to the end point doesn't mean you shouldn't move in the right direction," says Pimm. But, he says, "it means that as we go out and destroy nature, we need to be able to record what's there before we lose it."

In the years after Packard's article on the rediscovery of the savanna appeared, he and Pimm struck up a working relationship in which they often shared insights and information, an exchange that advances both theory and practice. It is exactly the kind of interchange that Bill Jordan had in mind when he began promoting the idea of restoration as a medium in which field experience could nourish theory, and vice versa.

But on the more particular question of the character of the savannas, Packard's article touched off a scientific furor, all the more so because his ideas and the successes of the North Branch Prairie Project had begun to appear more broadly in the scientific "gray literature," aimed at both scientists and interested laymen like conservation land managers, and in the general press.

Dr. Roger C. Anderson of Illinois State University, who came out of the Curtis school of thought at Wisconsin, challenged Packard's idea that there is a group of plants characteristic of the savanna. In his view, the savanna represented a transition between forest and prairie and was without any distinctive grouping of species. He argued that in presettlement times, the distribution of plant species formed a continuum from open prairie to savanna to forest. While some species may have reached their highest abundance in the savanna, he said, many were distributed across much more of the continuum; for example, bottlebrush grass is adapted to oak forests as well as savannas, and shooting stars are found on both prairie and savanna. It is impossible, Anderson argued, to separate the savanna, on the basis of floristic composition alone, from forests on one end of the continuum and treeless prairies on the other; on a floristic basis, there were simply no sharp dividing lines with which to distinguish the savanna. Any attempt to separate it out would be purely arbitrary, he argued.

As a general proposition, the continuum concept is widely accepted by ecologists. It says that within broadly defined habitats, species of plants and animals gradually replace one another along gradients of physical conditions like soil quality, moisture, and amount of sunlight. Packard accepted the continuum concept as applied to prairie, savanna, and forest, but not a corollary asserted by a number of academic critics: that the savanna was not a community in its own right, but merely a transition—an "ecotone," in the jargon of the profession—between prairie and forest. Critics often based their argument on the conclusion of Curtis that the savanna as it existed in the 1950s contained relatively few species—only six, in fact—that were more abundant there than anywhere else. Curtis called these "modal" species, and found that prairies and forests each contained many more modal species than did savannas. "Everyone repeated Curtis when you tried to make a case for the savanna," Packard would say later. He concluded that academic critics dismissed the savanna "in part because it didn't fit the categories they were used to thinking in, i.e., forest and prairie," but more especially "because Curtis's data seemed to show that nothing special lives there."

Actually, he thought, Curtis was right in his characterization of savanna as essentially a prairie with trees if, as Curtis did, one considers only the more open part of the savanna: Down at that end of the continuum, the savanna would have more prairie species than any others. But Packard had been working with the savanna definition used by Jack White in his 1984 survey of Illinois prairie and savanna remnants. This revision of Curtis's definition considered anything with a canopy cover of between 10 and 80 percent to be savanna. This seemed more useful for conservation purposes, since it included all the territory between open prairie and closed forest. And if that definition is followed, Packard believed, Curtis was probably wrong in concluding that the savanna had very few characteristic species.

To Packard, the question was much more than a mere academic quibble over definitions. He feared that if the savanna were defined away, there would be no imperative to conserve it, and with it, species that even Anderson conceded may be most abundant there. "Why put a lot of conservation effort into something that is already preserved, essentially, in the prairie preserves and the forest preserves?" is how Packard put the conventional wisdom.

But even though the savanna had once consisted of perhaps 30 million acres in total and covered half the landscape in southern Wisconsin and northeastern Illinois—pretty big, maybe, to dismiss as an ecotonal transition zone—the critics persisted. As might be expected, as Bill Jordan said with perhaps some understatement, "Steve's stuff at first wasn't welcomed with any great evident interest" up in Wisconsin, the citadel of Curtis's disciples.

Scientists in Madison and elsewhere had been researching savannas for years, and it would have been natural for them, as one Madisonian suggested, to resent the sudden appearance of a major conceptual revision from an uncredentialed nonresident of academia, especially one who was beginning to have a public and policy impact they never had. (An Environmental Protection Agency official described reading a newspaper account of Packard's savanna work as "one of those eureka experiences.") Packard had become adept at dealing with the press, taking pains to think through reporters' questions and come up with good quotes. As the savanna issue gained prominence, in fact, there was some grumbling in Madison to the effect that Packard was just a glory hog. It is the same kind of grumbling that scientists have sometimes directed at members of their own profession who have been a little too articulate, or too public, or too popular in their appeal. One Madisonian scornfully dismissed Packard as nothing but a publicity hound.

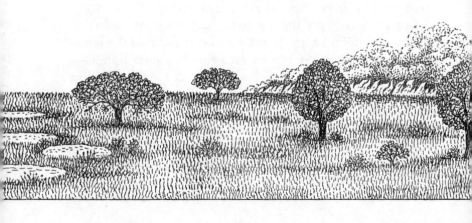

Another Madisonian, Bill Jordan, bristles at such suggestions and defends Packard with some heat. Others in Madison were generous as well. "What [Packard] has done is publicize the need for savanna restoration, which is very good," said Dr. Virginia Kline, a plant ecologist who as of 1993 managed the University of Wisconsin arboretum's research program. While Packard has not published much data and "gets chided for his lack of publications," she said, she was "appreciative of his efforts" in bringing savanna restoration to the fore. Moreover, she said, "if you read Curtis, he says in several places there will be new discoveries in certain areas, and I expect that if he were living he would welcome Steve's ideas."

Another University of Wisconsin scientist, Dr. Thomas Givnish, a botanist, accepted Packard's challenge to Curtis on the issue of savanna species composition as a serious

one and set out to learn experimentally who was right about savannas' special character or lack of it. Because the savannas had been so transformed by human impact by the time Curtis investigated them, Givnish wrote in a monograph describing his experiment, his account of savanna composition may indeed be "seriously misleading." He found Packard's argument "stimulating and highly original," but not yet proved by rigorous scientific testing. Givnish asserted that such a test was fundamental to any attempt to restore savannas; to determine, as he put it, "the proper target for a savanna restoration" and "the appropriate pool of plant species to be used."

"I think Packard is onto something," Givnish said in 1993. "He's got some good ideas, and he's made a major contribution to reviving interest in this area. But it really is not compelling yet, because he presents almost no quantitative data on any issue." Givnish set out to get some of the data by devegetating thirty five-by-forty-foot strips of ground stretching from tree trunks to open sites in what once were oak savannas in the Wisconsin arboretum. The strips were sown with about thirty-five species characteristic of the forest-prairie continuum. How the species naturally rearrange themselves over time along the sun-shade gradient will test the competing Curtis-Packard hypotheses. The experiment, in which a hypothesis generated by on-the-ground restoration is being tested in a traditional scientific manner, was still under way in 1993: another example of Jordan's hoped-for interplay between practice and theory.

Neither Packard's restoration work nor the debate swirling about it had been proceeding in a vacuum. Since the early 1980s, other restorationists had been working on less degraded savannas of a type other than those on the North Branch. Still others were getting seriously into the act, both as restorationists and investigators, and were learning much about savannas and how they function, by the time Vestal Grove burst forth in its first green blaze of savanna species in the spring of 1986. That same spring, Vicki Nuzzo published the savanna paper she had been working on when Packard came to her and Marlin Bowles for criticism of his own first effort at publishing. The Nuzzo paper was a comprehensive treatment of what was known about midwestern savannas at the time, incorporating the Curtis view of savanna species composition, and many came to use it as a basic reference and a conceptual framework. Broadly descriptive of the extent and status of the oak savannas, the paper reported that 27 million to 32 million acres of savanna covered parts of Minnesota, Iowa, Missouri, Illinois, Wisconsin, Michigan, Indiana, and Ohio in presettlement times. By putting together surveys from the individual states, Nuzzo determined that in 1985, less than 6,500 acres—.02 percent of the original—remained in relatively undegraded, high-quality condition. All but about 100 acres were on dry, sandy, or rocky soils unlike the rich soil of the classic bur-oak, tallgrass savannas of northern Illinois and southern Wisconsin. No state reported any intact, high-quality examples of tallgrass savanna.[20]

In Wisconsin, Alan Haney of the University of Wisconsin at Stevens Point and Steven I. Apfelbaum, a private consulting ecologist who was Haney's former student and present collaborator, had undertaken extensive investigations of the structure and dynamics of oak savannas, also starting in 1986. In one study, performed with several collaborators at twenty-four sites in northeastern Illinois, Indiana, and southern Wisconsin, they confirmed that fire was indeed a major factor in the establishment and maintenance of the savannas, and that periodic fire also appeared to favor a rich mixture of birds, insects, and spiders. They also found that in the most degraded savannas, the oaks were failing to reproduce. But they went on to pinpoint a likely mechanism for recovery of both the oaks and the larger ecosystem. Savanna oaks, they discovered, grew up in distinct, uniform age cohorts. They interpreted this to mean that periodic intense fires were interspersed with several years in which light fire or no fire occurred. During that hiatus, young oaks sprouting from "grubs," big root masses hundreds or even thousands of years old, grew to fire-resistant size. When the next fire came through, it destroyed brush and less fire-resistant trees, allowing the oaks to create the savanna canopy, and savanna grasses and flowers to proliferate richly under them. Haney and Apfelbaum concluded that frequent fires are usually necessary for several years to restore savannas, but that later on, hot fires should be limited to five-year or ten-year intervals to allow new oaks to be "recruited."

By 1993, Haney and Apfelbaum were studying and experimenting with restoration at some one hundred sites representing a range of savanna types across the Midwest. In Indiana, for instance, they teamed up with state conservation officials to help produce a savanna management plan. Indiana may have more acres of a particular type of savanna—with black oaks in dry, shallow, or sandy soil—than any other state. Because this type of savanna was less attractive to farmers, it has been less degraded than the tallgrass savanna. Under John A. Bacone, director of the Indiana Department of Natural Resources' Division of Nature Preserves, the state is restoring a number of sand-savanna tracts.

In Missouri, restorationists are learning the peculiarities of still other types of savannas, different from those of both Indiana and northeastern Illinois. Missouri's savannas in presettlement times ranged from those dominated by post oaks on well-drained, shallow soils in the Ozarks, to poorly drained post oak flatwoods that were wet for brief periods and dry the rest of the time, to deep-soil wet savannas on floodplains, to shallow-soiled savannas dominated by chinquapin oaks. It is turning out that in contrast to the tallgrass savannas farther north, these savannas, like the sand savannas of Indiana, are easier to restore. They, too, were less disturbed and fragmented by agriculture than were the tallgrass savannas. It is believed that under these conditions a viable supply of wild seeds often remains in the ground, and competing weeds find it harder to establish themselves than they would on land suitable for farming. The Missourians have found that the vegetation usually comes back naturally once a fire regime is reestablished.

Thousands of acres of this kind of savanna, most of it the post oak variety in the Ozarks, are being restored through efforts of the Missouri Department of Natural Resources, The Nature Conservancy, and the U.S. Forest Service. The main technique, according to Ken McCarty, a natural resource manager for the D.N.R., is the prescribed burn, with some removal of invasive trees to let in light. Replanting has been done in a few places, but in McCarty's words, "you don't have to start from ground zero" in most cases. Though some volunteers are involved, most of the work is done by paid state employees.

The Missourians find that their savannas recover in predictable stages: first with brush dominant, then brush mixed with some wildflowers and grasses, then the development of a rich, dense herbaceous understory with some of the more sensitive plant species characteristic of a mature community. The work has convinced McCarty and his colleagues that large stretches of Missouri savannas can be restored, and that significant results can show in as little as ten years. "It's really starting to pick up a lot of steam," said McCarty.

Apfelbaum and Haney have found in their research that sites vary in the ease with which they can be restored. Many will respond well without having to reintroduce plants or sow seed if the tree canopy is opened up somewhat to allow in enough light. But while vegetation might grow back on some sites, it may not be native plants, and reintroduction may be necessary in these cases. Other sites contain only a few small patches in which the natural seed bank is intact. Sites most severely degraded by erosion, grazing, and invasion by brush may not respond at all in the absence of planting.

Amid all this bubbling of ideas about savannas and savanna restoration, people on all sides of the question gathered in Chicago in the cold depths of February 1993 for a conclave that turned out to be something of a watershed.

Clearly, the savanna issue was reaching some sort of critical mass, creating an atmosphere of increasing urgency about protecting the remaining savannas and their species assemblages. One thing led to another and the conference was called. Its key organizers were Steve Packard and Karen Holland, the North Branch volunteer who also happened to work for the U.S. Environmental Protection Agency's Chicago regional office, which sponsored the meeting, and Alan Haney. Two other E.P.A. officials, William Franz and Milo Anderson, worked closely with them. Haney and Packard were the moderators and tone setters for the meeting. Many who would attend the conference were the same ones who had helped bring prairie preservation to the fore at conferences in previous years. The Chicago group was particularly prominent.

As planning proceeded, the meeting's purpose was broadened, at Packard's initiative, to include a larger and wider array of people with conflicting ideas on the savanna issue than had originally been proposed by Haney, and to produce a regional plan for biological recovery of the entire oak savanna ecosystem at large. Conservationists were beginning to think in terms of entire ecosystems rather than individual species, and Packard saw the concept of ecosystem recovery as a way to enlist the power of federal and state agencies in an ecosystem-wide effort parallel to those being made on endangered species.

By coincidence, the savanna conference convened the day after the Clinton administration's new interior secretary, Bruce Babbitt, announced that, in a shift in federal conservation policy, he would try to prevent what he called "national train wrecks" over the protection of endangered species by practicing preventive medicine. This, he said, would require focusing not on individual species but on entire ecosystems. Ecosystem protection and recovery plans would be developed before species actually became endangered and options became so limited that collisions between developers and conservationists became inevitable. "Just when we're meeting to talk about a savanna recovery plan!" Packard exulted when he read about the Babbitt announcement.

The group of about one hundred invited experts who convened in Chicago was a yeasty mixture: academic scientists, conservation land managers, volunteer restorationists, field practitioners, and ivory-tower theoreticians. It was the academy sitting down with the green-thumbers on equal terms. Packard later called it "a participatory democracy of science."

To Alan Haney, it represented a bridging of the gap between university ecologists and nonacademic field practitioners who have become so expert as to be de facto professionals. Haney remarked especially on what he called the "kind of peculiar" circumstance of Roger Anderson, "a Ph.D. regional ecologist who was trained at the University of Wisconsin, debating with a Steve Packard, who has very little training in ecology at all." That, he said in a side conversation early in the conference, "says a lot for Steve Packard, in my view."

And while Packard may be exceptional, Haney said that "everywhere I've gone throughout the country you run into people like that. They're the local experts in taxonomy. They're the local experts in control of noxious weeds. It's amazing what you find. Some of them are specialists in reptiles and amphibians, some in birds, a lot of them in insects. If we can keep pulling that energy and focusing it, I think there's a lot of knowledge out there we haven't taken advantage of. One of the things that bothers me is the degree of arrogance you see among the so-called scholars and researchers who have gotten the notion that they have all the answers and who often look down with disdain at people who are just walking encyclopedias of bits of knowledge." In many cases, he said, the volunteers and land managers in some ways know more than the scientists because they "have been out there worrying and thinking and working with oak savannas for several years" and often understand ecosystem processes and structure better than academics, who "may not have seen that many examples of real life out there in the field." Also, he said, "we have a lot of armchair ecologists who publish like crazy in the theoretical journals but who really have a very, very poor understanding and maybe even a lot of ignorance about the actual management and problems that managers face."

All that from one who is himself an academic scientist.

So there in Chicago were Anderson, Givnish, and many of their academic colleagues conferring with Packard and dozens of other nonacademics, hoping to synthesize their views in the interest of resurrecting the savanna. A tall order, since so many arrived with different pictures in their heads of what a savanna was. "I'm tired of hearing about this open, grassy, beautiful parklike savanna," one conferee groused. "That's stupid. They may have that up in Wisconsin, but not where I come from in Illinois. There it's brambles and shrubs and hazelnuts."

That, in fact, was one big lesson emerging from the meeting: The oak savannas of the mid-continent in pre-settlement times were an infinitely complex array of types, varying significantly from time to time and place to place depending on soils, climate, fire history, and stage of succession. But together they constituted a vast landscape stretching down through the country's midsection all the way from the Great Lakes to the Gulf Coast. For that matter, many other ecosystems in other parts of the country are really savannas, too, based on their ecological characteristics. These include oak savannas in California, pine barrens in New Jersey and at high elevations in the Appalachians, and the entire sweep of the longleaf pine-wiregrass landscape whose remnant Greg Seamon and company were restoring in Florida.

A second big lesson was that arguments over what defines a savanna can obscure what the presettlement landscape was really like. Almost everybody at the conference had his or her own idea of how to define a midwestern savanna. Much of what Curtis had called forest (50 percent or more tree canopy cover) for instance, others called savanna. In 1993, Packard and The Nature Conservancy considered 0 to 10 percent to be prairie, 10 to 25 percent savanna, 25 to 65 percent woodland (formerly called closed savanna), and more than 65 percent forest. The conference itself considered the range from 10 to 80 percent as the focus of conservation concern, thus for all practical purposes excluding only out-and-out prairie at one end of the continuum and out-and-out closed forest at the other.

Haney, who proved himself an exceptionally able and articulate synthesizer, offered a summary analysis at the end of the meeting that put the question of arbitrary definitions in its place.

One of the most salient facts about savannas, he said, is that as they actually arranged themselves on the land, they were so interlaced with forests, prairies, and wetlands that it was impossible to separate these arbitrary categories from each other. Moreover, this was not a static arrangement. All the elements shifted their positions on the landscape from time to time as climate changed. It is this entire shifting mosaic that ought to be the target of restoration and conservation. "It's important to recognize that we're dealing with a dynamic landscape," Haney said.

One result of this dynamism, he said, was that the savanna became unusually rich in biodiversity: "It provided an opportunity for the preservation and persistence of species that spent part of their time in the wetlands, part of their time in the forest." If elbow room cannot be provided for these population shifts to happen, Haney said, and if all the critical pieces of the landscape cannot be restored in relation to each other, "we probably can't restore the savanna as we would like to have it; it will be only a fragment of a real savanna that was once here." This means, he said, that "we need to place a very high priority, perhaps the highest priority, [on trying] to restore as large a block of landscape as we can, certainly one that contains the mosaic of community types."

If large enough segments of the total Texas-to-Canada mosaic can be acquired or dedicated to restoration, Haney said, it becomes less important to determine exactly what plant species must be included for restoration to work. To "the extent to which we can focus on the landscape mosaic and run the fire events and disturbance events [like grazing by elk and bison] through the landscape and let it kind of sort itself out," he said, "then we become less preoccupied" with questions of savanna composition.

In the end, the sense of the conference seemed to be that conservation plans must move ahead and cannot wait for every academic "i" to be dotted and "t" to be crossed; and that by thinking in all-encompassing terms, scientific distinctions become less important.

With one very, very big caveat: It will probably be some time before a landscape-wide conservation plan can be put into effect. In the meantime, the burden of savanna conservation will have to be borne by relatively small, incomplete fragments of the landscape mosaic—places like the North Branch. And because many of these fragments are specific, narrow, and unforgiving in the conditions of soil, moisture, and sunlight that they display, it will remain necessary in these cases to find out exactly what plants grew there; the question of the species mixture—of definitions—does not lose its importance after all. This Haney conceded: "To the extent we have to work with these little fragments, then these become pretty important questions."

Those little fragments, like Vestal Grove and its Somme surroundings and their counterparts in other locales and states, remain only beachheads. As a result of the Chicago conference, agencies, scientists, conservationists, and land managers launched a serious effort to move beyond the beaches. Once, Steve Packard had worried lest the savannas be defined away. The definition question was not settled in Chicago, but now savannas seemed to be solidly on the conservation agenda and in the forefront of consciousness.

PRAIRIE
WHITE-FRINGED
ORCHID

APPALACHIAN
BROWN

EASTERN
BLUEBIRD

12

NATURE
RECOVERS
(FITFULLY)

Seven years after the first tender green shoots showed
their fresh new faces in a reborn Vestal Grove, a rich
and colorful slice of the savanna-prairie-woodland mosaic
was reconstituting itself, however imperfectly, there and
on the remaining eighty-five acres of Somme Prairie
Grove. By 1993 the North Branchers' fires and saws had
removed the suffocating buckthorn, tartarian honeysuckle, and other invaders from about 60 percent of the
overall site, allowing wildflowers and grasses representing
most of the prairie-to-forest continuum to flourish. Of the
total Somme acreage, perhaps 10 percent was now prairie,
30 percent was open savanna, and 20 percent, including
most of Vestal Grove, was woodland (or closed savanna)
with smidgens of wetlands here and there. Young oaks
appeared to be present in large enough numbers to assure
that they will replace brush in the long run, given periodic
fires. Out in the open areas, big bluestem grass, northern
dropseed grass, yellow coneflowers, wild quinine, blazing

star, and other classic prairie plants created a summertime feast for the eye. In the woodlands, a thick herbaceous ground cover dominated by woodreed, sweet black-eyed Susan, purple Joe-Pye weed, and elm-leaved goldenrod developed. Here and there, the yellow-orange tubular blossoms of the rare hoary puccoon, transplanted from Preston Spinks's garden, grew in one stretch of open prairie. In a patch of open savanna surrounded by woodlands, the brilliant yellow five-petaled flowers of the rare great St. Johns-wort swayed atop their tall stalks in sunny profusion. In a wet swale, the delicate white blooms of the federally endangered prairie white-fringed orchid broadcast their charm. Packard had gotten their seeds from another site in Chicago, where, as of 1993, they had not been seen in eight years. The former site was so degraded ecologically that the hawk moth, which pollinates the orchid, had disappeared from it. Packard laboriously hand-pollinated the plants and introduced them to Somme, where the hawk moth now lives in sufficient abundance. The reintroduction was continuing in 1993 in cooperation with Marlin Bowles at the Morton Arboretum under a grant from the U.S. Fish and Wildlife Service.

Steve Apfelbaum and Alan Haney, in their savanna studies, found not only that plant species declined from around three hundred to about twenty-five when savannas were degraded, but that birdlife plummeted as well, from about twenty-eight species of breeding birds in one example to merely four—one of which, the ubiquitous European starling, was an exotic intruder. When the savanna becomes shaded by invading trees in the absence of fire, for instance, populations of ground-foraging birds decline as shade eliminates plants that produce the seeds and harbor the insects they eat. Flycatchers that perch in the trees of an open savanna, from where they can fly out to nab insects, also decrease as the savanna becomes choked by brush that would not be there if fire were allowed to have its way. "What this suggests," Apfelbaum told the Chicago savanna conference in 1993, "is that if we don't take the [ecological] degradation seriously in savannas, we're on the brink of a major collapse in the breeding-bird species of this region."

If Somme is any indication, restoration may be reversing that trend. A 1992 survey there by Jerry Sullivan identified more than thirty species of birds thought to have once inhabited the savannas. Included were a number of abundant species familiar to many suburban householders, like robins, bluejays, crows, mourning doves, cardinals, field sparrows, and song sparrows. But also on the list were the red-tailed hawk, the great crested flycatcher, the woodcock, the blue-gray gnatcatcher, American kestrel, cedar waxwing, blue-winged warbler, yellow warbler, rose-breasted grosbeak, and indigo bunting. The Cooper's hawk has been spotted there during the breeding season, too, as has the increasingly threatened American bluebird. "We see them," Sullivan said of the bluebirds, "but we have yet to confirm nesting. They drive us nuts. You see them going in and out of a nesthole [in a dead tree], and you think, 'Oh, boy.' But the next day they're gone, and you don't see them again. We have them [down] as probable nesters."

Insects make up the bulk of the fauna in any ecosystem, and Ron Panzer, an insect biologist at Northeastern Illinois University, believes on the basis of twelve years of study in the Chicago area that perhaps 80 percent of insect species originally found on prairies and savannas have adapted to the disturbed modern environment. The other 20 percent, more or less, need help. At the Fermilab project, where Bob Betz re-created the prairie flora virtually from scratch, the insects "haven't yet come back in any major way," Panzer said in 1993. Somme is a different story. "Fermi's a re-creation; at Somme, it was in bad shape but Steve [Packard] had a lot to work with." The rare hairstreaks, Appalachian browns, and fritillaries that appeared like magic at Vestal Grove probably were nearby "in ridiculously small numbers," Panzer said, and came back in force only after the plants they depended on were restored. "Steve and these guys probably rescued them from the brink on that site," Panzer said. "There's no doubt about it. They were there, and Steve made his move in time for these species." But he was probably too late for some species, like the silvery blue. It and other relatively uncommon species that should have lived at Somme are conspicuous by their absence. "We'll probably try to restore these," said Panzer. "At Somme that's do-able, but it's a pretty daunting task at Fermilab."

Bringing the insects back may turn out to be the toughest assignment of all for restorationists. With bigger animals it might be easier. Foxes and snakes, for instance, are pretty adaptable. "I'm quite certain that if I could take a couple hundred smooth green snakes and bring them in at the right time of year and day, I could do it," said Panzer. Plans were already under way in 1993 to return wild turkeys to two large restoration sites in Cook County forest preserves. Coyotes were returning naturally to the area, with a number of sightings made at Somme Prairie Grove between 1989 and 1994. Packard believes that at least one group of coyotes has made Somme its home base. While it was uncertain whether they were becoming permanent, breeding residents, it was likely that they would have an ecological impact. They eat rodents, which meant that the coyotes might reduce the rodent predation on plants and seeds. They also drive foxes from their habitat. Since foxes rob duck and songbird nests, the appearance of coyotes might allow bird populations to increase. Wiley Buck, a North Branch volunteer, in 1993 organized and headed a project to study the coyotes' movement and behavior.

There are, of course, limits to the degree to which large animals can be restored. Given the fragmentation and small size of restoration sites, it is probably never going to be possible to restore some big animals to the Chicago area. There is probably not enough room for bison, for instance. The reintroduction of historic predators like wolves and cougars is obviously out of the question in inhabited areas, though one of the most majestic of original savanna denizens, the elk, may be a feasible candidate for restoration.

Insects are another matter altogether. They are difficult to collect in large enough numbers, they must be handled delicately, and they don't necessarily stay where you put them. In what may be the first effort of its kind in the United States, Panzer and his associates have nevertheless experimented with translocating insects. Some have been moved successfully. But the first butterflies he tried to translocate "flew right out of the preserve: I watched them disappear over the horizon." Collecting some species is a challenge as well. The caterpillar of one species of fritillary, for instance, feeds on violets but only at night. "Try going out with a flashlight looking for a tiny little insect," Panzer said. "It forces us to work with adults, and they're delicate and have wings and can fly off the site." On top of that, he said, "a lot of insects are like wolves—alert, good vision, they hide, and you can't find them. You're lucky on your best day to find four or five individuals."

In restoration, Panzer said, "plants are the easy part." In restoring fauna, he said, "we're decades behind the plant people. No one is rearing butterflies in the backyard. There are no comparable or analogous things going on, and that bothers me."

All in all, the reemergence of Somme and its centerpiece, Vestal Grove, as a wild place in 1993 testified dramatically to both the promise and potential of ecological restoration. But it also offered an object lesson in how hard it is to put Humpty Dumpty back together, and therefore why it is all the more important, at least in this early state of the restoration art, to keep ecosystems from being destroyed or degraded in the first place.

Even with savanna plants there is much uncertainty.

With nature in constant flux, the Somme experiment, per-haps as good a laboratory as exists for the purpose, is raising innumerable questions about the course of succes-sion—the floristic community's gradual, ever-changing composition and movement, in phases, toward a more or less stable, mature state—in the prairie-savanna-woodland mosaic. Packard suspects that succession there is proceed-ing more slowly and is more complicated than he had at first hoped. In one area of open savanna at Somme, for instance, the North Branchers removed brush to reveal bare ground. They planted a mixture of seeds including yellow coneflower, wild bergamot, tall bellwort, and some prairie grasses, as well as the rare great St. John's-wort. Many of the species took hold strongly at first, but then shrank back to minor roles as the St. John's-wort prolifer-ated and dominated the area. "I think the jury's out about what that's going to look like" if and when the plant com-munity stabilizes, Packard said. The main reason, he said, is that none of the grasses have built up to the point where they provide a good source of fuel for fires. At the time of the original planting, the North Branchers did not have access to enough seeds of savanna grasses. If the grasses had been planted more thickly, the great St. John's-wort might not have been so dominant and succession might have taken a different course.

For that matter, said Packard, "we don't yet know if the savanna areas had thick matrices of grass like the prairies have." If the forbs—wildflowers, as distinguished from grasses—continue to dominate the community after sev-eral years of burning, he said, "and if those forbs don't make enough fuel to burn, then maybe we have a more complex successional process" than was thought. A num-ber of species that flourished early in the game "don't seem to be in it for the long haul"; bottlebrush grass, for instance, lives four or five years and then dies, at least under the conditions the restorationists have established. While some bottlebrush grass will probably always grow in Vestal Grove, Packard said, "it doesn't reseed [in large quantities] into the stage of succession that the community has reached," Packard explained, "and we lose our fuel matrix."

In the case of the great St. John's-wort, he said, the mixture of plants where it was growing in 1992 and 1993 "doesn't strike me as a mix that would hold its own" in the long run. Something else is probably going to take over. "It might be satin grass, for example, or it might be shrubs. And it may stay unburned for a long time until a real hot fire goes through and burns off all the shrubs, and we start off again with bergamot and bellflower and great St. John's-wort and eventually go back to shrubs again. There are a great many 'experiments' going on [at Somme], and some of them are going to stabilize. We don't know which ones, and we don't know what they're going to stabilize as. But when that happens, certain ones will turn out to be the dominant fuel species, and we'll start emphasizing those in our plantings." Some of the slow starters, he said, may be most important in the long term—or, the savanna's grass composition may always be more changeable than that of the prairie. "It's too early to speculate about it."

One of the most perplexing successional developments was the aggressive proliferation in Vestal Grove and elsewhere on both North Branch and other Chicago-area restoration sites of a native plant called tall goldenrod. Would it choke out other, more prized species in the long run? Or would it, like many another early-successional weed, retreat in time as more conservative species became established? The hope and expectation was that the tall goldenrod would ultimately lose out to other species. But the jury was out on that, too, and the restorationists were beginning to consider strengthening the competition by introducing more legumes and other savanna plants, like New Jersey tea, that require symbiotic nitrogen-fixing bacteria in their roots to flourish. The North Branchers had

Somme Prairie Grove

Plant communities and quality of vegetation, 1993

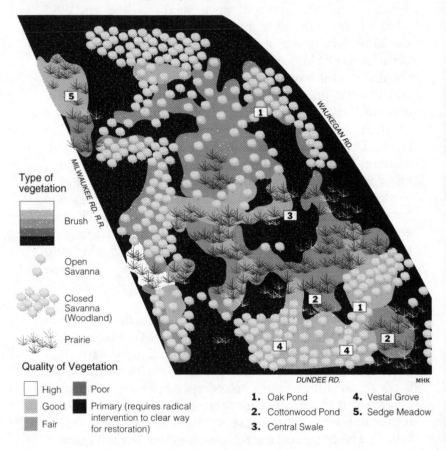

Type of vegetation

Brush

Open Savanna

Closed Savanna (Woodland)

Prairie

Quality of Vegetation

High | Poor
Good | Primary (requires radical intervention to clear way for restoration)
Fair

WAUKEGAN RD.

MILWAUKEE RD. R.R.

DUNDEE RD.

MHK

1. Oak Pond
2. Cottonwood Pond
3. Central Swale
4. Vestal Grove
5. Sedge Meadow

discovered that these plants are difficult to grow; they must be inoculated with the bacteria.

Despite the uncertainty, the North Branchers had teased out a number of ecological secrets during their seven years of work at Vestal Grove, and they were beginning to do so throughout the Volunteer Stewardship Network. All over the Chicago area, the volunteers were collecting data and building up an information base that over the long term would provide grist for a broader understanding of how ecological communities are put together and how they function. Here, Packard believes, the volunteers fill a special niche: Long-term studies are essential in community-level ecology, but the grants on which most scientists depend are almost always for the short term. "But when you have the luxury to do this stuff in your free time because you love it," Packard says, "the power and excitement of the study just gets greater and greater over time. And basically that's our niche: science that is fun but not attracting grants." By 1993, a variety of volunteer studies were under way, including, for instance, detailed biological mapping of restoration sites and a seven-year-old continuing effort to monitor and describe the butterfly population of the Chicago area.

At Vestal Grove, a number of conclusions were emerging from seven years of studies. The restorationists had learned, for example, that:

- In a closed savanna or woodland, an assemblage of nonprairie grasses and sedges, including woodreed, Virginia rye, downy rye, satin grass, and nodding fescue, along with a great many sedges, combine to make a characteristic turf wholly unlike that of the prairie turf's composition.
- Some forbs, like figwort and white snakeroot, should not be planted in the early stages of succession because they are too aggressive.

- Even though the prescribed fires in a closed savanna are small compared with those that sweep an open prairie, they are nevertheless large enough to kill exotic buckthorn, still the most stubborn and common plant in Vestal Grove. While the buckthorn continually sprouts anew, the fires control it; the trend is steadily downward. Without fire, the buckthorn would surely come back and kill everything else. But as the plant community becomes richer and richer, there can be longer intervals between burns, thereby making it easier on the invertebrates that live there. In 1993, some parts of Vestal Grove looked good even though they had not been burned in three years.
- On a site so completely degraded by invasive plants as Vestal Grove originally was, no natural seed bank remains. "The seed bank idea was absolute gospel, and people were very critical of us for planting anything, and some people still are," Packard said.
- Some plants otherwise rare in the region, including Canada milk vetch, big-leafed aster, and sweet black-eyed Susan, do spectacularly well in the restored setting; whatever insects depend on these plants have more raw material than they need after only seven years.
- Even in the originally degraded condition of Vestal Grove, many rare invertebrates, like the Edwards's hairstreak butterfly, were still hanging on, though no doubt in very precarious numbers. Restoration was sufficient to reestablish substantial populations.
- The forest-savanna-prairie continuum has many more components and complexities than some people's mental models might suggest. "People have liked to imagine that plant communities

were uniform, and you have one big chunk, and it's all the same, and another chunk and it's all the same," said Packard. On the ground, it is not that neat; just as patterns of light, soil, and moisture are distributed randomly and haphazardly, so the communities dictated by them are haphazardly and complexly intermixed.

All in all, Vestal Grove, as a continuing experiment, was promising to be a bountiful source of both questions and answers.

Whatever the successional sequence at Vestal Grove, it was thrown seriously out of kilter in 1992 by yet another consequence of postsettlement transformation of the northern Illinois ecology—an explosion of the white-tailed deer population. As happened in many other places across the country, the elimination of predators like wolves and cougars (and in this case the Indians for whom deer were a staple of life) allowed numbers of white-tailed deer to expand far beyond what they were, relative to the rest of the ecosystem, in presettlement times. The modern population is kept partially in check by winter stress. But a series of unusually mild winters removed this check in the upper Midwest in the late 1980s and early 1990s. And as development continued to eliminate privately owned deer habitat, the forest preserves of the Chicago area became ever more attractive to the white-tails.

At Somme Prairie Grove one hazy summer evening in 1992, with the sun setting and a peaceful hush settling over the savanna and prairie, the deer strode confidently across the open savanna and into the closed savannas and woodlands, pausing to gaze at a human visitor. Two bucks with magnificent racks of antlers posed majestically together. Stately and serene, the very embodiment of nature's beauty (though bucks occasionally will challenge humans, snorting and stamping and urinating), they nevertheless had such an impact on vegetation that a possible ecological disaster loomed.

Deer are very selective browsers, and they especially love wildflowers like those that predominate in Vestal Grove. "Anything in the lily family or the orchid family goes first," said Chris Anchor, a wildlife biologist for the Cook County Forest Preserve District. The deer show a particular fondness for plants in flower, often waiting until the blooms burst and seeds are in evidence before eating them. The deer eat mostly leaves early in the growing season, but when the flowers appear they seem to concentrate on them.

Since the understory of Vestal Grove was made up mostly of flowering plants, it was hit especially hard. In the prairie part of the Somme mosaic, such prominent species as the big, leafy prairie dock and the sunflowerlike compass plant were decapitated, the prairie lily simply no longer turned up in samplings, and the rare cream gentian no longer was able to produce seed. But although the prairie was "clobbered," as Packard put it, many flowers still spread a colorful summertime carpet over the gentle swales. In Vestal Grove in the midsummer of 1992, however, not a single flower was to be seen. The maple-leaved goosefoot and the great blue lobelia were two of the first to be cropped. The Michigan lilies also went out early on. The sweet black-eyed Susan did not bloom at all, the deer having eaten every one of the tens of thousands of individuals of this species down to four to six inches from the ground. It normally grows to a height of three or four feet. The Canada milk vetches, which had been going great guns and were becoming common in the grove, turned out to be a favorite of the deer. They ate them all. The purple Joe-Pye weed, which had been on the verge of dominance in part of the grove, was still there. But instead of growing to six feet, it grew to only a foot and did not look like much of anything. While Vestal Grove still maintained its lush, thick green understory, and the experiment was still basically intact, it seemed clear that if the problem became chronic, many of the plants would ultimately be unable to reproduce and would disappear, threatening the entire restoration enterprise. Already the explosion of the deer population had seriously muddied the succession picture at Somme, since it was now difficult if not impossible to tell whether some of the early successful plants whose numbers were now seriously reduced were naturally making way for other species that followed them in the succession cycle or were simply victims of the deer.

What to do? The question is perplexing and dividing many communities across the country, often pitting animal-rights activists against suburban homeowners, who don't like deer eating their garden plants and defecating on their lawns, and wildlife biologists, who in the eyes of the activists are sometimes regarded as callous killers who approach the problem like exterminators approach cockroaches and rats. The activists have many sympathizers with no direct stake in the controversy, particularly among urban people, who see deer as lovely and gentle creatures to be protected at all costs.

That all happened in the Chicago area, too, where the forest preserve districts were the focus of the emotional dispute. The district staffs proposed, as have wildlife managers in many communities, to thin the deer population simply by killing some of the animals. Activists argued that contraception should be given a chance. A hormonal contraceptive method has been developed, but many wildlife biologists argue that no way has yet been devised to deliver it to enough deer to reduce populations. "You'd have to inject 80 percent of the does," said Chris Anchor, the wildlife biologist, but it is impossible to catch that many. In Lake County, which is covered by the Volunteer Stewardship Network, animal-rights activists mounted strong protests, in some cases courting arrest for interrupting the deer-control program.

In Cook County, things went differently. When the forest preserve district and officials of some suburban towns announced that they were going to control deer, the expected polarization between animal-rights advocates on one hand and wildlife managers and upset homeowners on the other did develop. But in this case a third, more moderate force surfaced as well. One of its most visible adherents, by virtue of her speaking and writing, was Cynthia Gehrie, a Winnetka resident who had left her position as a college professor of urban ethnography to raise her children. She and other members of a small citizens' activist group opposed the killing of deer within the Winnetka town limits to protect people's lawns and gardens, as had been proposed. But she did not want to see the argument become an emotional, polarized, paralyzing dispute that shuts off any possibility of a rational solution, as she thought the abortion argument had done. "I thought, my god, we'll spend the next twenty years fighting this issue and find no common ground," she said.

It so happened that Gehrie and some other members of her group were undergoing their own awakening on the question of revitalizing natural areas and the relationship of urban humans to nature. For them, the deer were a powerful connector to the natural world. "When you're in an urban setting" she says, "it's very hard to touch this other force that you know has to be rekindled, so the deer for us were kind of symbols of that—beautiful, wild, exciting, and they were there; they were visible." But the views of Gehrie and others in the Winnetka group were evolving, and the philosophical context within which they saw the deer problem was broadening. Gehrie had heard Edward Wilson speak on biodiversity at a conference at the Chicago Botanic Garden. At that conference, representatives of the North Branch project also gave a talk and showed slides about their restoration work. "I saw there was not only this terrible [biodiversity] problem, but that there was room to participate, and that humans could be not just an erosive force in nature but could be a positive force," says Gehrie.

Steve Packard, meanwhile, had been impressed by an article Gehrie wrote in a local environmental publication called *Conscious Choice*—"a beautiful article about this deer stuff," Packard said, "a hard-line animal-rights kind of article, but very sensible. She came at it in a profound, wise way." The article explored the issue from many angles and put it in the context of humans' impact on the environment. Among other things, Gehrie wrote that the issue is "not merely a question of animal rights, it is about the human presence on earth and our relationship to other species. . . . It is about wildlife and shrinking habitat. It is about our fear of wild things and about our need for control." Packard remembers thinking, "I need to meet this person." The Forest Preserve District "urged me to stay away," he said, "because nothing good could come from it. But one of the strong points in her article was that the Forest Preserve District refused to meet with her group and take anything they said seriously. This approach inflamed the animal-rights folks. It confirmed their impression that the 'Bambi killers' are inhuman bureaucrats with no ethical arguments on their side."

Packard's natural tendency was to line up on the side of those who want to protect wild animals. But he also believed that many animal-rights activists in the deer controversy had an unrealistic view of nature. "I often quote Bill Jordan, who said a very wise thing when asked why he thought this deer question had become a hot topic. He said, 'I think it's something that's been raised by urban people who are out of touch with nature.' That's what it's all about." Many animal-rights people, Packard said, imagine a world where the laws of ecology and of animal behavior, of prey and predator, of ecological interdependence, do not exist. "What happens," said Packard, "is that these people have begun to think of these creatures as pets." But they also, he believed, "really do share many values with the people who want to save endangered species, and yet sometimes these two groups seem to be the biggest enemies of each other."

Gehrie's article suggested to Packard that there could be some common ground. He sought a meeting with her and soon found himself invited to an entire day of get-togethers in which he talked to different groups with different interests; the fact that he was "known and respected," Gehrie said, meant that everyone in the community wanted to take part. Packard visited a school whose teachers and students wanted to plant a buckthorn-choked patch of land across the street with prairie plants and helped them get the project going. Another group wanted to burn a prairie remnant but was wary of the neighbors' potential opposition; Packard explained it to a key neighbor and eventually the burn went off without a hitch.

At a potluck lunch at a home in Glencoe, he talked with some thirty-five women about how to go about changing over their gardens from ornamentals dependent on pesticides and fertilizer to native plants. The meeting was not mostly about deer. Packard remembers a lot of it being about ecology and restoration: "We talked about our problems and what we believed in, and there was a lot we shared."

But a number of the women were animal-rights activists, and the deer question did come up. "I agreed with them that the people who had contempt for the animals just wanted plastic deer in their yards," Packard recalls. "I said I wanted them to understand that I shared their caring about animals, but I encouraged them to look at large numbers of species of animals, not just one, and at rare butterflies that are wonderful animals being driven to extinction because the deer are eating the plants they utterly require, so that there's not enough left for them, and at birds that can no longer live in habitats being made uninhabitable by the deer because the deer eat out all the shrubbery that the birds nest and forage in, and that there are snakes and frogs which require that understory. These people care about that kind of thing, plus there's the fact that overpopulation is not really good for the deer, either. The deer thrive among all those other species, and it's downhill for the deer, for everything, once the ecosystem starts to fall apart."

In the public debate, Gehrie and Packard had been placed on opposite sides. But now they agreed that the question of preserving biodiversity was paramount, that this was where the focus should be. Gehrie said that "for my money, restoration is the most hopeful way of involving more people in the process, and we kind of left it at that." Gehrie and her allies in Winnetka undertook to try to inform their fellow villagers about the degraded state of the forest preserves, about biodiversity, about the need to reestablish the ecosystems—trying, she said, to get people to view the deer issue in the broader perspective. As part of this effort, Packard and Laurel Ross were invited to help set up a program to educate parents and teachers about restoration. Some thirty-five Winnetka residents, Gehrie included, became volunteers under the Volunteer Stewardship Network.

In Gehrie's view, the fact that people were taking part in restoration helped break down polarization. Of the restorationists who see control of the deer as essential, she said: "You see that these are people who love the land, and they're sick about killing the deer." This, she said, creates "an atmosphere of compassion for one another's point of view, and people are much more likely to listen to somebody who's chopping out brush right next to them than to somebody who's [merely] showing up at a meeting."

Gehrie herself now believes that there is no one universal solution to the deer problem, but many local ones. She and other members of her group still adamantly oppose the killing of deer in their town. She hopes that there, where the deer numbers are not so high, measures short of killing, like contraception, barriers, and spraying plants to repel deer, will suffice. But she and her group have reluctantly accepted the killing of deer at Somme Prairie Grove—as long as it is part of the restoration program and as long as it is only a temporary, short-term measure designed to put the deer population back into balance with the rest of the ecosystem.

In an article in a Winnetka newspaper in March 1993, she put forth a concept and a word to describe what must be done: "We do not want to kill deer, but there they are, crowded into the last wild lands because we have torn apart all the other places. If we are to begin to fix things, some deer must be . . . sacrificed. *Sacrificed*—'the giving up of some valued thing for the sake of something of greater value or having a more pressing claim.'"

The upshot of all this was that in Cook County, at least, the Forest Preserve District went ahead with its deer-control plans essentially unimpeded. In the winter, forest preserve crews capture deer in nets, shoot them, and donate the meat to a food program for the homeless. Their goal at Somme in 1992 was to reduce the population by fifty deer; they reduced it by only 10. This nevertheless had an impact: While Vestal Grove in 1993 did not flower as spectacularly as it had before the deer population got so destructively out of hand, it did rebound strikingly, as will be seen.

13

THE CHICAGO WILDERNESS

As the North Branch project headed toward its third decade, restoration had gained such a foothold in the Chicago area and had attracted so many committed people that its future prospects seemed safe and solid. Some 10,000 acres of the Cook County Forest Preserve District's 67,000 acres of degraded oak savannas and prairies had been targeted for restoration, about one fifth of the district's potentially restorable acreage. By 1992, volunteers in the stewardship network were putting in nearly 30,000 hours a year on restoration activities in the district, almost triple the amount of work two years earlier. "People have really taken to restoring our nature preserves by leaps and bounds," said Chet Ryndak, the district's superintendent of conservation. The district stepped up its commitment, too, assigning $75,000 a year and hiring a land manager and volunteer coordinator to work with the volunteer stewards.

By 1993, the North Branch project had become widely known, and it drew a constant stream of visitors from other states and countries who sought to take its lessons home. The question was raised in some quarters as to whether the enterprise could work as effectively if Packard were to move on for any reason. It seemed likely, however, that the North Branch and the volunteer network had long since grown beyond any single person, that leadership was both strong and decentralized enough to carry on. The organization "would certainly be under stress for a while" in Packard's absence, said Karen Holland, "but we have a great many good leaders, and we could do it." Holland herself had grown into one of those leaders. So had Laurel Ross. The Balabans had established themselves as very models of the citizen-scientist who both learns from the ecosystem and turns that knowledge toward its restoration. As co-leaders of the North Branch work group on ecological management, they played key roles in decisions about what specific management steps should be taken. To free up more time, Jane in 1992 cut her work schedule at the pharmacy in half.

Larry Hodak in 1993 was the leader in longest standing except for Packard. His wife, Chris, had insisted that he take a few years off to attend to family matters as his two young daughters were growing up, and he had done so. Fifteen years after Hodak and Packard had tramped the North Branch sites with Eisenbeis and Betz, hoping against hope that Betz would not sink the project and rejoicing when he gave his imprimatur, all four Hodaks were now in the picture, Larry reassuming a major leadership role as chief steward of Sauganash Prairie and Chris occasionally attending workdays. Daughters Eleanor and Hannah, ten and eight years old in 1993, came along, too. Larry would give them a quarter a bag for pulling garlic-mustard weeds, and they loved it. They adopted a great bur oak and called it their climbing tree. (The girls and the tree were featured on the family Christmas card one year.) They took watercolors to the site to draw and paint, they picked up trash, they collected seeds. "They're really dying to go to a burn," Chris said in the summer of 1993. "They've seen the prairie [after a burn], and lots of slides of burns, and [Larry] comes home smelling so good" after a fire. "But Larry doesn't think they're old enough yet." Larry said he was wary of pushing them: "Sometimes that's counterproductive."

Hodak offered this personal retrospective on his North Branch experience:

> After a couple of years, it's kind of an interesting hobby. But after fifteen years it starts to define your life a little bit. I can't imagine what my life would be without this. It's provided me with a real connection to the landscape, and with this place in northeastern Illinois, and to call it a hobby seems to demean it. I really feel like it's my second job. Hardly a day goes by where I don't think about it, some aspect of it. I don't know how I'd define myself environmentally, politically, any other way, even religiously, without my fifteen years on the North Branch.

That sense of identity and commitment, in various forms and degrees, was at the heart of the political impulse that gave birth to the North Branch project, secured the assent and then the support of skeptical landowners, built a constituency that shielded the restoration effort from attack and gave it negotiating credibility. As a result, the project that began so inconspicuously in 1977 had by 1993 brought about an important change in both the culture and politics of conservation. "The key thing," Packard said, looking back, "was getting all those people out on the land."

Despite all this, or perhaps in part because of it, Packard and the Volunteer Stewardship Network were hit by a major challenge to both the scientific and philosophical rationale for the entire savanna restoration movement. Restoration sometimes throws basic questions about humans' relationship to nature into especially sharp relief, and this was such a case. The challenge came from Dr. Jon Mendelson, a professor of environmental science at Governors State University in Illinois; Stephen P. Aultz, chief naturalist of the Will County, Illinois, Forest Preserve District; and Judith Dolan Mendelson, a member of the Illinois Endangered Species Protection Board.

The Mendelson paper, as it became known, appeared in the Winter 1992–93 issue of *Restoration & Management Notes*.[21] The authors described Packard's idea of a savanna as being that of a distinct community with a unique set of plant species. This idea, they wrote, was the most influential concept in savanna restoration. They called the "postulated uniqueness of the savanna flora" an illusion. (Packard had not said that characteristic savanna species are unique to the savanna, but merely that they predominate there.) They dismissed the very name savanna as "no more than a name applied to an arbitrarily defined segment of a particular continuum," representing "an ecotone of uncertain width and uncertain stability lying between grassland and forest." Whatever portion of the continuum is defined as savanna "depends on the definer; it is not inherent in the vegetation. Seen in this light, the management activities so popular today lose some of their romance."

Moreover, the paper went on, the restoration activities "are not so much noble attempts to restore a unique savanna community as they are increasingly destructive efforts to shove existing assemblages of species in one direction or another along a vegetational continuum." In particular, the article contended, the restorationists were trying to create a savanna out of a forest. The authors based their conclusion on observations of restoration efforts at a Cook County Forest Preserve site called Cap Sauers Holding, where Volunteer Stewardship Network restorationists were working. That site, the Mendelsons and Aultz charged, "is currently being heavily managed to give it a savannalike appearance, even though in topography and soils (to say nothing of the existing vegetation itself) it is a landscape clearly favoring the establishment of closed woodland."

Relying especially on soil type as "the best indication of the prior extent of all vegetation types in the region," the authors argued that the soil at Cap Sauers Holding and many other sites was clearly of a woodland type. Furthermore, they said, managers at Cap Sauers Holding were burning north-facing slopes of ravines; but since prevailing winds were from the southwest, it was unlikely that north-facing slopes burned with much frequency in presettlement times. Thus they had probably been forested.

And, the article pointed out, restorationists were cutting and burning white ash, basswood, black cherry, hawthorn, dogwood, and northern arrowwood, all native to northeastern woodlands. The restorationists believe that these trees, which were present in the presettlement savanna, have become overabundant in the absence of fire, to the point where they are choking out many other elements of the community. But the Mendelson article said the elimination of these trees demonstrates not only questionable value judgments but also "an incomplete understanding of woodland ecology." They further criticized the way in which fire was being used, charging that "the systematic burning of small areas within larger communities by managers has the effect of increasing fire intensity and coverage." They argued that "nature does not operate in such a nonrandom manner." In fact, they wrote, restoration interferes with natural processes. While it is true that the first European settlers' suppression of fire disturbed the natural community, they argued, the major effect of fire suppression was largely limited to the early years after settlement.

All of which led to the following conclusions:

The existing shrubs and saplings are not an unnatural assemblage that should be removed but, instead, represent "a healthy, vigorous recovery from disturbance, a recovery that should be allowed to continue unhindered." There is little or no value in choosing "a single moment in time as the aim of a restoration effort." Any human conception of how the areas being restored were constituted "is only a human approximation of reality," and its end product is "not the limitless creativity of nature, but a form of landscape architecture limited by the imagination of the manager."

"We're not opposed to restoration out of hand," Mendelson said in a conversation after the article appeared. "We took a pretty extreme position, [but] I think we were operating in a climate of near totally unanimous support" for restoration in the Chicago area. "The question," he said, "is where are you doing [restoration] and at what cost?" He said it is possible, as early surveys might indicate, that what now appear to be closed-canopy woodlands were more open and savannalike in presettlement times. Nevertheless, he said, what exists now is legitimate in its own right: healthy systems representing an "explosion of life" that could be considered "a wonderful recovery phase" from postsettlement disturbance.

By manipulating an ecosystem, he said, you might allow a diversity of plant species to return to it. But if this means taking a postsettlement woodland with a healthy, increasingly forestlike canopy on purely woodland soil, on topography that suggests a woodland, and cut out everything in the understory, and burn it and "poison things that are resistant to slashing and burning, then the cost is too high." Even if this provides a home for some rare and endangered species, he said, opening up the canopy might decrease the microhabitat for many other organisms.

But Mendelson's bottom line seemed as much philosophical as scientific: "I don't think the cure [for postsettle-ment disturbance] is to return to those woodlands and chop the hell out of them. It offends my sense of rightness. We've done enough messing around in the world. These places ought to have a chance to breathe."

Two years earlier, Douglas Ladd of The Nature Con-servancy's Missouri chapter had published a paper that seemed to go against Mendelson's assertion that postset-tlement disturbed woodlands are undergoing a "natural succession." In it, Ladd cited many accounts from early settlers that, taken together, thoroughly documented the Indians' annual burning of Missouri's oak savannas, which he termed woodlands. The burning had shaped the open aspect and ecological character of the woodlands for at least 10,000 to 12,000 years, or since the last ice age, he suggested. Suppressing fires on the grounds that they were set by humans and were therefore unnatural, and then calling the result "natural succession," may be philo-sophically interesting, Ladd continued. But he argued that as a practical matter, "to allow midwestern woodlands to degrade and become depauperate [species-poor] in the name of 'natural succession' would result in continuing loss of biodiversity without any possibility of correspond-ing gains."[22]

Despite the Ladd paper and the growing popular and scientific groundswell for savanna restoration, Packard saw the Mendelson article as a potential threat. Bill Jordan, recognizing its implications not just for savanna restora-tion but for restoration generally, offered Packard the chance to reply. He did, in the Summer 1993 issue of *Resto-ration & Management Notes*.[23] The result was something of a manifesto not only for restoration and for what might be called the New Conservation, but for the emerging new view of humans' relationship to nature on which both are based.

Many of Mendelson's arguments, he wrote, "are logical within the framework of conservation ethics and scientific thinking that have prevailed over much of the twentieth century." Mendelson's thinking is characterized by some elements of this conventional wisdom, he wrote, among them these:

- Nature is best defined as "animals and plants un-affected by people."
- Biodiversity thrives if we just leave nature alone.
- When brush or weeds overrun a preserve, that is "natural succession."

While most people probably would agree with those concepts, at least at first glance, Packard continued, hard experience has convinced many field conservationists that they are "fundamentally inadequate. They haven't worked in practice."

What is nature?

Packard offered this elaboration of the philosophy that had undergirded the efforts of the whole restoration movement:

In most parts of the world, certainly in Illinois, the human species has played an important role in the landscape for thousands of years. Native peo-ple, through hunting, gathering, and burning, were as much a part of nature here as were the beaver, buffalo, bear, and bumblebees. The fact that people helped make or perpetuate these prairies didn't mean that prairies weren't nature. . . . [I]t is the communities of species that have gradually shifted their relationships and their positions on the landscape over millennia in response to all sorts of influences—human and nonhuman—that are na-ture. In fact, . . . the loss of people from a natural system in which we have played an essential role can be as destructive to the functioning and sur-vival of that community as the loss of a key preda-tor, pollinator, herbivore, or any other key species.

This understanding needs to be worked into a

clear definition of the word *nature* as used by conservationists. There are other definitions of nature, of course. The community of microorganisms in the bowels of a healthy person, the stars, flirting teenagers, the successional processes of an abandoned city lot are all nature by one legitimate definition of nature or another. So is everything else—as in Random House definition number 6: "the universe, with all its phenomena."

But the nature that needs preserving . . . is better defined as *complex assemblages of species as they have evolved in their environments over the ages.* Whether people have played a role in this evolution is not key. [But] if people—or anything else—change the environment sufficiently rapidly so that substantial numbers of species die instead of evolve, then what we have is degradation (or "development") rather than nature. . . . [R]egardless of whether Homo sapiens is or is not present, if nothing causes changes so rapid as to eliminate species from any long-evolved community, this is nature. In fact, if people intervene and go to great lengths to restore the conditions of relative stability which allow the continued existence and evolution of those ancient lineages and interdependencies, the result is still nature.

Packard argued that if exotic species or native weeds or brush are allowed to take over an area because humans have disturbed it, and if in this course of events a rich array of native plants and animals are consequently driven out, the result is a diminishment of natural biological diversity. This, he said, is not natural succession but rather artificial succession; and for many species inhabiting the oak woodlands and savannas, the threat posed by artificial succession has become potentially lethal: "The system continues to evolve. But it has lost thousands to millions of years of evolved prairie richness."

As to whether the savanna restorationists are misguidedly trying to convert forest to savanna, Packard disputed Mendelson's contention that Cap Sauers Holding was a forest in presettlement times. First, he wrote, the presettlement public land survey found that the vegetation was composed of oaks, a few hickories, and no maple or basswood; that in many places the oaks were widely spaced; that even relatively closed-canopy oak communities have long been known to be fire-dependent; that since both the northern and southern (uphill and downhill) edges of the preserve were prairie, at least the edges of the woodland would have ignited whenever the prairie burned.

Moreover, he wrote, Cap Sauers Holding supports what may be the state's largest population of the endangered savanna blazing star (*Liatris scariosa*), a plant so characteristic of the savanna that it had disappeared from floristic manuals with the vanishing of the savannas. The species survives only in parts of oak woodlands where the trees are widely spaced—and on precisely the type of soil found at Cap Sauers, indicating that these soils would be appropriate for a closed savanna rather than the non-oak forest it would become if left alone. "Without restoration of its open woodland habitat," Packard wrote, "this plant would probably soon vanish from the earth."

Why pick a single moment in time past as a restoration target? The reason for going back to early land surveys as a starting point is simply that "typically they are our best single source of information" on what the presettlement ecosystem was like. "Taking the land back to 1738 or 1438 or 2,000 B.C. would serve just as well—if we knew how," he wrote. Quoting David Brower, the former head of the Sierra Club, he wrote that "we are in the position of lost hikers trying to relocate the last spot at which they still knew where they were; once we get back on track, the idea is not to stand still but to proceed. The restoration goal is to have natural processes, including evolution, proceed, with the bulk of the biodiversity surviving."

And in response to Mendelson's reassertion that the savanna is merely an unstable ecotone, or transition zone, and an arbitrarily defined segment of a continuum, Packard wrote:

> The fact that a community is part of a continuum does not diminish its significance. . . . Most if not all communities are part of continua. Biotic continua of many types may be described: dry-wet, hot-cold, light-dark, young-old, rich soil-poor soil, etc. The dry-wet continuum might be articulated as:

> desert . . . chaparral . . . shortgrass prairie . . . mixed grass prairie . . . tallgrass prairie . . . tallgrass savanna . . . oak woodland . . . beech-maple forest . . . swamp . . . marsh . . . stream . . . river . . . estuary . . . inshore ocean . . . open ocean.

> Except for the end points no part of this continuum is more or less "ecotonal" than any other part. For successful conservation we would want to maintain healthy examples of all parts. Defined communities, though arbitrary, are useful in designing and monitoring fragmented preserve systems.

> In fact, if we could rely on landscape-scale burning, natural processes would then maintain the whole continuum, and whether people applied one name or another to various parts of it wouldn't matter. Instead, it is precisely because managers must find and restore isolated remnant components of the continuum that we have to watch our definitions. Back when many managers thought simply in terms of prairie and forest, our preserves were being envisioned as, and managed to become, one or the other.

To Mendelson's charge that restoration is "limited by the imagination of the manager," Packard replied:

". . . [E]very restorationist knows the ecosystem will respond in unpredictable ways that rise out of itself. That's precisely what we want to liberate. . . . The goal of restorationists is precisely to set in motion processes we neither fully control nor fully understand. A restorationist, like a parent, needs to protect an unsteady being from certain great insults to its health or existence. Similar to good parenting or coaching or teaching, the goal of restoration is to help some life go forward on its own— and in the process become more truly itself."

As 1994 approached, the academic argument about the character of oak savannas was nowhere near settled. But Packard's ideas were at least beginning to be cited in the professional literature. A few years earlier, Bill Jordan had expressed concern over the possibility that the ideas might at first be ignored by the academy, and later appropriated by it without acknowledging Packard's contribution. Now that seemed less likely, but whether Packard's view would become integrated into the body of ecological knowledge was a tale still to be told. While some scientists like Stuart Pimm were expressing admiration for his work, others continued to express skepticism pending the publication of supporting data. Packard conceded the need to publish, and was preparing to offer a number of papers, including data from Vestal Grove, for publication as 1994 began. Whether they would satisfy his academic critics remained to be seen.

In his fiftieth year, Packard had emerged as a trailblazer and groundbreaker to be reckoned with in American conservation, and one who excited great emotion—positive and negative.

"He's had a terrific impact; we think he's a real leader

in our organization," John Sawhill, the president of The Nature Conservancy, said in 1993.

On the other hand, some critics charge him (not to his face) with practicing salesmanship more than science. And after a favorably received presentation by Packard at a conference, one participant was heard to remark in the corridor, "Have they canonized Steve yet?"

"People tend to be either very pro or very anti. He is an unusual personality; he's not a neutral character," said Wendy Paulson, who by 1993 had completed a ten-year term on the board of the Illinois Conservancy and was starting another on the Conservancy's national board. "I think that in any kind of creative effort, and I consider this a unique creative effort, there are all kinds of hurdles to be crossed, and some of them are personality conflicts. And usually when one individual is largely associated with a movement like this, it's almost inevitable that jealousy creeps in."

Packard, in Russ Van Herik's experience, has been the kind of person who can drive supervisors to the aspirin bottle. Van Herik, who in 1993 was a national vice president of the Conservancy, was Midwest regional director from 1988 to 1991.

Packard "is not an institutional type," Van Herik said, "and that means that every time you look into what Steve's doing, the lawyer in you gets queasy, the institutional vice president in you quakes, the scientist in you starts asking a lot of hard questions to which he, Packard, doesn't have answers, and the political scientist in you is intrigued, and you finally realize the best thing you can do is leave him alone and hope for the best. And that was my management technique. That's the simple truth. You can't manage a Steve Packard, and if you do, you throw him off his rhythm.

Packard "researchers and experiments aggressively with a scientist's eye but a politician's heart," Van Herik said, "that means he doesn't take advice. At most he'll listen to it. He's acting on his own instincts and he trusts his own instincts." (Packard says he seeks lots of advice and does indeed reject some, but that he takes lots of it, too.)

In any case, Van Herik said, when a "vector for change" like Packard appears "you let him run with it. . . . It's hard for an organization to have its change agents out front contradicting its accustomed values. But you've got to do it. Otherwise you don't get break-throughs." The Conservancy, in Van Herik's view, is basically a format and a forum "for creative people to experiment with methods of saving biodiversity that can be tested in a relatively rigorous way. What Packard was doing was a social-environmental experiment that deserved all the elbow room in the world.

"If biodiversity is going to be saved in this country or anywhere, it has to become part of the value system of the landscape's dominant species, namely the human species. And that's exactly what Packard was tinkering with." It would be "grossly irresponsible of any of us not to applaud or at least not to allow that kind of testing of the system. The science will be better for it, but it's messy."

Packard chose to play in two rough arenas at once, Van Herik pointed out: "Any time you mess around in the sciences and certainly any time you mess around in Chicago politics, your moves are going to be interpreted and misinterpreted by a cast of thousands." Steve Packard, he said, "deserves all the praise he gets, and he deserves pretty much all the criticism he gets." But he is "making use of the Conservancy to do some fascinating experiments."

"It is a guy fighting the past and helping to midwife the future."

After fifteen years, the North Branch volunteer stewards knew their individual sites pretty thoroughly, and certainly better than anyone else. But by 1993 their attention had moved beyond the original North Branch sites to include other areas of the North Branch ripe for restoration, making a total of eleven sites. The volunteers had watched some of these areas steadily deteriorate. But could the volunteers afford to devote sufficient time to them? Their workload had increased as the restoration effort expanded. In the project's early years, workdays had been scheduled only on Sundays, and only in the spring and fall. By 1993 they were scheduled year-round and most weekends on Saturday as well as Sunday. Many weeknights were by then given over to seed processing or, when the light lasted long enough, to still more restoration work on the sites.

Even so, the North Branch effort was becoming somewhat diluted; instead of forty people working a given site on a given weekend as before, for instance, there might now be thirty at one time, twenty at another, and fifteen at a third. Many, including Packard, were feeling that the North Branchers were spreading themselves thin. One result, Packard said, was that some sites where restoration was on "a pretty good trajectory" were now getting less attention. This posed a difficult question of priorities. If an urgent problem became apparent somewhere else, should work on existing restoration sites be slowed to attack it? "Everyone would like to finish Somme off," said Packard. "It's such a wonderful place. On the other hand, is it more important to finish off a 20-percent brushy corner there or to attack brush at another site that's going downhill fast?" So in 1992, the group undertook a comprehensive survey of the North Branch flora with the aim of establishing priorities.

With funding from the Forest Preserve District and the Conservancy, four young interns—college students and recent graduates—were hired to map the total plant community of the North Branch and take detailed samples in each present or potential restoration site. The interns did indeed find lots of plant colonies and a number of potentially restorable communities of which the North Branchers had been unaware. Working out of the Balabans' house, they produced data that Hodak translated into an elaborate ecological map. At a series of meetings in 1993, key North Branch stewards gathered to go over the maps and the data. Susanne Masi called it a "family powwow." The purpose was to rank all of the potential North Branch restoration sites in terms of the attention that should be paid to them. "It's a tricky list to make because it means balancing what's urgent and what will do okay if we don't get to it too quickly," said Packard. The making of the list was supervised by John Balaban and Drew Ulberg, now the North Branch science committee chairman. Somme Prairie Grove was among three sites eventually assigned highest priority.

The effort to set priorities signified a broadening of vision and purpose. Previously, the North Branch site stewards had operated pretty much independently in making management decisions. Now they were trying to create a common strategy and approach that would treat the North Branch as an ecologically integrated unit. That unit in turn would be part of a grander strategy still.

For the goal of the Volunteer Stewardship Network, of which the North Branch was the archetype, was now to restore nothing less than 100,000 acres of largely degraded habitat, much of it savanna, in the Chicago area as part of a regional "bioreserve"—the Chicago Wilderness, as Packard, ever attentive to symbols, dubbed it. Chicago? Wilderness? At first glance it is an oxymoron. But why not? No wilderness is pristine anymore, and the components certainly exist in the Chicago area for fashioning an "archipelago" of authentic ecological islands adding up to a substantial slice of the savanna-prairie-woodland mosaic. These islands might eventually be connected by natural corridors, or "greenways," to allow animals to move freely between them. And while ecologically sound, they would be interwoven with the life of metropolitan Chicago. If conservation does not treat humans as part of the ecosystem to be restored and maintained, it will fail, according to the new thinking that was taking over the world of conservation, a philosophical shift in which the Conservancy had been a leader.

The bioreserve concept idea would, in effect, treat the entire northeastern Illinois region as an integrated unit for conservation purposes. The concept, which is being pursued by the Conservancy in several parts of the country and by at least one state government, in California, is simple: At the center of the bioreserve, in theory, is a "core" preserve, a relatively intact swatch of the ecosystem in question, where human activity is either prohibited or restricted. Surrounding the core is a buffer zone where ecologically friendly activities—tourism and recreation, for instance, or commercial fishing—are allowed. But the theoretical concept does not always fit reality so neatly. In Chicago, the bioreserve would have three essential elements, none of them classic core or buffer:

- Scores of high-quality nature preserves, most of them in the forest preserve districts, set aside as inviolable. Somme Nature Preserve, a near-pristine prairie remnant next to Somme Prairie Grove and Vestal Grove, is one of these.

- A much larger acreage of recreational land in forest preserve districts, adding up to some 100,000 acres, capable of being restored to high ecological quality. These are sites where human activities with a light impact, like hiking, biking, bird-watching, and photography, blend with nature. The North Branch restoration sites, and similar tracts where restoration has not yet begun, are examples of these.

- A third category of places where more intensive human use blends with ecologically important habitat. Essentially, this land represents an extension of wild habitat into the human domain. Examples include corporate office parks where large populations of waterfowl settle in retention ponds; forest preserve district golf courses and picnic grounds where animals hunt and nest; housing subdivisions in oak woods next to forest preserves, where birds like the red-shouldered hawk breed in people's yards; farmland that, if managed properly, can provide habitat for prairie and savanna creatures; and homes where people give parts of their yards or gardens over to prairie plants. The Conservancy's seed gardens are a step in that direction.

In the long term, the "core" of the Chicago Wilderness will be the 100,000 acres of restored habitat. The extension into human-occupied territory will depend on how much public interest there is and whether it can be sustained. "It's either the beginning of a trend, or it's a fad that will go away," says Packard.

A wide range of public and private agencies were involved in planning the Chicago Wilderness. The planning was initiated by the Conservancy and included the U.S. Environmental Protection Agency, the U.S. Fish and Wildlife Service, the U.S. Forest Service, the Illinois Department of Conservation, all the forest preserve districts of the Chicago area, the Illinois Nature Preserves Commission, the Northeastern Illinois Planning Commission, the Morton Arboretum, the Brookfield Zoo, the Chicago Botanic Garden, and the Openlands Project.

Packard believes that the 100,000 acres of prairie-savanna-woodland mosaic could be under restoration in twenty years at the outside. Ten years may be technically possible, he said, but may not be logistically feasible: "There are a lot of people to train, a lot of funds to raise, a lot of permits to get." Once the restoration is under way, "high quality may elude us for some time," Packard said.

The Chicago Wilderness would be just one of a number of large restored chunks of the prairie-savanna mosaic contemplated under the midwestern savanna recovery plan developed as a result of the February 1993 savanna conference in Chicago. The plan, whose details were still being ironed out at this writing, will provide an overall framework and strategy. The organizers of the conference were only beginning to develop a mechanism for putting it into effect. Early plans called for the creation of a regional "recovery team" of scientists, agency representatives, and conservationists to negotiate land-use arrangements. Their goal would be to assemble enough tracts that, when restored and managed properly, can guarantee the long-term maintenance of an ecologically viable chunk of the prairie-savanna mosaic. How much land this requires is uncertain; some scientists think 5 percent of the original landscape might be sufficient.

Some potential chunks of such a complex were already materializing outside northeastern Illinois. One is the Walnut Creek project in Iowa, where the U.S. Fish and Wildlife Service by 1993 had assembled 5,000 acres of a planned 8,654-acre tract, about half of which was comprised of degraded prairie and half was made up of a prairie-savanna-sedge meadow mosaic. Most of the site had been plowed and row-cropped, and the rest had been used as pasture. Pauline Drobney, the biologist in charge, estimates that about 100 acres consisted of restorable remnants, and that dribs and drabs of prairie-savanna vegetation were hanging on in isolated patches totaling perhaps 800 acres. In 1992 the volunteers gathered enough seed to sow 4 acres of new ground, and from that harvested enough to escalate the planting to 400 acres in 1993. Some 300 volunteers took part. Drobney hopes and believes that, eventually, the Walnut Creek site will be the largest tract to date to be reconstructed virtually from scratch using remnants of prairie and savanna flora.

Restoration activities were still proceeding in Indiana and Missouri, and in the latter state the Department of Natural Resources alone was actively restoring 16,000 acres of savanna with a goal of expanding to more than 60,000 acres over the next decade.

And in the spring of 1993, The Nature Conservancy burned nearly 26,000 acres in northeastern Oklahoma, squarely in the southern reaches of the presettlement tall-grass prairie-savanna complex, in the most ambitious prairie restoration effort undertaken until then. In October of that year, in a moment fraught with both historical and ecological significance, 300 bison were released there on the Conservancy's Tallgrass Prairie Preserve. It was the first attempt to recouple fire and bison grazing and thereby re-create the conditions that maintained the prairies' biological diversity before Europeans and their descendants arrived.

The Oklahoma project had a leg up in that the tallgrass preserve had never been plowed, and more than 500 species of prairie plants, though suppressed over the decades by overgrazing of cattle and by the lack of fire, appeared after the first burn. No reseeding was necessary. Ultimately, 1,800 free-ranging bison are to roam the preserve, there to help reestablish the original prairie dynamic in which fires set by lightning and Indians (restorationists now stand in for them) burned random patches of grassland each year. The buffalo would graze in the young green growth that appeared after the fire, meanwhile leaving other, unburned patches to mature through different stages of succession. When another patch burned, they would move. This produced a quiltlike pattern of patches in different stages of succession, each with its own combination of plant species and attendant fauna, that gave the prairie its rich diversity. Reviving this elegant interdependency promised to be a special experiment in the annals of restoration.

The Chicago Wilderness promised to be just as special in other ways.

"I imagine, supposing we do a good job with this, that the Chicago Wilderness will be one of the great hallmarks of the region; that it will be part of the global image of Chicago," Packard says. "They'll think of this as the metropolitan area where people first learned to live in harmony with a rare natural ecosystem."

If that happens, there will be good reasons. First, because of a historical quirk, nature in Illinois survived better in the metropolis than it did in rural areas. In the midwestern corn belt, almost every available acre of black-soil prairie and savanna was converted to agricultural or livestock use. But in the metropolitan areas, especially Chicago, early foresight in creating nature preserves combined with failed subdivisions and the sale of relatively undisturbed estates to provide substantial public preserves in largely degraded but restorable condition—adjacent to the public preserves. Further, interest in nature developed strongly in the Chicago area, with its relatively close proximity to the North Woods. City living and indoor jobs created a hunger to get out, and a rich array of educational institutions and conservation organizations fed the preservationist impulse. Chicago had the raw material, the people, the will, and the basic institutions.

It may be, Packard said, that because so many elements of the ecosystem—the larger predators, for instance—can never be reintroduced, management may always be necessary. If so, the manpower and the expertise to do it exist primarily in urban areas. In the case of the tallgrass savanna, he said, "it could be that the Chicago metropolitan area will always have the best there is."

But he hopes not. "I would hope that we would want to restore vast acreages somewhere outside the metropolitan area, where the land is all contiguous, and put back the mountain lion, the bear, the wolf, the bison, the prairie chicken, and all the rest, and that restoration technology will improve so that sometime, far into the future, there may be big, wonderful preserves that are better than what we have here, because they are contiguous and you can let catastrophic fire blast through." If that happens, "it will be because the interest was raised here and the genes were saved here and the restoration techniques were worked out here and the education proceeded from here."

Somme Prairie Grove

Plant communities and quality of vegetation, 2013 (anticipated)

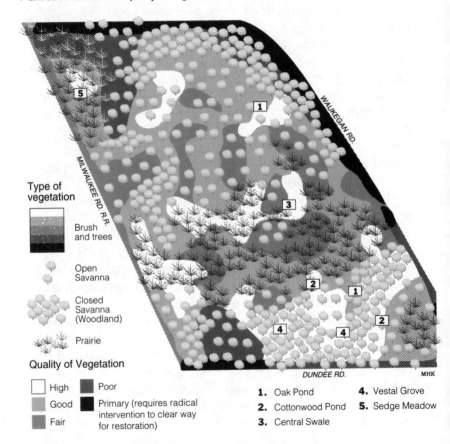

Type of vegetation

Brush and trees

Open Savanna

Closed Savanna (Woodland)

Prairie

Quality of Vegetation

High

Good

Fair

Poor

Primary (requires radical intervention to clear way for restoration)

1. Oak Pond
2. Cottonwood Pond
3. Central Swale
4. Vestal Grove
5. Sedge Meadow

MILWAUKEE RD. R.R.

WAUKEGAN RD.

DUNDEE RD.

MHK

14

VESTAL GROVE: PRESENT AND FUTURE

Septuember. Tag end of the day. Not a breeze stirs. The first crisp hint of autumn chill is in the air. Somme Prairie Grove, resplendent in bronze and gold against a deep green backdrop of oaks, is in full reproductive flush. A sea of Indian grass and big bluestem, more than six feet tall with seed heads rapidly ripening, shimmers in the rays of a fading sun. The delicate heads tickle the face. There are more of them than ever—millions of seeds with which to enlarge the steadily expanding reach of restored ecosystems in metropolitan Chicago. Crowds of bright yellow sawtooth sunflowers, chest-high, punctuate the grassland of the open savanna.

Off to one side, near a little dab of wetland probably created out of the depression left by a melting chunk of glacial ice, unprepossessing little brown stems, long past flowering, jut up behind two screens of chicken wire fashioned in the shape of overturned wastebaskets to protect the plants from deer. The stems display rows of fat pods, each containing perhaps 7,000 seeds of the endangered prairie white-fringed orchid.

Farther along, at the top of a slight rise in the cozier confines of Vestal Grove, a profusion of sweet black-eyed Susans, little yellow sunbursts erupting from a thick carpet of green, nestles at the foot of a bur oak whose trunk at chest height is nearly four feet in diameter. A foot-wide strip of light brown running the length of the dark trunk shows where recent lightning has struck. The tree could be three hundred years old. Black Hawk himself, as Gerry Wilhelm says, might have sat under it.

As counterpoint to the season's dominant theme of gold and green, delicate little pinkish magenta blossoms of the false dragonhead, clustered in rows along a spikey stalk like the blooms of a snapdragon, assert themselves in the dappled pattern of light cast by the partially open oak canopy above. Its other name is the obedient plant: People find to their delight that if they turn one of the blossoms in a given direction, it will stay there.

There is no sound except for the deer that warily inspect a human visitor from twenty feet away and then, taking alarm, bound off with white tails flashing like warning flags. Here and there, small woody plants droop over, broken in half when the deer used them as rubbing posts for removing velvet from antlers. Although the deer browse freely, damage to vegetation is much less than a year earlier, and many more flowers are in bloom; early efforts to thin the herd have evidently had some effect.

Into this scene a few hours later, on a glorious, breezy Sunday morning in 1993, come a dozen or so North Branch volunteers. Most are veterans. Steve Packard is there, and John Balaban and Karen Holland. But there is a newcomer, too: six-year-old Madeline Mansfield, whose mother, Karen Mansfield, is attending her first North Branch workday since she gave it up two years earlier upon the birth of a second child. Packard, as the chief steward of the site, calls the group together in the circle that traditionally opens each work session. He reports on the progress of the prairie white-fringed orchids transplanted to Somme: "It takes four or five years to grow big enough to flower; that's something to look forward to." Balaban reports that at Harms Woods, a site where he is steward, efforts to cut out "weedy trees" and open up an oak woodland have resulted in a wonderful surprise: a proliferation of turtlehead plants, a rare species so named because its white flowers are shaped like a turtle's head. Turtlehead seeds from Harms Woods have been planted in Vestal Grove to expand the species' population, it is reported.

Packard outlines the work for the day. One group will mount a search-and-destroy mission against black locust, a native invader that almost ranks with buckthorn as a choker of savanna plants. The black locusts are on the run, but there are still some to be cut down. The second group will pick seed. The grasses are not quite ripe yet. But leadplant, blazing star, nodding wild onion, and purple prairie clover are ready. Packard offers the group's members a choice of joining either the brush-cutting team or the seed-picking team. Most choose seed picking. Packard interrupts business to point out a red-tailed hawk flying overhead and note that the hawks fledged two young at Somme this year. In short order the two groups of workers are off, one carrying saws and a herbicide to kill the locust stumps, the other carrying clear plastic bags, marching to work among the wind-rippled grasses while squadrons of dragonflies dart by overhead.

Balaban leads the seed pickers. The first target is purple prairie clover, a member of the pea family whose tiny purplish pink flowers appear in summer. Now it is identifiable by brownish seed heads that look like miniature pineapples sitting atop slender, parsleylike stalks hidden among the much taller stalks of Indian grass. "Just smash the head, and the thing will break apart," Balaban instructs the pickers. "If it crumbles in your fingers, it is clearly ripe." He urges the pickers to tread softly, to "try to go through without looking like a herd of buffalo; the ideal is to walk above the ground." Failing that, he says, the pickers should walk carefully, stop and plant their feet, and keep them from moving while picking the seeds. "In presettlement times," asks a relatively new volunteer, Rinda West, who teaches English at a community college, "would there not have been herds of buffalo?" Balaban concedes there would have been. "So we don't have to feel too guilty," West says playfully.

So they set to work, picking the seeds of purple prairie clover and those of any other ripe species they can find. Karen Mansfield roams among the Indian grass, three plastic bags in hand. Into one she puts seeds of blazing star, into another purple prairie clover, and into another, wild bergamot. She works quickly, expertly, the two-year layoff apparently having dulled neither her eye nor her technique. Six-year-old Madeline works, too. Her mother says it would be good if more children would get out and do it; it would be a good way to get them to appreciate and learn about nature. By the end of the morning, Madeline is thirsty and ready to quit; but she says she would like to come back again. Rinda West finds seed picking "very satisfying; sort of lovely; it satisfies parts of the spirit." But, she says "it's not easy on your back."

"When we started here," Packard says, surveying the swells and swales of the open savanna between Vestal Grove on the south and other woodland stretches to the north, "there was not a stalk of Indian grass," and certainly none of the rare plants that grow among it. Mostly it was dense brush with a small open area. Now little purplish stiff gentians are everywhere among the tall grass. So is the equally rare cream gentian, though it has been hit hard by the deer. And Kalm's brome. Little bluestem grass, though not rare, in a month or so will be, in Packard's description, "the knockout of the site" with its "ethereal, creamy wine color." Many of the species in these open areas are prairie plants, but Packard says he considers the area not prairie but savanna. For one thing, small young oaks have begun to grow in the open spaces. Nor is the open area big enough for prairie birds to nest there safe from predators; the oak branches of Vestal Grove and other closed-savanna copses nearby are close enough to provide vantage points and launching points for attack by hawks and parasitism by cowbirds.

Everywhere, to Packard, there are reminders of people and events past: Here, blazing stars transplanted by Pete Baldo from his garden; over there, brown-eyed Susans whose seeds were spread by Mim—"I feel a touch of her when I look at them."

From the direction of the black locusts comes the sound of surgical mayhem: saws biting into wood.

Along the trail comes Wiley Buck, the volunteer who is investigating the presence and role of coyotes in the reemerging ecosystem. "Anybody see the coyote scat on the trail?" he asks, with some excitement. A short discussion ensues in which Buck says that although coyotes will pick off fawns and attack adult deer in packs, it is doubtful that they are having much impact on the deer population. He was hopeful that some clues may emerge once scats are collected and the hair they contain is analyzed.

By noon the volunteers are back at the gravel parking lot where the day began, the seed pickers bearing their clear bags of ecological treasure. One of them, containing seeds of nodding wild onion, so named because its little, white bell-shaped flowers cluster on the tops of drooping stems, smells like a delicatessen. Which is where some of the North Branchers head to fuel up for the afternoon activities.

Chief among these is making the fall sampling of the permanent transect established in 1985 to keep track of how the plant community is evolving in Vestal Grove—at once the showcase and primary scientific monitoring arena for the entire savanna restoration effort in the Chicago area. Packard and Balaban stretch a measuring tape between metal stakes left permanently in the ground to mark the swath through Vestal Grove along which the semiannual counts of plant species are taken. Then they put down the one-meter hoop marking the sampling quadrat at intervals along the tape, exactly one meter from it. Then Balaban and Packard identify each species inside the hoop and estimate its relative abundance, easily and familiarly calling off the Latin names and numbers to Holland, who records them.

But no formal survey is necessary to see that a healthy, biologically diverse ecosystem is developing. It is true that tall goldenrod, asserting impressive bravado, seems present everywhere, its general adaptability enabling it to rush into disturbed areas ahead of more conservative species. And the vegetation is not as lush as it might be once the deer population is under better control. "It would have been so much better without those deer," Packard says, surveying the scene. "It set us back a couple of years—I hope. It knocked out some species, but I hope we can restore them."

The place is nevertheless abloom and abuzz with far more color and biotic variety than a year earlier, at the height of the deer depradations. Young oaks are sprouting. Old ones are growing new leaves on the lower parts of trunks that earlier had been bare, enclosed and choked by twelve-foot-tall buckthorn. "I like that," says John Balaban. On the open savanna just adjacent to Vestal Grove, monarch butterflies alight daintily on yellow blossoms in search of nectar to fuel their fall migration to Mexico. Flycatchers swoop and dart. Where trees become more closely spaced on the northeastern edge of Vestal Grove, bumblebees work their way deeply into the elongated, tightly clustered, bluish purple blooms of the bottle gentian, so named because they look like small, cylindrical bottles nearly closed at the tip. They also look much like a certain type of Christmas-tree bulb. The bees entirely disappear within the blossom, which pulsates as the insect draws out its nectar and exchanges its pollen.

Here, where open savanna grades into closed savanna (or woodland, take your choice), is a truly special spot, the *pièce de résistance* of Vestal Grove, the very embodiment of its magic, of a miracle wrought by workings of nature that humans cannot duplicate or fully understand, but can only liberate and foster. Within the space of a few feet, virtually the full range of the prairie-to-woodland continuum appears. It is a place where the overhead canopy has conspired to let in just the right pattern of light, in just the right amounts and from the proper angles, to assure a mixture of plants found on the prairie, in the woods, and on the savanna in between. The mixture follows no smooth, linear gradient on the ground but is instead a beautifully chaotic, infinitely fine-textured jumble, a marvel of apparent disorder within an underlying invisible order, dictated by the unique pattern of light, soil, and moisture that distinguishes each square millimeter of ground, a pattern partly created when the North Branchers opened up the canopy somewhat by eliminating trees that would not have grown there under the fire regime of presettlement times.

As one moves from the open sea of Indian grass into this special place, a cluster of bright red berries at ground level announces Jack-in-the-pulpit, an inhabitant of damp woods and swamps. At the same time, isolated stems of Indian grass and big bluestem—denizens of the prairie and open savanna—wave in the breeze just feet away. They are accompanied by other representatives of the relatively sunny end of the continuum: rattlesnake master, the big green leaves of prairie dock, false dragonhead, cowbane, Culver's root, the feathery-leafed wood betony, brilliant yellow blossoms of sneezeweed, grass-leafed goldenrod, and the bottle gentians. But mixed in with them are many species from the shady end of the savanna spectrum: sweet black-eyed Susans, Virginia rye, satin

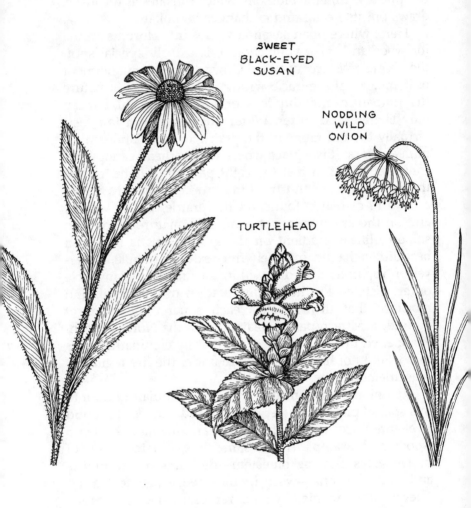

SWEET
BLACK-EYED
SUSAN

NODDING
WILD
ONION

TURTLEHEAD

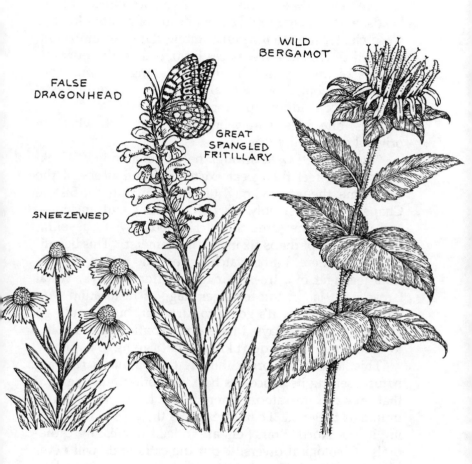

FALSE
DRAGONHEAD

WILD
BERGAMOT

GREAT
SPANGLED
FRITILLARY

SNEEZEWEED

grass, mullein foxglove, tinker's weed (wild coffee), wild lettuce, bottlebrush grass, and the delicate woodreed. A few feet away, sweet black-eyed Susan, woodreed, turtle-heads, and the big moplike seed heads of spotted Joe-Pye weed cluster in casual beauty among the dead limbs of a downed tree. And a few paces beyond that, the purplish blooms of the savanna blazing star, long missing from midwestern botanical manuals but now secure in Vestal Grove, grace a sunny opening.

This, one feels, surely begins to approach what the original community was like.

"Every time I walk through here I get all tingly," Pack-ard says. "I feel this great excitement and peace at the same time, the way you might feel walking into the Sistine Chapel. It's almost holy. It's rich, healthy, and ancient—and young at the same time." He nods toward a young tree, its trunk perhaps six inches in diameter. "This beauti-ful bur oak here, I'll be watching that the rest of my life. It's a teenager of a tree." For that matter, he says, Vestal Grove itself is "in the teenager stage of restoration; you get a sense of how it's going to turn out, but it could go in many different ways. I have every confidence it's going to change a lot. But I don't know what's going to happen."

This is both the price and the fascination of reviving nature, setting its processes back in motion, making sure that they can operate unfettered, and then letting things unfold as they will. That, after all, is the object. In pursu-ing it, the North Branchers are indeed re-creating cathe-drals of biological diversity. But the cathedrals will never be finished; evolution and the sheer changeability and in-stability of nature will see to that.

It is hard, with the breeze rippling through the Indian grass and the kaleidoscopic beauty of Vestal Grove on dis-play, to imagine the day when it all will be buried again under half a mile of ice. Yet that will surely happen if prevailing scientific opinion is right, and all the works of humans in and around what is today called Chicago, including the ecological achievements of the North Branchers and their thousands of compatriots, will be ground to dust. It is also hard at such a time to envision the much more immediate possibility—unproved at this writing—that carbon dioxide poured into the air by humans' burning of fossil fuels created out of the plants of another epoch will warm the atmosphere and create conditions too hot and dry, too quickly, for Vestal Grove's finely tuned ecology to survive.

The prairie-savanna ecosystem has outlasted the comings and goings of the ice many times in the last 3 million years or so by migrating as the climate changed. And the evolutionary ancestors of the grasses and wildflowers whose habitat is so lovingly being restored today go back many millions of years before that. Clearly, life has been resilient in the face of the planet's larger rhythms.

But now, in what could be a drastic departure from the past, humans threaten both to disrupt the ancient chain of being by extinguishing much of the raw material of evolution, and to accelerate the natural rhythms to which ecosystems have become attuned. The magnitude of this threat to biological diversity and to the global ecosystem is unclear. Uncertainty is a double-edged sword, however: It seems just as possible that ecological disaster lies ahead as that it does not. Humanity's record until now in dealing with the rest of nature offers little encouragement, and the virtually certain prospect of at least a doubling of the global population offers even less. Prudence, it would seem, requires a serious and sustained effort to be ecologically safe rather than sorry. Preservation of natural areas, even though it may constitute a rearguard action, is essential to such an effort. Restoration, both by reviving damaged and destroyed ecosystems and re-creating others in new and more hospitable places if future climatic change makes it necessary, may well provide the means for an effective counterattack. The twenty-first century could indeed turn out to be the era of restoration in ecology and conservation, especially if restoration becomes more science and less art, as it undoubtedly will.

The future of the enterprise is by no means certain. Many challenges of science and politics lie ahead. Homo sapiens' transforming and often ruinous impact on the natural world is great, while the restorative response at this point is still comparatively small. The history of the midwestern prairies and savannas vividly illustrates how ecosystems are so easily disrupted, degraded, and destroyed and how difficult and imperfect their recovery will be.

Vestal Grove nevertheless makes it possible to imagine that some humans, through vision, knowledge, skill, and will, can help keep the evolutionary drama on its natural course despite other humans' disruptive and destructive impulses.

That is perhaps the least and the most anybody can do. It is a lot.

Contact List for Volunteers

Ecological restoration programs welcome volunteers in many parts of the United States. The following list of contacts was current as of 1994. The Society for Ecological Restoration can supply updated information. Its address is 1207 Seminole Highway, Madison, WI 53711. The telephone number is (608) 262-9547. The Nature Conservancy can also furnish fresh information. The address of its national headquarters is 1815 Lynn St., Arlington, VA 22209. The telephone number is (703) 841-5300.

What follows is divided into two categories: Offices of the Nature Conservancy that operate volunteer restoration programs, and other contacts by region of the country.

NATURE CONSERVANCY CONTACTS

As of 1994, the Conservancy operated its most extensive volunteer programs in Illinois, California, and Florida. Fewer than one hundred volunteers a year were employed in other states, but this was expected to grow in some instances.

ALABAMA:
Betty Donovan
2821-C 2nd Ave. S.
Birmingham, AL 35233
(205) 251-1155

ARIZONA:
Linda Brewer
300 E. University Blvd., Suite 230
Tucson, AZ 85705
(602) 622-3861

ARKANSAS:
Amy Bradshaw
601 North University
Little Rock, AK 72205
(501) 663-6699

CALIFORNIA:
Southern
Norma LaMadrid
P.O. Box 83658
San Diego, CA 92138
(800) 733-1763

Northern
Sarah Blanchette
6500 Desmond Rd.
Galt, CA 95632
(800) 733-1763

COLORADO:
Sarah Clausen
1244 Pine St.
Boulder, CO 80302
(303) 444-2950

CONNECTICUT:
Jean Cox
55 High St.
Middletown, CT 06475
(203) 344-0716

FLORIDA:
Florida Regional Office
Emillie Peck
2699 Lee Rd., No. 500
Winter Park, FL 32789
(407) 628-5887

GEORGIA:
Pat Lynch
1401 Peachtree St., NE, Suite 136
Atlanta, GA 30309
(404) 873-6946

HAWAII:
Jan Eber
1116 Smith St., Suite 201
Honolulu, HI 96817
(808) 537-4508

IDAHO:
Cindy Lunte
P.O. Box 165
Sun Valley, ID 83353
(208) 726-3007

ILLINOIS:
Laurel Ross
79 W. Monroe St., Suite 900
Chicago, IL 60603
(312) 346-8166

LOUISIANA:
Richard Martin
P.O. Box 4125
Baton Rouge, LA 70821
(504) 338-1040

MAINE:
Suzanne Drew
14 Main St., Suite 401
Brunswick, ME 04011
(207) 729-5181

MARYLAND:
Linda Kramme
Chevy Chase Metro Bldg.
2 Wisconsin Circle, Suite 600
Chevy Chase, MD 20815
(301) 656-8673

MASSACHUSETTS:
Julie Richburg
79 Market St., Suite 300
Boston, MA 02110
(617) 423-2545

MICHIGAN:
Nancy Sferra
2840 E. Grand River, Suite 5
E. Lansing, MI 48823
(517) 332-1741

MINNESOTA:
Nancy Falkum
1313 5th St., SE
Minneapolis, MN 55414
(612) 331-0750

MISSOURI:
Susanne Greenlee
2800 South Brentwood Blvd.
St. Louis, MO 63144
(314) 968-1105

MONTANA:
Glenn Johnson
32 South Ewing
Helena, MT 59601
(406) 443-0303

NEW HAMPSHIRE:
David Van Luven
2½ Beacon St., Suite 6
Concord, NH 03301
(603) 224-5853

NEW JERSEY:
Ben Silverbarb
17 Fairmount Rd.
Pottersville, NJ 07979
(908) 439-3007

NEW MEXICO:
Kristi Echols
107 Cienega St.
Santa Fe, NM 87501
(505) 988-3867

NEW YORK:
Adirondacks
Bill Brown
P.O. Box 65
Keene Valley, NY 12942
(518) 576-2082

Central and Western
Melissa Friscia
315 Alexander St., Suite 301
Rochester, NY 14604
(716) 546-8030

Long Island
Bonnie Verrine
250 Lawrence Hill Rd.
Cold Spring Harbor, NY 11724
(516) 367-3225

Eastern
Peter Kahn
1736 Western Ave.
Albany, NY 12203
(518) 869-0453

South Fork/Shelter Island
Danielle Nevel
P.O. Box 2694
Sag Harbor, NY 11963
(516) 725-2936

Lower Hudson
Chris Harmon
223 Katonah Ave.
Katonah, NY 10536
(914) 232-9431

NORTH CAROLINA:
Maura High
Carr Mill Mall, Suite 223
Carrboro, NC 27510
(919) 967-7007

OHIO:
Marleen Kromer
1504 W. 1st Ave.
Columbus, OH 43212
(614) 486-4194

OKLAHOMA:
Sara Wilson
320 S. Boston, Suite 1700
Tulsa, OK 74103
(918) 585-1117

RHODE ISLAND:
Ginger Carpenter
45 S. Angel St.
Providence, RI 02906
(401) 331-7110

SOUTH CAROLINA:
Sallie Carvalho
P.O. Box 5475
Columbia, SC 29250
(803) 254-9049

TENNESSEE:
DeeAnn Harris
2002 Richard Jones Rd.
Suite 304-C
Nashville, TN 37215
(615) 298-3111

TEXAS:
Sharon Reynolds
P.O. Box 1440
San Antonio, TX 78295
(512) 224-8774

UTAH:
Lupine Jones
P.O. Box 11486
Pioneer Station
Salt Lake City, UT 84147-0486
(801) 531-0999

WASHINGTON:
Kristin Mishler
217 Pine St., Suite 1100
Seattle, WA 98101-1572
(206) 343-4344

WISCONSIN:
Benita Walker
333 W. Mifflin, Suite 107
Madison, WI 53703
(608) 251-8140

WYOMING:
Rick Studenmund
258 Main, Suite 200
Lander, WY 82520
(307) 332-2971

The following is a list of people likely to be informed on restoration activities as the activities evolve and develop. Most are not themselves connected with volunteer programs, though some are. Most are associated with the Society for Ecological Restoration. All should be able to provide guidance.

William R. Jordan, III, editor of *Restoration & Management Notes*, University of Wisconsin Arboretum, 1207 Seminole Highway, Madison, WI 53711. (608) 262-9547.

Donald Falk, executive director of Society for Ecological Restoration, c/o Society for Ecological Restoration, 1207 Seminole Highway, Madison, WI 53711. (608) 262-9547.

Andre F. Clewell, president of the Society for Ecological Restoration. A. F. Clewell Inc., Route 7, Box 1195, Quincy, FL 31351. (904) 875-3868.

Eastern States

James Allen, 109 Sue Circle, Youngsville, LA 70592. (318) 856-8057.

Leslie Sauer, Andropogon Associates, 374 Shurs Lane, Philadelphia, PA 19128. (215) 487-0700.

Clare Billet, Wissahickon Stewardship Program, 102 W. Mermaid Lane, Philadelphia, PA 19118. (215) 242-3427.

Mary Robertson, board member of Pennypack Watershed Association, 1955 Edge Hill Rd., Huntingdon, PA 19006. (215) 784-9767.

John Mickelson, president of northeastern chapter of Society for Ecological Restoration, P.O. Box 865, Storrs, CT 06268. (203) 487-4350.

John Munro, Munro Ecological Services, Inc., 990 Old Sumneytown Pike, Harleysville, PA 19438. (215) 287-0671

William A. Niering, editor of *Restoration Ecology*, official journal of the Society for Ecological Restoration, Department of Botany, Connecticut College, New London, CT 06320. (203) 447-1911.

Tom Chase, regional ecologist for The Trustees of Reservations, Box 115, Oak Bluffs, Martha's Vineyard, MA 02577. (508) 693-3678.

Dennis Burton, Central Parks Conservancy, 830 5th Ave., New York, NY 10021. (212) 242-3427.

Ed Garbisch, Environmental Concern Inc., P.O. Box P, St. Michaels, MD 21663. (301) 745-9620.

Russ Lea, College of Forestry, North Carolina State University, P.O. Box 8002, Raleigh, NC 27695.

Amy Bowers, chairperson of Society for Ecological Restoration education committee, 756 Darden Place, Nashville, TN 37205. (615) 352-5487.

George Gann-Matzen and Noel Gerson, Ecohorizons, Inc., 22601 SW 152nd Ave., Goulds, FL 33170. (305) 248-0038.

MIDWESTERN STATES

Steve Packard, director of science and stewardship, The Nature Conservancy, 79 W. Monroe St., Chicago, IL 60603. (312) 346-8166.

Robert F. Betz, Department of Biology, Northeastern Illinois University, 5500 N. St. Louis, Chicago, IL 60625.

Gary Eldred, Southwest Wisconsin Prairie Enthusiasts, 4192 Sleepy Hollow, Boscobel, WI 53805.

Alan W. Haney, College of Natural Resources, University of Wisconsin–Stevens Point, Stevens Point, WI 54481. (715) 346-2955.

Steven I. Apfelbaum, research and consulting ecologist, Applied Ecological Services Inc., Route 3, Smith Road, P.O. Box 256, Brodhead, WI 53520. (608) 897-8547.

John A. Bacone, director of Division of Nature Preserves, Indiana Department of Natural Resources, 402 W. Washington St., Room W267, Indianapolis, IN 46204. (317) 232-4052.

Ron Bowen, Prairie Restorations Inc., P.O. Box 327, Princeton, MN 55371. (612) 389-4342.

Neil Diboll, Prairie Nursery, P.O. Box 306, Westfield, WI 53964. (608) 296-3679.

Pauline Drobney, Walnut Creek National Wildlife Refuge, P.O. Box 399, Prairie City, IA 50228. (515) 994-2415.

Ken McCarty, natural resource steward, Missouri Department of Natural Resources, P.O. Box 176, Jefferson City, MO 65102. (314) 751-8660.

Gerould Wilhelm, Morton Arboretum, Lisle, IL 60532. (708) 719-2419.

Bob Welch, Lansing Community College, Dept. 31, 41 N. Capital Ave., Lansing, MI 48901. (517) 483-9675.

Karl Smith, Cleveland Metroparks, 9305 Brecksville Rd., Brecksville, OH 44141. (216) 526-1012.

Molly Fifield-Murray, University of Wisconsin Arboretum, 1207 Seminole Highway, Madison, WI 53711. (608) 262-5522.

Laura Jackson, Department of Biology, University of Northern Iowa, Cedar Falls, IA 50614. (319) 273-2456.

WESTERN STATES

Gail Newton, Department of Conservation, 801 K Street, M509-37, Sacramento, CA 95814. (916) 323-8567.

Edith Allen, Department of Botany and Plant Science, University of California, Riverside, CA 92521. (909) 787-2123.

David Bainbridge, Department of Biology, San Diego State University, San Diego, CA 92182. (619) 594-4409.

William Halverson, National Park Service Cooperative Studies Unit, 125 Biological Sciences East, University of Arizona, Tucson, AZ 85721. (602) 670-6885.

John Rodman, member of board of Society for Ecological Restoration, Pitzer College, Claremont, CA 91711. (714) 621-8000.

Anne Sands, Riparian Systems, 5755 State Route 1, Bolinas, CA 94924. (415) 868-1618.

John Stanley, Habitat Restoration Group, 6001 Butler Lane, Scotts Valley, CA 95066. (408) 439-5500.

Tim White, president of Northwest Chapter of Society for Ecological Restoration, 12940 S.E. 185th St., Renton, WA 98058. (206) 453-5000.

James MacMahan, Department of Biology, Utah State University, Logan, UT 84321.

Patrick Burke, Bitterroot Native Growers, P.O. Box 566, Hamilton, MT 59828. (406) 961-4702.

Deborah Keammerer, member of board of Society for Ecological Restoration, Keammerer Ecological Consultants, 5858 Woodbourne Hollow Road, Boulder, CO 80301. (303) 530-1783.

Native Plants Growing in Vestal Grove, 1993

Scientific Name	Common Name
Actaea pachypoda	White baneberry
Agastache nepetoides	Yellow giant hyssop
Agrimonia gryposepala	Common agrimony
Agropyron trachycaulum unilaterale	Bearded wheatgrass
Agrostis perennans	Woodland bent
Allium canadense	Wild garlic
Allium cernuum	Nodding wild onion
Allium tricoccum	Wild leek
Ambrosia artemisiifolia elatior	Common ragweed
Ambrosia trifida	Giant ragweed
Amphicarpaea bracteata	Hog peanut
Andropogon gerardi	Big bluestem grass
Andropogon scoparius	Little bluestem grass
Anemone quinquefolia interior	Wood anemone
Anemone virginiana	Tall anemone
Antennaria neglecta	Cat's foot
Antennaria plantaginifolia	Pussytoes
Apocynum sibiricum	Dogbane
Aquilegia canadensis	Wild columbine
Arabis glabra	Tower mustard
Arabis laevigata	Smooth bank cress
Arenaria lateriflora	Grove sandwort
Arisaema atrorubens	Jack-in-the-pulpit
Arisaema dracontium	Green dragon
Asclepias exaltata	Poke milkweed
Asclepias purpurascens	Purple milkweed
Aster ericoides	Heath aster

SCIENTIFIC NAME	COMMON NAME
Aster laevis	Smooth blue aster
Aster lateriflorus	Side-flowering aster
Aster macrophyllus	Big-leaved aster
Aster novae-angliae	New England aster
Aster pilosus	Hairy aster
Aster praealtus	Willow aster
Aster sagittifolius Drummondii	Drummond's aster
Aster Shortii	Short's aster
Astragalus canadensis	Canada milk vetch
Baptisia leucantha	White wild indigo
Bidens frondosa	Beggar's-tick
Brachyelytrum erectum	Long awned wood grass
Bromus kalmii	Kalm's brome
Bromus purgans	Woodland brome
Cacalia artiplicifolia	Pale Indian plantain
Cacalia tuberosa	Tuberous Indian plantain
Calamagrostis canadensis	Blue joint grass
Camassia scilloides	Wild hyacinth
Campanula americana	Tall bellflower
Cardamine Douglassii	Purple spring cress
Carex cephaloidea	(no common name)
Carex cephaloflora	Woodbank sedge
Carex laxiflora	Wood sedge
Carex normalis	Scale wood sedge
Carex pensylvanica	Pennsylvania sedge
Carex rosea	Tuffed wood sedge
Carex tenera	Flexed wood sedge
Carya cordiformis	Bitternut hickory
Carya ovata	Shagbark hickory
Ceanothus americanus	New Jersey tea
Celastrus scandens	Climbing bittersweet
Chelone glabra	Turtlehead
Chenopodium boscianum	Woodland goosefoot
Chenopodium hybridum gigantospermum	Maple-leaved goosefoot
Cicuta maculata	Water hemlock
Cinna arundinacea	Common woodreed
Circaea quadrisulcata canadensis	Enchanter's nightshade

SCIENTIFIC NAME	COMMON NAME
Cirsium altissimum	Tall thistle
Cirsium discolor	Pasture thistle
Claytonia virginica	Spring beauty
Comandra richardsiana	False toadflax
Coreopsis palmata	Prairie coreopsis
Coreopsis tripteris	Tall coreopsis
Cornus racemosa	Gray dogwood
Corylus americana	Hazelnut
Cryptotaenia canadensis	Honewort
Danthonia spicata	Poverty oats
Dentaria laciniata	Toothwort
Desmodium canadense	Canada tick trefoil
Desmodium paniculatum	Panicled tick trefoil
Dodecatheon meadia	Shooting star
Elymus canadensis	Canada wild rye
Elymus villosus	Satiny wild rye
Elymus virginicus	Virginia wild rye
Epilobium coloratum	Cinnamon willow herb
Erechtites hieracifolia	Fireweed
Erigeron philadelphicus	Marsh fleabane
Erigeron pulchellus	Robin's plantain
Eryngium yuccifolium	Rattlesnake master
Erythronium albidum	White trout lily
Eupatorium maculatum	Spotted Joe-Pye weed
Eupatorium perfoliatum	Common boneset
Eupatorium purpureum	Purple Joe-Pye weed
Eupatorium rugosum	White snakeroot
Euphorbia corollata	Flowering spurge
Festuca obtusa	Nodding fescue
Fragaria virginiana	Common strawberry
Galium circaezans hypomalacum	Wild licorice
Galium concinnum	Shining bedstraw
Gentiana Andrewsii	Bottle gentian
Gentiana crinita	Fringed gentian
Gentiana flavida	Cream gentian
Gentiana quinquefolia occidentalis	Stiff gentian
Geranium carolinianum	Carolina cranesbill
Geranium maculatum	Wild geranium
Gerardia grandiflora pulchra	Yellow gerardia

SCIENTIFIC NAME	COMMON NAME
Gerardia purpurea	Purple false foxglove
Gerardia tenuifolia	Slender gerardia
Geum canadense	White avens
Geum laciniatum trichocarpum	Rough avens
Glyceria striata	Fowl manna grass
Hackelia virginiana	Stickseed
Hedeoma pulegioides	American pennyroyal
Helenium autumnale	Sneezeweed
Helianthus divaricatus	Woodland sunflower
Helianthus grosseserratus	Sawtooth sunflower
Heliopsis helianthoides	False sunflower
Heracleum maximum	Cow parsnip
Hypericum perforatum	Common St. John's-wort
Hypericum pyramidatum	Great St. John's-wort
Hypoxis hirsuta	Yellow star grass
Hystrix patula	Bottlebrush grass
Impatiens capensis	Spotted touch-me-not
Iris virginica Shrevei	Blue flag
Juglans nigra	Black walnut
Juncus dudleyi	Dudley's rush
Krigia biflora	False dandelion
Lactuca canadensis	Wild lettuce
Leersia virginica	White grass
Liatris scariosa	Savanna blazing star
Lilium michiganense	Michigan lily
Lobelia siphilitica	Great blue lobelia
Lycopus americanus	Common water horehound
Lysimachia ciliata	Fringed loosestrife
Monarda fistulosa	Wild bergamot
Muhlenbergia mexicana	Leafy satin grass
Oenothera perennis	Small sundrops
Orobanche uniflora	One-flowered broomrape
Oxalis stricta	Common wood sorrel
Oxalis violacea	Violet wood sorrel
Oxypolis rigidior	Cowbane
Panicum latifolium	Broad-leaved panic grass
Parthenium integrifolium	Wild quinine
Parthenocissus inserta	Thicket creeper
Pedicularis canadensis	Prairie betony

SCIENTIFIC NAME	COMMON NAME
Penstemon Digitalis	Foxglove beardtongue
Perideridia americana	Thicket parsley
Phlox divaricata	Woodland phlox
Phlox glaberrima interior	Marsh phlox
Physostegia virginiana	False dragonhead; obedient plant
Phytolacca americana	Pokeweed
Podophyllum peltatum	Mayapple
Polemonium reptans	Jacob's ladder
Polygala sanguinea	Field milkwort
Potentilla simplex	Common cinquefoil
Prenanthes alba	White lettuce
Prunella vulgaris lanceolata	Self-heal; carpenter's weed
Prunus americana	Wild plum
Prunus serotina	Wild black cherry
Pycnanthemum virginianum	Common mountain mint
Pyrus ioensis	Iowa crab
Quercus alba	White oak
Quercus ellipsoidalis	Hill's oak
Quercus macrocarpa	Bur oak
Ranunculus septentrionalis	Swamp buttercup
Ratibida pinnata	Yellow coneflower
Rhus glabra	Smooth sumac
Rhus radicans	Poison ivy
Rubus allegheniensis	Wild blackberry
Rubus flagellaris	Common dewberry
Rubus occidentalis	Black raspberry
Rudbeckia hirta	Black-eyed Susan
Rudbeckia subtomentosa	Sweet black-eyed Susan
Rudbeckia triloba	Brown-eyed Susan
Sanguinaria canadensis	Bloodroot
Sanicula gregaria	Clustered black snakeroot
Scrophularia marilandica	Late figwort
Scutellaria lateriflora	Mad-dog skullcap
Senecio pauperculus balsamitae	Balsam ragwort
Seymeria macrophylla	Mullein foxglove
Silene stellata	Starry campion
Silphium integrifolium	Rosinweed
Silphium terebinthinaceum	Prairie dock
Sisyrinchium albidum	Blue-eyed grass

Scientific Name	Common Name
Sisyrinchium angustifolium	Stout blue-eyed grass
Smilacina racemosa	False Solomon's seal
Smilacina stellata	Starry false Solomon's seal
Smilax ecirrhata	Upright carrion flower
Smilax lasioneura	Carrion flower
Solidago altissima	Tall goldenrod
Solidago caesia	Blue-stemmed goldenrod
Solidago flexicaulis	Broad-leaved goldenrod
Solidago gigantea leiophylla	Late goldenrod
Solidago graminifolia nuttallii	Grass-leaved goldenrod
Solidago juncea	Early goldenrod
Solidago nemoralis	Old field goldenrod
Solidago riddellii	Riddell's goldenrod
Solidago rigida	Stiff goldenrod
Solidago ulimfolia	Elm-leaved goldenrod
Sorghastrum nutans	Indian grass
Spartina pectinata	Prairie cordgrass
Spenopholis intermedia	Slender wedge grass
Taenidia integerrima	Yellow pimpernel
Teucrium canadense	Germander
Thalictrum dasycarpum	Purple meadow rue
Thalictrum dioicum	Early meadow rue
Thaspium trifoliatum flavum	Meadow parsnip
Tovara virginiana	Woodland knotweed
Tradescantia ohiensis	Ohio spiderwort
Trillium grandiflorum	Large-flowered trillium
Trillium recurvatum	Prairie trillium
Triosteum aurantiacum	Early horse gentian
Triosteum perfoliatum	Late horse gentian
Verbena urticifolia	White vervain
Veronicastrum Virginicum	Culver's root
Viola papilionacea	Common blue violet
Zizia aurea	Golden Alexanders

Source: John Balaban, Steve Packard, North Branch Prairie Project.

1. Robert F. Betz, introduction to Torkel Korling, *The Prairie—Swell and Swale* (Dundee, IL: Torkel Korling, 1972), pages unnumbered.

2. John T. Curtis, *The Vegetation of Wisconsin: An Ordination of Plant Communities*. (Madison, Wisconsin: University of Wisconsin Press, 1959, pp. 325–337.

3. Steve Packard, "Just a Few Oddball Species: Restoration and the Rediscovery of the Tallgrass Savanna," *Restoration & Management Notes*, The University of Wisconsin Press, Vol. 6, No. 1 (Summer 1988), p. 18.

4. Curtis, op. cit. p. 332.

5. Packard, op. cit. p. 19.

6. Packard, op. cit. p. 19.

7. Edward O. Wilson, *The Diversity of Life*. (Cambridge: Harvard University Press, 1992), p. 340.

8. Daniel H. Janzen, "The Neotropics," *Restoration & Management Notes*, Vol. 10, No. 1 (Summer 1992), p. 10.

9. Laura L. Jackson, Joseph R. McAuliffe, and Bruce A. Roundy, "Desert Restoration," *Restoration & Management Notes*, Vol. 9, No. 2 (Winter 1991), p. 78.

10. William R. Jordan, III, "The Reentry of Nature; Ecological Restoration," in *Chronicles*, Rockford Institute, Rockford, IL (August 1990), pp. 20–21.

11. Edward O. Wilson, *Biophilia* (Cambridge: Harvard University Press, 1984), p. 65.

12. Ibid. pp. 85, 139.

13. Ibid. pp. 109–112.

14. Ibid. pp. 10, 139.

15. William R. Jordan, III, Michael E. Gilpin, and John D. Aber, *Restoration Ecology: A Synthetic Approach to Ecological Research.* (New York: Cambridge University Press, 1987), p. 6.

16. Stuart L. Pimm, *The Balance of Nature? Ecological Issues in the Conservation of Species and Communities.* (Chicago: University of Chicago Press, 1991), p. xi.

17. D. W. Schindler, "Comments on the Sustainable Biosphere Initiative," *Conservation Biology,* Vol. 5, No. 4 (December 1991), p. 550.

18. Packard, op. cit. p. 13

19. Andre F. Clewell, "Observations Corroborate Savanna Community Concept," *Restoration & Management Notes,* Vol. 7, No. 2 (Winter 1989), p. 82.

20. Victoria A. Nuzzo, "Extent and Status of Midwest Oak Savanna: Presettlement and 1985," *Natural Areas Journal,* Vol. 6, No. 2 (April 1986), pp. 6–36.

21. Jon Mendelson, Stephen P. Aultz, and Judith Dolan Mendelson, "Carving up the Woods: Savanna Restoration in Northeastern Illinois," *Restoration & Management Notes,* Vol. 10, No. 2 (Winter 1992), pp. 127–131.

22. Douglas Ladd, "Reexamination of the Role of Fire in Missouri Oak Woodlands," *Proceedings of the Oak Woods Management Workshop,* Eastern Illinois University, Charleston, IL (1991), pp. 67–80.

23. Steve Packard, "Restoring Oak Ecosystems," *Restoration & Management Notes,* Vol. 11, No. 1 (Summer 1993), pp. 5–16.

SELECTED REFERENCES

Bretz, J. Harlen. *Geology of the Chicago Region, Part II: The Pleisto-cene.* Urbana, Illinois: State of Illinois (Geological Survey), 1955.

Cronon, William. *Nature's Metropolis: Chicago and the Great West.* New York: Norton, 1991.

Curtis, John T. *The Vegetation of Wisconsin: An Ordination of Plant Communities.* Madison, Wisconsin: University of Wisconsin Press, 1959, 1987.

Edmunds, R. David. *The Potawatomis: Keepers of the Fire.* Norman: University of Oklahoma Press, 1978.

Hoffmeister, Donald F. *Mammals of Illinois.* Champaign Illinois: University of Illinois Press, 1989.

Imes, Rick. *The Practical Botanist.* New York: Simon & Schuster/ Fireside, 1990.

Jordan, William R., III, Michael E. Gilpin, and John D. Aber. *Restoration Ecology: A Synthetic Approach to Ecological Research.* New York: Cambridge University Press, 1987.

Leopold, Aldo. *A Sand County Almanac.* Oxford University Press, Oxford and New York: 1966.

Madson, John. *Where the Sky Began: Land of the Tallgrass Prairie.* San Francisco: Sierra Club Books, 1982.

Markman, Charles W. *Chicago Before History: The Prehistoric Archaeology of a Modern Metropolitan Area.* Springfield, Illinois: Illinois Historic Preservation Agency, 1991.

Masi, Susanne. *"Prairie Restoration Management and Vegetation Change.* Miami Woods Prairie: A Case Study," Master's thesis. Northeastern Illinois University, 1991.

National Research Council. *Restoration of Aquatic Ecosystems: Science, Technology and Public Policy.* Washington: National Research Council, November 1991.

Niering, William A., and Nancy C. Olmstead. *The Audubon Society Field Guide to North American Wildflowers, Eastern Region.* New York: Knopf/Borzoi, 1979.

Peattie, Donald Culross. *A Natural History of Trees of Eastern and Central North America.* Boston: Houghton Mifflin, 1966.

Peterson, Roger Tory, and Margaret McKenny. *A Field Guide to Wildflowers of Northeastern and North-central North America.* Boston: Houghton Mifflin, 1968.

Pielou, E. C. *After the Ice Age: The Return of Life to Glaciated North America.* Chicago: University of Chicago Press, 1991.

Pimm, Stuart L. *The Balance of Nature? Ecological Issues in the Conservation of Species and Communities.* Chicago: University of Chicago Press, 1991.

Pyle, Robert Michael. *The Audubon Society Field Guide to North American Butterflies.* New York: Knopf/Borzoi, 1981.

Willman, H. B. *Summary of the Geology of the Chicago Area.* Illinois State Geological Survey, 1971.

Wilson, Edward O. *Biophilia.* Cambridge: Harvard University Press, 1984.

———. *The Diversity of Life.* Cambridge: Harvard University Press, 1992.